THE BOOK OF THE
Everglades

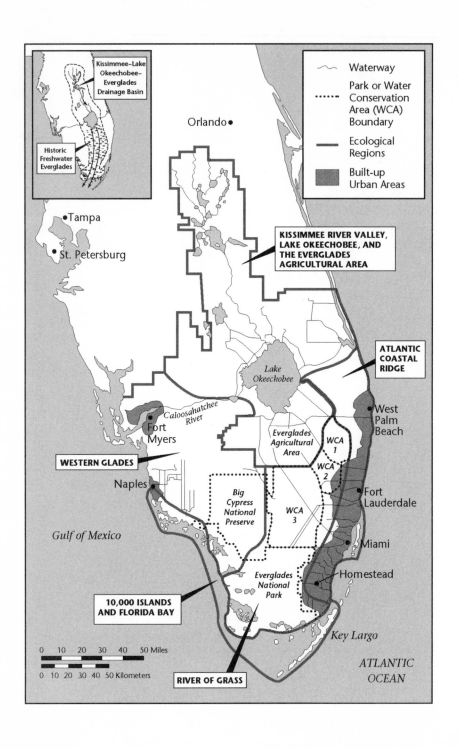

THE BOOK OF THE
Everglades

Edited by

SUSAN CERULEAN

MILKWEED
EDITIONS

Published 2002 by Milkweed Editions
Printed in Canada
Cover and interior design by Dale Cooney
Cover paintings, "Confluence (2001)" and "Cypress (1996)," by James M. Couper
Interior map by Patti Isaacs
The text of this book is set in Stone Serif.
02 03 04 05 06   5 4 3 2 1
First Edition

Milkweed Editions, a nonprofit publisher, gratefully acknowledges support from the Bush Foundation; General Mills Foundation; Marshall Field's Project Imagine with support from the Target Foundation; McKnight Foundation; Minnesota State Arts Board through an appropriation by the Minnesota State Legislature and a grant from the National Endowment for the Arts, and a grant from the Wells Fargo Foundation Minnesota; A Resources for Change technology grant from the National Endowment for the Arts; St. Paul Companies, Inc.; Target Stores; and generous individuals.

Library of Congress Cataloging-in-Publication Data

The book of the Everglades / edited by Susan Cerulean.— 1st ed.
        p.   cm.
    Includes bibliographical references (p.).
    ISBN 1-57131-260-9 (pbk.)
    1. Natural history—Florida—Everglades.   2. Endangered ecosystems—Florida—Everglades.   3. Nature conservation—Florida—Everglades.   I. Cerulean, Susan.

    QH105.F6 B66 2002
    508.759'39—dc21   2001044932

This book is printed on acid-free, recycled paper.

For my father,
Charles R. Isleib

Thank you for setting me on the path.

THE BOOK OF THE EVERGLADES

Part Five

THE TEN THOUSAND ISLANDS AND FLORIDA BAY

FOREWORD

Al Burt

It works this way.

Late one May or June morning, thunder growls. Winds begin making clouds out of the heat and moisture. The clouds billow into airy, blackening mountains. The process builds, as if the Everglades are shaking out of a lethargy. Lightning cracks. By afternoon, the atmosphere explodes into a thunderstorm. For an hour or two, rain bursts hard upon the Everglades. Then all is quiet again. The wet season has begun.

After drying out and drowsing through the winter, the Everglades welcome it. Scorched saw grass enlivens and greens. Mud flats, cracked and dry while winter tourists frolicked on the coasts, turn into nourishing ooze again. Turtles and frogs, and an immense variety of other visible life-forms as small as tadpoles and as large as alligators, take on renewed wriggle. The hot, wet rituals of summer begin.

The cities, bumping against the edges of the Everglades, love the cool, dry winters and hate the hot, wet summers. Tourists come in fewer numbers. Many residents flee to the mountains. Summer turns into a bittersweet time, even though most threats from Everglades flooding were removed from city streets years ago by system-altering canals and dikes; even though the rains deliver a brief puff of cooler air and sometimes a freshening hail; and even though they drop free sweet water out of the sky on a land that somehow manages to parch despite all that water around it. It is a land whose highest points seem to have a hankering to be desert.

The conflict, humans versus the Everglades, always has been as basic as that. Historically, there has been little more than lip service applied to any common cause among the general population to preserve and protect the Everglades. Full recognition of interdependence always falls short. No true response ever was made to scientists' warnings about foreseeable disasters that could alter and cripple the whole region, spoil the South Florida scene. Average folk in highly urbanized Florida do not, for the most part, get emotional about the Everglades one way or the other. The "big swamp," as close as it is, still seems too remote from most day-to-day lives. This single most significant patch of Florida, ecologically important enough to compare to any other similarly sized region in the United States, perhaps in the world, is out there like the sky and the ocean, too big and too complex for working folk to measure by the rule of their nine to five schedules. They tend to fret more about the discomforting downside of the weather system than to cheer for the fluctuations that keep alive some chance that the Everglades can survive. Many folks are not comfortable with the idea that they should share a shaky water supply with what they see as a big swamp because somebody tells them that the big swamp in turn will make the water supply less shaky. So they do not rejoice over the rains, except in emergencies, when smoke from wildfires darkens the skies and makes the air hard to breathe, or when the faucets flow so weakly that swimming pool levels dwindle. Most everything about the Everglades that intrudes into their lives seems to come as a distraction or a common nuisance.

City folk are more likely to curse the annoyances than to cheer the benefits of the geography and the weather that make South Florida and the Everglades one. The rains slicken the streets and cause accidents; they douse clothing and interrupt ball games and recreation; and in the smothering heat they cause a constant, uncomfortable wetness and a persistent mildew. The Everglades take up real estate that could be dried and developed. They force highways to take longer, circuitous routes to cross the state. They create homes for millions of mosquitoes and bugs that fly into places where they are not wanted. The Everglades? So what.

Most of Florida is filled with folk who learned how to live their lives in cities foreign to the peculiarities of South Florida, even if they were located within the mainland United States. Though the Everglades rank as a romantic presence—while reading Marjory Stoneman Douglas's defining words or Peter Matthiessen's fictional illuminations of land and history, while hearing champions Nathaniel Reed or Art Marshall thunder about the future like wounded evangelists, or while seeing those blue-gray rain smudges gracefully moving in bent columns across saw grass plains in the inspiring paintings of James Hutchinson—for most folk they still remain pesky, at least in nose-to-nose encounters. In casual approach few find the Everglades easy to love or to understand. You have to work at give-take relations, and from that wise and essential and sometimes onerous labor often emerges something grander than you could first imagine.

The Everglades deserve rank as one of the world's great marvels, and their interdependent, conjoined-twin relationship with the cities takes on as mysterious and tangled a politics as you can find. The body of South Florida makes war against itself—the natural Everglades trying to defend itself against the overdeveloped yet still insatiable urban coast. In the resulting conflict they seem like two small and feisty nations bumping borders, clashing, threatening, literal opposites dependent on lifestyles that bleed away each other's great gifts. So different they seem, and yet so joined and inseparable.

The constant Everglades are like a giant puddle—inches deep, miles wide—migrating through the grasses (hence, Marjory Stoneman Douglas's *River of Grass*) for most of the year, repeatedly renewing itself on rains and spillover from Lake Okeechobee. The puddle moves down the slight incline of South Florida toward the ocean, refreshing the water-storing aquifer below as it goes. The flow of the water is a cumbersome thing of great utility, difficult to view and not easily appreciated.

The Everglades are an irregular jewel, too big and too conventionally ugly for pleasure seekers looking for packaged wonders, people who are conditioned to emit instantly delighted exclamations at first sight of the neatness, convenience, and store-bought prettiness of a theme park. The Everglades, instead, are somewhat like body innards appearing on the outside, an earth-connected heart or a liver hanging out there and working in the open, where it might be admired by the scientists and marveled at by the academics, but where it tends to look a bit yucky to the common gawker.

The Everglades make their own dimensions. Most of the sights don't sweeten the eye immediately. Everglades vistas loom so huge that the eyes do not seem capable of assessing them all at once, and the mind does not easily compute their encyclopedic message. Neither do the smells (odors, actually) immediately charm the nostrils, not like the fragrance of orange blossoms. Not until you can inhale and with informed imagination picture where that smell comes from and why, do the odors begin to properly fascinate. The sounds of the Everglades, too, have their own scores. They cannot easily be put to lyrics—the rush of the wind on the marsh, given scale by its range of strengths; the rain with its varied percussions; the soprano calls of the birds; perhaps the cry of a panther on a difficult hunt, lamenting that its world narrows dangerously; occasionally the grunt of an alligator or the whines of mosquitoes. All of these can be heard. Yet, there is mostly the silence to hear and the heat to feel and the sweat to taste.

The delicacy, complexity, and quietly logical savagery of a wilderness launch many mysteries and some answers. Frogs eat insects, snakes eat frogs, egrets eat snakes, gators eat egrets. Birds rise on the thermal currents. Gators dig water holes that become little oases. Wading birds and their feathered kin need the water that the aquifer needs, but not too much water that it interferes with nesting. When the water rises too high, deer drown. Farms need the water, but not all the time. As the water is managed up and managed down to accommodate human needs, it accumulates unnatural runoff. The quantity and quality and timing of the managed water cannot please all the needs. What seems right for the farms rarely seems right for the Everglades and its creatures. When the locked canals drain off a wet season surplus into the coastal estuaries, those natural hatcheries deteriorate. The complications are endless. When levels are low, salty ocean water intrudes inland into the sweet water. Around the edges, that briny mixture can nourish shore-saving mangroves and small sea creatures can flourish, but if the salt intrudes too far, it kills the Glades system. It seems a hopeless task to try to beat nature at its own balancing game, but historically that has been the plan.

The Everglades and all of South Florida merge, and they require that balance. There needs to be some of all, just enough, not too much of any. Land and water join one into the other so subtly that they have no clear boundaries; they create new definitions. Subtropical influences lean into the temperate zone and empower immense variety, fresh and different arenas of life. All of it is a delicate improvisation.

In 1970, there were seven million people living in Florida; in 2000, there were more than sixteen million, and most of them lived in South Florida, crowding around the perimeters of the Everglades and yearning for more elbow room. Can the Everglades and that many neighbors survive healthily side by side? Will there always be public servants who note uninformed public appetites and doubt the realities of the "big swamp"? Even now, after all this time, will some of them always want to buy the notion that they can tinker with it, somehow short-ration it, tidy it up for the forty million tourists who come to Florida each year looking for sun and fun?

The flat Everglades, the monotonous marshes, the land-marking hammocks staked out by cabbage palms, the wide sky, and the monstrous weather have their own grandeur. The scenes gladden the eye of old-time Floridians. They require knowledge and imagination for full appreciation; experience multiplies it. The eye finds joy in the marvel it understands. The Everglades have an essential, adult beauty that comes from truth and significance. Strangers, visitors, might not be able to see the beauty until someone explains that they should look closely, because here lies some kind of barefooted, bewitching miracle.

This book does that.

When **AL BURT** *ended his forty-year association with the* Miami Herald, *the newspaper titled his full-page retirement story with a headline that suggested his place among Florida's homegrown interpreters: "A Legend Rests." As a roving columnist, his words joined Florida's past, present, and future to the real lives of real Floridians. He wrote movingly of the joys and dilemmas of living on the long peninsula while its extraordinary natural heritage eroded before development. Burt has written five books, and regards the last three as a trilogy that grew out of his newspaper experiences. They are* The Tropic of Cracker *(University Press of Florida, 1999);* Al Burt's Florida *(University Press of Florida, 1998); and* Becalmed in the Mullet Latitudes *(Florida Classics Library, 1984).*

THE BOOK OF THE
Everglades

THE EVERGLADES

AN ECOLOGY IN FIVE PARTS

Susan Cerulean and Jono Miller

Grand Canyon, easy. Niagara Falls, no problem. Yellowstone's Old Faithful, got it.

But despite the Everglades' ranking on a par with these natural wonders, it's a landscape very hard for most people to visualize or appreciate. Florida naturalist Archie Carr described the phenomenon as well as any:

> Visitors still arrive expecting to see a dim, mysterious swamp-forest full of reptiles, exotic birds and eerie noises, a sort of Hollywood jungle set in which boa constrictors or bands of apes would not come as a total surprise. This probably accounts for the let-down look park rangers see in the faces of some newcomers as they gaze out over the saw grass plain for the first time.

Maybe the flat ecosystem is too subtle. Perhaps it is a cultural blind spot. Possibly, as Carr intimates, Hollywood is to blame. But the inability of Americans to appreciate this system has resulted in far more than disappointed tourists. After roughly a century-long binge of drainage, diking, dredging, canalization, and agricultural conversion, the State of Florida has wakened with a tremendous headache, mostly self-inflicted, confronting a set of tantalizing, expensive, and

3

unproven palliatives. The Everglades has experienced the effects of an unparalleled paradigm shift as Floridians have moved from a situation of wanting something we didn't have (a drained Everglades), to having something we don't want (a drained Everglades).

Second to Marjory Stoneman Douglas's "river of grass" metaphor, the most common descriptor of the Everglades is that it is the only one of its kind. While no doubt true in the specific sense, it is also quite possible that had the Bangladeshis, or the peoples of the Okavango Delta, or those of the seasonally flooded forests of the Amazon basin colonized Florida, rather than northern Europeans, the treatment of the landscape might have been quite different. Instead of seeming inhospitable and useless, the Everglades might have been viewed with a certain familiarity, even nostalgia.

In an ancient Hindustani parable, five blind men encounter an elephant, but each one a different body part—trunk, leg, tusk, tail, or belly. Each in turn make different assumptions about the whole creature, based on the nature of the limb they examine through touch. The Everglades system is another such elephant. In the course of a weekend one could: float out of sight of land in the center of the largest freshwater lake occurring wholly within a state; stand in a densely shaded cypress cathedral waist deep in cool dark water; drive through miles of intensively managed, diked, and drained farmland; ride an airboat through a shallow freshwater sea nearly hidden by saw grass; drift over shallow salty marine meadows; or swat mosquitoes in a dense maze of mangrove islands.

A single enormous watershed, sprawling three hundred miles from Orlando to Florida Bay, underlies all of South Florida's Everglades ecosystem, an ecology in five parts. What we often think of as the true Everglades, Douglas's "river of grass," is only a piece of this complicated landscape mosaic. Adjacent, to the north, south, east, and west, lie its relations—the Kissimmee-Okeechobee basin, the coastal Atlantic upland rim, the mangrove coast and Florida Bay, and the Big Cypress landscape. The contours of each dovetail intricately with the others, and the flow of freshwater links them all.

SUSAN CERULEAN AND JONO MILLER

South Florida is a relatively young terrain, its basement rock formed from the carbonate remains of marine algae and shells drifted and deposited on the floor of an ancient sea. When the sea level fell, the marine sediment was exposed to freshwater and cemented into limestone. Then, about fifteen thousand years ago, sea level rose once more as the polar ice caps melted. And then began the development of the Everglades as we know it today.

Freshwater historically entered the Everglades ecosystem just south of present day Orlando in the wide river plain of the Kissimmee, with its eighteen chained lakes, broad prairies, and braided wetlands. Kissimmee waters filtered into the great Lake Okeechobee, which periodically sent some of its excess east and west, creating productive lagoons and estuaries on both coasts of the peninsula. But most of Okeechobee's waters tilted south, forming a forty- to fifty-mile-wide saw grass marsh studded with tree islands that sloped ever so gently top to bottom, south to Florida Bay. To comprehend the subtle tilt of the landscape and the almost infinitesimally slow movement of water that links the system north to south, lay this book on a flat surface and then slide a piece of paper under one end. The lift provided by that paper mimics the relative difference in elevation between Orlando at the top of the system and Florida Bay, 250 miles to the south. The system allows a delayed delivery of the wet season's watery bounty by a good two or three months, after the rains taper off in October and the dry season begins.

An exposed rock rim—where most of South Florida's major cities lie today—interrupted any eastward flow of shallow surface waters to the Atlantic, redirecting the movement of freshwater to the southwest. A similar ridge to the west of the river of grass delineates the interconnected habitats of Big Cypress, Fakahatchee Strand, and Corkscrew Swamp.

At the base of the peninsula, fresh Everglades waters mingle with the salty gulf in a tangled maze of mangrove forest before giving way to the open sea grass meadows of Florida Bay. The southern boundary of the bay is the Florida Keys, an ancient coral reef.

All of this country is known as the Everglades. Before European contact, the vastness of this landscape—about nine million acres—offered the large ranges required by the region's top predators, the Florida panther and the black bear, as well as room for adaptation to, and recovery from, the hurricanes and fires that regularly swept across the land.

Two hundred years ago, South Florida supported only a smattering of tiny hamlets—mosquito-besieged outposts awaiting the next hurricane on Key West and on the coastal ridge paralleling the Atlantic. Little was known about the state's interior: there was not reliable information that Lake Okeechobee existed until 1837, when 130 soldiers marching with Colonel Zachary Taylor (later President) were wounded or killed on Christmas Day. Taylor and his men were trying to remove Native Americans—Seminole Indians—who themselves were relatively new to South Florida.

The would-be white settlers who trickled into South Florida in the 1800s had virtually no experience adapting to life in the humid, seasonally flooded subtropics. For the most part, the region was viewed as uninhabitable in its natural condition. Throughout the Glades, people made scant livings harvesting alligator skins, wading bird plumes, and various animals and fish for food, including catfish from Lake Okeechobee. Agricultural export was modest; the clear-cutters hadn't yet made much progress on the state's ancient pine and cypress forests. By 1900, a lucrative, open-range cattle industry had evolved on the interior prairies, but the practice was so disorganized that, purportedly, even the honest cow hunters had to rustle a few cattle to keep their herd size up.

Newcomers continued to apply lessons learned from the temperate northern states and the Mediterranean, without much success. The Spanish, for example, were largely unsuccessful in their attempts to transplant the flora of the Mediterranean to the Everglades region. The only success was an example of the exception proving the rule. Where grapes and olives perished, citrus exploded, precisely because citrus was more at home in the subtropics than in the Mediterranean.

One thing on everyone's mind as they jostled into this new

frontier was that if South Florida could ever be drained, all that frustrating interior land would open to venture, including the deep muck soils south of Lake Okeechobee.

When engineer Hamilton Disston arrived in 1881 to finally "solve the problem" of the Everglades, the system began to give way. Disston purchased four million acres of land from the state for twenty-five cents an acre, and was encouraged by the government to drain the land. The next year he set out to massively reshape and drain the Everglades, gouging, dynamiting, and eventually completing a canal to the west coast from Okeechobee by way of the Caloosahatchee River. This canal allowed boat access to the interior but didn't effect much drainage.

In 1905, the powerful, oratorical governor of Florida, Napoleon Bonaparte Broward, picked up where Disston had left off, with the construction of three enormous canals, the first one angling northward from the lower east coast, through the river of grass, toward the great lake. Broward's canals and their connectors sliced through the landscape, indifferent to the natural lay of the land, diverting and impounding the freshwater flow from the north and dumping much of it in the Atlantic Ocean. By 1925, the St. Lucie Canal was completed, desiccating the land further. Broward linked the drainage of the Everglades, what he called the "pestilence-ridden swamp," to the virtues of the people of Florida. In an open letter to the citizens, Broward wrote:

> It would indeed be a commentary on the intelligence and energy of the State of Florida to confess that so simple an engineering feat as the drainage of a body of land 21 feet above the sea was above their power. . . . Shall the sovereign people of Florida surrender . . . and supinely confess that they cannot knock a hole in a wall of coral and let a body of water obey a natural law and seek the level of the sea? To answer "yes" to such a question is to prove ourselves unworthy of freedom, happiness or prosperity.

By 1928, the infamous tradition of buying swampland in Florida was well under way. Most of the folks who bought so-called farmland along the south rim of Lake Okeechobee found out pretty quickly that their land was better suited for fishing than for farming and left. Those settlers who determined to tough it out, persisting in the effort to drain their watery new farms, settled in towns such as Belle Glade and Chosen, and even on islands within the lake.

A pair of grand, wet, devastating hurricanes killed nearly two thousand people on lands southwest of the lake's shore, establishing in the mind of the populace that they could not live safely or farm productively in the Everglades without considerably more "improvement." In the 1940s, the Army Corps of Engineers began to construct a system of canals, pumps, and levees—including the Hoover Dike rimming and constricting Lake Okeechobee—to prevent further flooding.

"Terraforming," a term that refers to sending people and machines to other celestial bodies to modify the landscape and atmosphere in a way that makes the planet, moon, or asteroid more supportive of human life, is the only word that adequately expresses the degree of annihilation the Everglades has endured. Sixteen hundred miles of canals, levees, and pumping stations, the most extensive water control project in the United States, have bent and restrained this watery wilderness into a more predictable, flood-free landscape that now supports a lucrative agricultural economy and massive coastal cities.

In our lifetimes, this unique landscape has been reduced to half its former size. We will never see the sparkling rapids of the Miami River, or the tropically abundant pond apple forests on Okeechobee's southern shore, or Lake Flirt to the west. Fewer than 10 percent of the untold millions of egrets, ibises, and herons that nested in the Everglades at the turn of the century can still be counted. The Florida panther, the Key deer, and the American crocodile are others among the fifty-six threatened and endangered species struggling to survive in the greater Everglades ecosystem. The once crystalline waters of Florida Bay have turned murky green, killing sponges and a myriad of other marine species, and many coral reefs, as well.

But, we must honor the fact that as the new millennium begins, the official voices of power have joined the call for Everglades restoration.

SUSAN CERULEAN AND JONO MILLER

It is something of a miracle that in South Florida, scientists, engineers, six state agencies, and the tribal governments have combined their efforts to plan jointly for the restoration of this ecosystem. The guiding document, published in April 1999, known as the "Restudy," claims as its overarching and primary purpose "the restoration, preservation, and protection of the South Florida ecosystem." That is good news indeed. A $7.8 billion, thirty-six year water supply project was approved by Congress in October 2000, which proposes to replenish and remap the moribund Everglades to meet the needs of the growing population and to tackle the environmental restoration as well. We are daring to mend what we so terribly destroyed, by purchasing lands, raising roads, plugging canals, and building safe passage for the waters to move once again across the landscape. The key to the new plan is based on the assumption that although we cannot restore the historic size of the Everglades, we can restore many of the ways in which water flowed and was stored in the remaining area. Getting the water right, by addressing four issues—quantity, quality, timing, and distribution—is the new mantra of the Army Corps of Engineers, now an indispensable partner in the restoration of the Everglades.

More than ever before, we can describe an emerging common vision of a landscape whose health, integrity, and beauty are restored and nurtured by its interrelationships with South Florida's human communities.

The Book of the Everglades, part of the Literature for a Land Ethic series published by Milkweed Editions, gathers together powerful voices, each one a committed student of the greater Everglades ecosystem, its cycles, and its creatures. Here you will encounter lament, celebration, inquiry, and a passionate call for an entirely more inclusive relationship with the land. Each author will escort the reader into this vast, fractured landscape with humility and infinite respect for the indigenous. Taken together, these essays offer us the bare outlines of a restoration rising from the ashes of unbearable loss.

Part One

THE KISSIMMEE RIVER VALLEY, LAKE OKEECHOBEE, AND THE EVERGLADES AGRICULTURAL AREA

Up that chain of lakes, the rains fall and brim the fine green-ringed cups. The waters begin again their southward flow. The Kissimmee River is swollen and strongly swirling between its wet marshy banks, but still the water does not move off fast enough. The banks are overflowing and the spongy ground between it and Fisheating Creek is all one swamp. The rains fling their solid shafts of water down the streaming green land, and Okeechobee swells and stirs and creeps south down the unseen tilt of the Glades.

THE EVERGLADES: RIVER OF GRASS, MARJORY STONEMAN DOUGLAS

The natural waters of the Everglades originate just south of Orlando in the Kissimmee Valley, swelling, during the wet months, a closely connected chain of lakes, then moving gradually through the twists and curves of the Kissimmee River and its braided floodplain, eventually emptying into Lake Okeechobee. The Kissimmee River Valley is actually a shallow drainage slough whose low relief provided an ideal trough for a slow-flowing, meandering river. Early white settlers recognized the valley as promising cattle country, and soon after the Seminole wars—in the 1830s and 1840s—the area began to go into ranches and is now the heart of Central Florida's cattle industry.

The river, meandering a mile west or east for every mile south, delivered its water and sediments to the 730 square-mile basin of Lake Okeechobee, and farther yet downstream to the northern river of grass. The lake in modern aspect did not actually appear until about four thousand years ago, after enough overflow of peat and muck created a sill impounding the lake's waters along the southern and eastern rim. This elevated, three-mile-wide natural levee supported a tropical forest composed of custard apple on the southern shore and cypress along the lake's eastern bank—a region noted for its remote and impenetrable beauty. During wet years, the lake expanded to perhaps 850 square miles, shrinking considerably in times of drought.

For at least a hundred years, the Kissimmee Valley has been subjected to drainage operations of one kind or another. Between 1958 and 1972, over half of the extending prairies and pinelands were drained and planted in pasture grasses at the expense of native land cover. But of all the insults to this landscape, surely the most grievous was the straight-reaming of the river itself. In 1970, Peter Matthiessen described the "River Eater" as an "awesome machinery of destruction that has settled on the Kissimmee like a black-and-yellow warship from another planet. The thing squats," Matthiessen wrote for *Audubon*, "in the murky water of its own desolation, a hundred feet high and two hundred feet long, not counting the huge underwater cutting head that sweeps back and forth before it like a blind proboscis, nor the hundreds of feet of extruded steel intestine a yard in diameter that squirts the residue of its monstrous appetite over the spill banks and across the ravaged marsh."

In this fashion, a quarter of a million acres of wild wetland habitat were destroyed in the name of flood protection, erasing more than 90 percent of the valley's abundant waterfowl population and leaving behind a lifeless artery that became known simply as "the ditch."

Similarly, the old south shore of the lake and its deep rich muck soils were among the first to be converted to successful agriculture in South Florida, after the entire lake's confinement within the Herbert Hoover Dike. The rare custard apple forests were virtually gone by 1930, and what was once the northern Everglades was completely transformed by ditch and plow into the seven hundred thousand-acre Everglades Agricultural Area.

THE RIVER AND THE PLAIN

Archie Carr

The Kissimmee River is the chief tributary of Lake Okeechobee and
the master stream for a vast complex of landscapes linked to the
Everglades system—prairies, marshes, sloughs, hammocks and pine
flatwoods. Parts of the Kissimmee Valley look very much like the
Everglades—so much so that some of it, the saw grass and wet prairies
in the valley's southern and western sections, is sometimes called the
Little Everglades. Before the Kissimmee River was channelized, when
it meandered through a hundred miles of meadows, its valley was
much wetter than it now is. Nevertheless, early visitors recognized it
as promising cattle country, and soon after the Seminole wars—in the
1830s and '40s—the region began to go into ranches. As these spread,
artificial drainage increased, and the water table went down markedly.
But it is still good country, and parts of it have hardly changed at all.

The flatlands of the Kissimmee basin, including the region loosely
known as Kissimmee Prairie, are a part of the coastal lowlands, the
series of sandy marine terrace plains that extend down both sides of
peninsular Florida and meet northwest of Lake Okeechobee. In the
north these terraces are mainly covered with pine flatwoods of several
different kinds. In the south they merge with the saw grass Everglades
below Lake Okeechobee and with the tree swamps, glade lands and
pine flatwoods of Big Cypress Swamp.

In Florida the word prairie is applied to two different landscapes, neither of which, except in flatness, resembles the dry Western country the term usually brings to mind. In northern Florida where I live, prairies are solution basins—that is, marshy lakes filled with emergent and floating herbaceous plants, and subject to abrupt drying up when water levels drop and the water drains through holes in the limestone bottoms. One season you may fish from a boat in one of these places; the next season you may walk across dry ground there. These northern Florida prairies are similar in general appearance to what are known as wet prairies in the Everglades, where they are one of the landscape variants in the saw grass plain.

Prairie means something different in the expanse of lowlands above Lake Okeechobee. The prairies here are low, flat, tremendous meadows, set with stands of saw palmettos, copses of live oaks, groves of cabbage palms or mixed hammocks of various temperate and tropical hardwood trees.

The dry prairie is the characteristic country of the Kissimmee Valley region; nowhere on earth is there a terrain just like those short grass and saw-palmetto savannas. A place it brings to mind is the grassy savanna land of eastern Africa. Kissimmee Prairie all but cries out for antelope, but lacking those, it has made do with white-tailed deer, wild Kissimmee ponies and box turtles. It is a land where long-legged birds stalk the uncluttered ground, or walk from pond to pond, and where once I saw wild turkeys, sandhill cranes and wood storks standing together on a burn. The storks were just at the edge of a drying pond, the turkeys and cranes not 50 feet away on fire-blackened grass.

Like most of Florida, the original prairie was almost surely a landscape shaped by fire. As in the saw grass Everglades—and in most of the big savanna lands of the world—fire is constantly in the background here, although its role is confused by other factors that help to keep the land as grassland. Periodic drought and periodic flooding, for instance, are both involved. Some of the original aspect of Kissimmee Prairie was no doubt due to seasonal soaking and a high water table and some to seasonal drought and baking of the surface. But the most fundamental factor that kept short-grass savanna here was probably the fires that intermittently or regularly crept or swept across the land and prevented the growth of broad-leaved trees except where some special local condition allowed patches of hardwood and palm to develop.

Before the white ranchers came, the prairie was Indian country. The Seminoles loved to burn the land—to flush out game, to kill ticks and rattlesnakes, or to make new grazing land for their cattle and ponies. When white men moved in they did the same, only worse, because they were more uneasy than the Indians about snakes, ticks and the black wolves that howled in the night. But the question is, how prevalent was fire before people of any kind came to the prairie? The answer obviously depends on how often you think lightning hit tinder at times when dry fuel lay on the land. It seems to me that this must have been often, and that you see a sign of it in the avid way each new generation of prairie birds quickly learns to crowd onto newly burned ground to eat the cooked animals there, especially the big grasshoppers that seem too dim-witted to flee from fire.

Two characteristic birds of the prairie community are especially fond of cooked victuals. One of these is Audubon's caracara; another is the Florida sandhill crane. There are two distinct subspecies of this crane in the state. One is migratory; it nests in Michigan and spends the winter in the South. The other is a year-round Florida resident, and its chief remaining stronghold is Kissimmee Prairie. Its feeding habits obviously evolved in a prairie environment, and its predilection for burned ground suggests a long association with fire. Anyway, back in the days when fires were more prevalent than they are today, if you wanted to find cranes the best thing to do was to ride a horse out to where a big smoke had been rising for a day or so.

When you got out to such a burn you nearly always found Audubon's caracara there. The caracara is as intrinsic a part of this landscape as the saw palmetto. Though it doesn't exactly look the part,the caracara is a kind of long-legged hawk. The name caracara is supposed to suggest the creature's voice, a peculiar grating croak that is uttered as the bird tilts its head back between its shoulders.

The third member of the avian triumvirate of Kissimmee Prairie is the burrowing owl. A small bird, standing about nine inches tall, it too has very long legs for its body. While this amiable owl is a characteristic occupant of Kissimmee Prairie, it also turns up in other parts of the peninsula that have a proper prairie look. Much of Florida has recently been put into short-grass savanna, in the form of pastures, golf courses and airports; and these are the habitats the little owls have colonized. Their settling at Miami International Airport stirred the Florida Audubon Society to have the airport designated a wildlife preserve.

Burrowing owls are gregarious, and if you come across one anywhere it is likely to be a member of a colony. The burrows are tunnels that, in Florida at least, usually seem to be scratched out by the owls themselves. They are about three inches high and five wide, and go down at a slant for several feet, the final depth often being determined by the top of the water table. The burrow serves as refuge, dormitory and nesting place. During leisure times outside, the owls stand about on little raised places, and bob up and down engagingly when approached.

Because the prairie landscape in its original form was unusually well suited to human needs, the man-made changes there seem a little less drastic than in other Florida terrain. The whole region is certainly much drier now than it was when the wolves and Indians left it, because of the increased drainage that came with the growth of the human population and the spread of the ranches. At the same time, the frequency of wildfire has been reduced. While this is clearly a blessing for snakes, quail, mice and box turtles, it is bad for cranes and caracaras, depriving them of the grasshopper bakes that brightened the days of their fathers. Both of these birds are as stimulated by the disaster of fire as storks are by the disaster of fish-stranding drought. It may be because of this change that cranes and caracaras are less numerous now in Kissimmee Prairie than, say, back in the 1930s when burning was practically a ceremonial practice among tenant farmers.

ARCHIE CARR *(1909–1987) was an eminent naturalist, writer, conservationist, and world authority on sea turtles. During his illustrious career, he won numerous awards and honors, including the Daniel Giraud Elliot Medal of the National*

Academy of Sciences, the O. Henry Award for short story writing, the Hal Borland Award of the National Audubon Society, and the designation of Eminent Ecologist by the Ecological Society of America. Throughout his life he wrote on many aspects of natural history, but he was particularly entranced by the wildlife and ecosystems of Florida, where he lived for more than fifty years. Among his many books are Ulendo, Travels of a Naturalist in and out of Africa, So Excellente a Fish, The Windward Road, *and* A Naturalist in Florida: A Celebration of Eden.

TWO HUNTERS

Betty Mae Jumper

On the edge of the Everglades lived two men from the Village of Many
Indians. These two men were hunters who went into the Glades for
months at a time. Sometimes, when the hunting was good, they came
back to the village within two weeks or less with lots of meat which
they would smoke and dry. They hunted deer and birds and picked
up as many water turtles as they could fit into their two canoes. They
only hunted when they had to, when the meat supply had run out.

Early one spring, the two hunters talked about the Big Lake and
how there would surely be lots of game around there at this time of
year. "We will return in two weeks or less," they assured their families.
"Now is a good time to hunt near the Big Lake."

They left in the morning and, on the second day, made camp
near the Big Lake. On the way, the two hunters talked about how the
hunting would be good, for they saw many animals around eating the
green grass. After making camp, they settled down to sleep.

As the sun rose the next morning, they hurried out and immediately killed a deer. It took most of the day to clean the large deer. They
dried and smoked the meat so it would keep until they returned home.
Both men were filled with happiness and good feelings for they were
sure there was plenty of game around and this trip away from the
village would be short. They would return soon with lots of meat for
their families.

They went to sleep early. When they awoke the next morning, they were surprised to see that it was raining very hard. The rain fell most of the day, so they stayed at the camp. In the late afternoon, the rain finally stopped and the sun came out. "It's too late now to hunt," said one hunter. "I guess we'll have to wait until tomorrow. I think I'll take a little walk along the lake."

The other hunter was feeling hungry, so he cooked some deer meat. Soon the hunter returned carrying two big fish. "Look what I found," he said. "Beautiful bass, big and fat."

"Where did you get those fish?" asked the other hunter. "I didn't see you take anything to fish with when you left."

"No," the hunter explained. "I found them jumping on the ground near the lake, so I picked them up. I guess they must have come down with the rain!"

"Go and put them into the lake," said the other hunter, "and let us eat the meat I am cooking."

"Oh no," his friend replied. "These fish are too good to throw away. I'm going to clean and cook them right away." And he did.

After the meal, they sat around the fire and talked. They agreed to start early the next day and maybe kill two deer and fix them before nightfall. Soon it was time to go to sleep. All the night birds were singing away. Somewhere near, in a tree, an old owl was laughing and crying throughout the night.

In the middle of the night, the hunter who ate the fish called and called, "Come here! Come here!" His partner awakened and yelled out: "What's wrong?" He stood up and walked over to his friend's mosquito net. He stared in fright as his friend spoke: "I think I'm turning into a snake. You told me not to eat that fish but I didn't listen to you. Now look at me!"

The hunter started a fire to get a better look at his troubled friend. His legs had already turned into a snake's tail!

"I want you to go home. Don't wait to see how I look. You can't help me now," said the man turning into the snake. "By daylight I will be completely turned into the shape of a snake. Go home and tell my wife and children what has happened to me. Also tell my parents, sisters and brothers. Tell them when the moon is full to come and see me.

"Bring all my family to the lake. Remember the big log near the lake? I want you to hit it four times when the sun is right in the middle of the day. I want them to see me and I want to talk to them. Tell them not to be afraid. I won't hurt them. Now go! Get out of here and run home!"

The other hunter left without looking back, taking with him the meat they had prepared. On the second day he reached the Village of Many Indians and told his friend's family the bad news.

Then the day came for the hunter to take his friend's family to the lake. They arrived at the lake beneath the full moon and camped out, waiting nervously for the next day. Finally, when the sun reached the middle of the day, he led them to the big log and fulfilled his friend's request. He hit the log once, twice, three times, four times. When he was finished, bubbles came up from the middle of the lake. Then up came the head of a large snake. The children were scared, but the older people told them to be quiet and listen to what the snake had to say. The snake floated to the top of the lake and slithered near the shore where his family stood.

Slowly, the snake moved toward them. "Come close," said the snake. "It's me. I wish to talk with you. Listen close to what I have to say, for after this I will never speak again."

When they had all moved close, the snake began to speak again: "I did wrong when I cleaned those fish, cooked them and ate them. I knew better, but I went against the forbidden law of our elders. I am paying for it now. When you leave, I want my family to never think bad about me. Think forward and go on with your life, for I will never be back. This lake is going to be my home. I will live in this water until I die. When you all go, never come back to this lake, for once you all leave, all my memories will be gone. I won't know you at all. I might be mean and I might hurt you. It is the life of a snake I'll be living. Just remember all the good things and forgive me."

The snake turned to his hunter friend: "I want you to please help my family and share meat with them. Teach my sons to be good hunters like you. Make sure they take care of their mother." The hunter friend promised he would.

"Now," said the snake, "I'm coming to the top. I want you to see all of me." And when he did, everyone could see that he was huge, longer than a large canoe. Then, suddenly, the snake went underwater. When he came back up, he was back where he started from, in the middle of the lake. The snake stuck his tail high out of the water and waved it at them. Then he went down deep, deep into the black waters of the Big Lake.

With sad feelings, his family turned and left the Big Lake, never to return again.

———————

BETTY MAE JUMPER *is currently director of communications for the Seminole Tribe of Florida. She was the first Seminole Indian to graduate from high school, and has spent most of her career in tribal government positions, including tribal chairman and editor of the* Seminole Tribune.

WELCOME TO DIKE OKEECHOBEE

Julie Hauserman

In the vast, green-fringed fields of Florida's sugarcane country, only newcomers seem surprised by the Lake Okeechobee dike.

I know I was. Fifteen years ago, a fresh-faced Yankee, I saw the huge blue blob on the Florida map and wanted to go there. Walk along the shores of America's second-largest lake (only Lake Michigan is bigger). Maybe take a swim.

After an hour's drive from the coast into Florida's middle, I dead-ended at a giant wall of earth and grass. It looked like the side of a landfill.

But as many travelers discovered before and since, I had indeed reached Lake Okeechobee's shore, or at least what passes for it these days. A steep, sodded mound, protected from the waves by piles of trucked-in rocks too treacherous to climb.

The Herbert Hoover Dike, as wide as a football field and as tall as a three-story building, stretches a whopping 140 miles around Okeechobee. It's a fat, earthen snake, with towering mechanical locks to let boats through and enormous gates to hold water in and let it out. It took 30 years to mow down the lakeside forests, dredge the marshes, and erect the mammoth dike. By the mid-1960s, the U.S. Army Corps of Engineers was done.

"It's weird," says Nancy Marsh, a grandmother from Lake Worth who paused on a cross-state drive to climb the dike near the town of

South Bay. "You can't imagine them putting a big dike around those Great Lakes up north."

You can't.

But you practically expect it in Florida. The wall around Lake Okeechobee is just one part of a massive manipulation: People came to this state because it was beautiful and, once they got here, promptly began hauling in equipment to turn it into something else. White sand beaches became condo canyons. Meandering rivers became unbending canals. The Everglades became ditched farmland.

And Lake Okeechobee became an artificial reservoir. Years later, we are realizing it wasn't such a good idea after all.

THE ARID LANDSCAPE

There are no longer any true "lakeside towns" around Okeechobee. Like an interstate slicing a neighborhood in two, the dike has cut them off from the 730-square-mile lake for good.

In Pahokee, a Burger King backs up to what would be a waterfront vista. Except it's just a giant, mowed berm looming above the restaurant's roof. Even the rich people in Clewiston, home to U.S. Sugar Corp., see only the giant dike when they look through the windows of their manicured mansions.

"It's what we planners would call a 'visual access problem,'" Palm Beach County planner Vicki Silver says dryly. "I've always thought it had the potential for marketing as 'Florida's Lost Sea.'"

The Corps' giant public works project has an eerie military order to it: ramrod-straight canals, buzz-cut levees, square irrigated fields with razor-sharp corners. But the communities that the flood control project is designed to protect look haphazard: rusty old school buses carry migrant workers through sugarcane and vegetable fields. Rundown shacks sit crumpled along the highway. And trucks rumble endlessly around the lake, taking the region's fertile fruits somewhere else.

Today, mowing and groundskeeping on the dike and the parks along it cost taxpayers $1.5-million every year. It costs another $9-million a year to operate the pumps and gates and other gizmos that the U.S. Army Corps of Engineers needs to keep this once-self-sufficient lake running in an artificial world.

"This monster had to be controlled by bigger levees and by bigger canals," trumpets a U.S. Army Corps of Engineers propaganda film from the 1950s called *Waters of Destiny*. "We've got to control the water and make it do our bidding."

Now, Corps engineers say the aging dike is leaking, and could breach in high water. The engineers estimate that fixing the first 22 miles will cost $64-million—a little less than $3-million a mile. That's on top of a staggeringly ambitious $8-billion—that's billion with a "B"—plan to replumb Lake Okeechobee and the Everglades.

The government has built skinny, steep roads with guardrails leading to the top of the dike. In some places, tax dollars have paid for flat parks on the inside of the dike, down where the lake is. You can't just drive around up there: most of the road is fenced off. Bicyclers hold an annual ring-around-the-lake ride.

Locals stand on overturned bait buckets and hang their arms over tall chain-link fences to fish—not in the lake, but in the artificial canals that stretch out like spider legs outside the dike. The fishermen cluster beneath the mammoth, industrial-looking concrete locks, standing on cement piers without a single shade tree.

I want to yell: "Hey! There's a lake right over there!"

After a rainstorm blew over the lake one sweltering evening in Clewiston, I saw a rainbow—but I had to peer through barbed wire and a chain-link fence to see it.

TEAR DOWN THE DIKE?

Over the years, Lake Okeechobee has acquired a nickname: "Florida's Liquid Heart." And one of the first assaults perpetrated against the Everglades was a very human one: Out of fear, we walled off Florida's heart.

There was plenty to be scared about. Two hurricanes, one in 1926 and one in 1928, turned Lake Okeechobee deadly. The 1928 storm killed about 2,000 people when the big lake broke through an old, five-foot farm dike and flooded towns and farm fields—a natural disaster rivaled only by the Galveston Hurricane and the Johnstown Flood. The wind howled at 160 miles per hour. Nobody in that remote part of Florida had adequate warning. Many of those killed were farm workers who didn't know how to swim. It took six weeks to collect the bodies. Anguished survivors and rescue workers piled up the dead people, burned the bodies, and buried many of them in a mass grave near the lake. For a long time afterward, farmers continued to find skeletons in their fields.

"We have not forgotten the hurricanes of the 1920s," says Clarence Anthony, the mayor of South Bay, a tiny, poor town of farm workers on the lake's southern shore that brags about its newest employer, a prison.

Several years ago, a South Florida planner came up with a scheme to tear down part of the dike, a proposal he later called "radical common sense."

The planner, Dan Williams of the University of Miami, was hired by the government to find a way to revitalize Belle Glade, an impoverished lakeside farming community.

A huge vegetable farming operation owned by U.S. Sugar Corp. shut down in 1994, leaving hundreds jobless. At the town limits, a sign greets visitors: "Belle Glade: Her Soil is Her Fortune."

Williams looked at the map, saw the lake, and asked the obvious question: Why is this community cut off from the water?

His idea: Tear down the dike to reconnect the town and the lake. Use the dirt to build up a new, higher Belle Glade with lakefront homes and water-based businesses. Allow the lake waters to once again run over the fields and build up the soil during the rainy season. Convert the town to a center for organic farming, a fast-growing market.

"Basically, I was run out of town on a rail," said Williams, who—for unrelated reasons—later moved to Seattle.

Belle Glade Mayor Harma Miller, who grew up in a migrant farming family, considered the plan an affront.

"This is a real place," she said. "There are extreme environmentalists who don't want any town here."

Williams believes the dike is really there to benefit the sugar industry south of the lake, which relies on Lake Okeechobee to irrigate cane fields that stretch off to the horizon, a green sea propped up by pesticides, irrigation canals, farm subsidies and cheap labor.

"Tell me: Why were there no dikes put up so that terrible Biscayne Bay wouldn't flood downtown Miami anymore? Because it was valuable waterfront property, and people knew it," Williams said. "There's really no threat now, with modern warnings, that the lake will rise up and kill people. And you're losing billions in ecotourism dollars. It's 140 miles of coastline, gone."

THE GOVERNMENT VS. NATURE

The Army engineers were not the first mound builders around Lake Okeechobee. On the lake's southwestern shore, near Fisheating Creek, archaeologists unearthed a complex of circular mounds built 2,000 years ago by Indians, possibly the Calusa tribe. Some of the circles were house pads, some were ceremonial. Others, the late South Florida archaeologist William H. Sears argued in a 1982 book, were round farm ditches to irrigate and drain crops of maize.

The mound builders left spectacular artifacts that symbolize ancient life around Lake Okeechobee: carved wooden birds, panthers and owls. Near Belle Glade, another mound excavated by the Smithsonian Institution in 1933 yielded ceremonial talismans: four-foot-high totem poles, hair pins carved from deer bones, daggers made from an alligator's jaw, and a bowl made from a human skull.

Today's mound builders, the Army Corps, operate out of an art deco building that sits next to a Clewiston graveyard in the shadow of the Lake Okeechobee dike.

Pete Milam, a towering, mustachioed Marlboro man who started out as a biologist, oversees the massive plumbing system that the Corps created here.

"It is sad that you do not have a lot of public out there" on the lakeshore, he admits, after some prompting. "We want to get people out there, driving across the state, we want to get them off the road and let them drive on the crest of the dike. Here we've got the largest lake in Florida—the second-largest lake in the United States—and you cannot see it."

Actually, it's even worse than that.

Manipulating the shallow lake—dredging up the marshy edges and replacing them with sterile rock; changing the water level to please farmers and thirsty cities; and polluting it with fertilizers, cow manure, and pesticides—has made it deathly ill.

"It's very bad. There's no two ways about it," says Al Steinman, a South Florida Water Management District ecologist. "The dike created an artificial system and allowed us to create a water-supply reservoir instead of a natural lake."

At most of the lakeside parks, there are bulletin boards, covered by glass. Neon orange placards are posted there: "TREATMENT NOTICE: AQUATIC PLANT TREATMENTS ARE PLANNED IN THE FOLLOWING AREAS—SEE MAP. USE OF REWARD/WEEDAR/RODEO."

Pesticides. The Corps and the state have to spray pesticides straight onto the weed-covered water, all the time, to keep exotic weeds from taking over.

The government uses poison, too, to kill Australian melaleuca trees that the Corps planted on artificial islands just inside the dike. Government workers spray pesticides from helicopters and hack into the trees to poison the flesh inside. The melaleucas are botanical invaders, muscling out native plants and gobbling up wetlands. So the Corps kills the trees it planted, then clears the dead trunks away.

"NOTICE: MELALEUCA CONTROL PROJECT IN MARSH AREAS OF THE LAKE. BOATERS WATCH FOR STUMPS," another lakeside notice says.

One day, while Florida Gov. Jeb Bush sat in front of the cameras at Everglades National Park signing a law to provide $2-billion to help re-plumb the Everglades, Pete Milam was in the Corps' Clewiston office, presiding over a controversial hydrological maneuver.

He was releasing water out of the lake to the sea.

When the lake gets high, the last remaining Lake Okeechobee marshes drown, hurting birds and fish. The Corps releases water down two canals: the St. Lucie to the east, and the Caloosahatchee to the west.

By building a system that's dependent on pumps and engineers instead of nature, the government has dug itself into a deep political hole.

The town of Okeechobee, which depends on bass fishing to help its economy, threatened to sue the Corps for drowning the marshes. Martin County, on the east coast, threatened to sue after lake water was blamed for actually eating the flesh off fish in a local estuary. Lee County, on the west coast, sued to stop the Corps from sending lake water its way, but lost in court.

To stop the wrangling over the lake's level, the Corps plans yet another giant, unproven engineering fix. It wants to build huge reservoirs and punch 300 wells deep into the stony aquifer around Lake Okeechobee and the Everglades. When the lake water swells, the Corps would pump water into the reservoirs and then down into the aquifer, a shadowy labyrinth that scientists barely understand. During drought, engineers would pump the water back out. No one has ever tried to use the so-called aquifer storage and recovery wells on such a large scale.

"I believe the lake's going to be better off," said Stu Appelbaum, who heads the Corps' Everglades restoration effort. "We're still manipulating it, but we're manipulating it in a way that mimics what nature did before we impacted it."

Before she died at the age of 108, author Marjory Stoneman Douglas offered a theory about the Corps of Engineers' endless dredging, diking and filling in South Florida:

"Their mommies," she suggested in a voice like Julia Child's, "mustn't have let them play with mud pies!"

WATERS OF DESTINY

In the 1950s, the U.S. Army Corps of Engineers produced a propaganda film to build support for the Central and South Florida Flood control project. Called *Waters of Destiny*, it has the same urgent tone as war propaganda films and even *Reefer Madness*, a famous 1950s anti-drug film.

Waters of Destiny features endless photos of dredges and bulldozers "taming" nature around Lake Okeechobee and the Florida Everglades.

"It's a cult classic," quips Stu Appelbaum, the U.S. Army Corps of Engineers official in charge of Everglades restoration today.

It opens with a shot of tourists frolicking on a South Florida beach:

"Beautiful, carefree, the land that nature always smiled upon—or so it seemed."

(Ominous, dramatic music rises, storm clouds form.)

"Nature was frowning."

(Film shows Florida's cycle of rain, drought, and wildfires.)

"Once lush farmland, now reduced to dry dust by the crazed antics of the elements.

"Central and South Florida just laid there, helplessly waiting to be soaked and dried and burned out again.

"Something had to be done, and something was.

"The going was tough, and many a drill point was dulled in attempts to burl the way for dynamite, foot by foot, mile by mile, the work went on: drilling, blasting, digging, bite by bite . . . slowly, persistently, gouging the bottom to build up the top."

(Photos of alligators and snakes, slithering away from the dredges.)

"You had to watch your step. Progress usually finds anger along its path."

(Patriotic music rises.)

"We've got to control the water and make it do our bidding.

"Water that once ran wild. Water that ruined the rich terrain. Water that took lives and land and put disaster in the headlines and death upon the soils. Now, it just waits there—calm, peaceful, ready to do the bidding of man and his machines.

"Oh, there are still heavy rains. Where the project's been completed, the dams will control them and the spillways release them and the canals take them on, sending them to the appointed areas. They lie there, waiting.

"So they wait—the waters, there in the great natural reservoir of Lake Okeechobee. They wait for the warnings of drought. Now, they come out to spread life on the dried-up soils. Life brought unto man.

"No longer do the waters saturate and destroy the riches of the land.

"Much has been done. Central and southern Florida is no longer nature's fool—the stooge for the impractical jokes of the elements.

"In fact, it's just really begun. . . . The great valley of the upper St. Johns is still somewhat defenseless.

"Was it worth it? Just look around you: What do you see? You see cattle country!"

(Peppy music rises, film shows scenes of a rodeo.)

"Look at it: Once upon a time, this land may have been under water."

(Film shows farmworkers in the fields.)

"Fifty million dollars in crop damage has been saved. Fifty million dollars. Think how much more will be saved, how many more hundreds of millions of dollars in the endless future before us?

"More tourists have come. Cities have grown. Sport has been better than ever. Families are safer than ever.

"For every dollar being spent, four dollars are coming back. As any business man knows, you can't do much better than that!

"Flood control must proceed as fast as humanly possible so that . . . everyone, everywhere, can share in the rich results of man's mastery of the elements."

(Patriotic music rises.)

"Then it shall be that the water—once the fierce, uncompromising enemy of this long, wild, low-lying land, will become its greatest ally.

"Rains may come, but there will be no fear in them. They are the waters of Florida's unfolding destiny, of Florida's glowing future!"

"WASN'T THAT OLD LAKE A FASCINATING PLACE"

"Welcome to Gloriously Natural Glades County!" a roadside billboard shouts.

A few miles down the highway, at the Belle Glade library, I find a 1964 book, *A Cracker History of Okeechobee*, by Lawrence Will, a local historian who survived the 1928 hurricane.

"Although the shores were, for the most part, black muck, low and flat, there were some sandy beaches too," he wrote. "Under leafy branches covered over with a solid blanket of white blossomed vines which made twilight at midday, you might walk for miles and scarcely glimpse the sky."

"The lakeshore's one-time natural beauty is gone, and man, wasn't that old lake a fascinating place."

I pull into one of the little parks inside the dike, my rental car snaking up the dike road and down the other side. Frankly, it's depressing here, even though the lake stretches out, water so big you can't see the other side. The wildness is neutered. Mowed. Edged.

I am thinking about the lost custard-apple forests, about the moon vines so thick they block out the sun. There's a boat ramp here, really just a road that dips into the lake.

A shiny red Chevrolet pulls up with Broward County plates and stops just short of the water. A man and his young son get out.

"There it is!" he tells the boy. They are driving across Florida. They stand there for a minute, by the car's front bumper. The boy picks up some gravel from the boat ramp and tosses it into Lake Okeechobee. There's nowhere to walk, or even wade, really.

They lean against the Chevy's warm hood.

"Well," the Broward County dad says. "You ready to go?"

They've been at Lake Okeechobee's shore for less than five minutes.

"Yeah," the boy says. He climbs in the front seat, and with a roar, they drive off toward somewhere else.

JULIE HAUSERMAN *has been writing about Florida's environment for fourteen years. She won the investigative journalism prize from the Institute for Southern Studies, and was nominated for a Pulitzer Prize for her stories about pollution in North Florida's Fenholloway River. She has been named Journalist of the Year by the Florida Audubon Society, the Florida Wildlife Federation, the Sierra Club, and the Florida Consumer Action Network. She has won the Florida Press Association's Public Service Award three times. Hauserman is a capitol bureau reporter for the* St. Petersburg Times *in Tallahassee and does commentary for Florida Public Radio. She is among eighteen Florida nature writers featured in* The Wild Heart of Florida. *Profit from the book is donated to the Nature Conservancy to help buy public lands. She is also a mom to one daughter, Colleen, and is committed to preserving some of the Florida she loves for her child.*

LOST GOURDS AND SPENT SOILS ON THE SHORES OF OKEECHOBEE

Gary Paul Nabhan

I.

I pulled the car over just past a road-killed possum, under a sixty-foot arching trunk of live oak veiled in Spanish moss. I had stopped near the place where naturalists John and William Bartram signed a treaty with the Creek Indians on November 18, 1765, thereby allowing the father and son to continue southward on their Florida Plant Survey. Walking across the country highway, I stared saucer-eyed at the St. John's River, which seemed a mile wide to a desert dweller like myself. Here, the division between river and forest was abrupt. On one side of me was open water; on the other, there was the shade of pines mixed with an assortment of hardwoods, all underlain by saw palmettos.

Nearby, however, the land and the river graded into tannin-stained sloughs. These backwater habitats reminded me of those described in William Bartram's journal. In 1774, the junior Bartram described an area upstream from where I stood, close to Lake Dexter:

> After going 4 or 5 miles, the land still Swamp and Marshes, observed abundance of Alegators almost every where bask in the sun on the banks. . . . Came to a high Bluff; here the main Land on the west side came to the River . . . went a shore & ascended the Hill . . . left

Palm hill & continued up the River, passing by Swamps & Marshes on each side . . . observed the Trees along the River Banks adorned with garlands of various species of Convolvulus, Ipomea, Eupatorium scandens, and a Species of Cucurbita which ran & spread over bushes & Trees 20 or 30 yards high, altogether affording a varied Novel scene exhibiting Natural Vistas, Labyrinths and Alcoves varied with fine flowering plants . . . all which reflect on the still surface of the River a very rich and Gay picture.

I watched ospreys flying out over the river and spotted a reclusive heron partially hidden in a small clump of cattails. Was the scene I saw today as rich and varied as that which the Bartrams saw two centuries ago? I knew that at least one element of the St. John's River flora was now missing; in fact, it was altogether rare in modern-day Florida. The garland had lost its species of *Cucurbita*, a vine that William Bartram described as "the wild squash climbing over the lofty limbs of the trees; their yellow fruit somewhat of the size and figure of a large orange."

This wild squash could have been the feral gourd, *Cucurbita pepo* variety *texana*. Although absent in Florida's wild vegetation today, it was recently identified from archaeological remains at Hontoon Island, near the St. John's headwaters. On the other hand, several Florida botanists have suggested that Bartram may have seen a different, more enigmatic wild gourd. These botanists suggest that Bartram was actually referring to a hard-shelled gourd later described as *Cucurbita okeechobeensis*, a tropical plant that reaches its northern limits in Florida. It is not closely related to the widespread pumpkins and gourds of the species *Cucurbita pepo,* such as those found prehistorically on Hontoon Island. It is more akin to a wild gourd of southeastern Mexico, first described as *Cucurbita martinezii*. Recently, geneticist Tom Andres and I have determined that the Mexican *martinezii* gourds and the Floridian *okeechobeensis* gourds should be considered distinctive subspecies of the same species, *Cucurbita okeechobeensis*.

These two subspecies share many characteristics; in fact, they are the only wild American gourds with cream-colored flowers. They are cross-compatible, but exhibit certain differences in their enzymes, in amounts of intensely bitter chemicals known as cucurbitacins, and in the oil content of their seeds. In addition, they have been geographically isolated from one another for centuries. While subspecies *martinezii* is locally common in habitats in eastern Mexico that have long been managed or disturbed by humans, subspecies *okeechobeensis* is rare, and has never been collected from more than a handful of localities. Oddly, these localities are places where gourds have had a long association with humankind.

That history of association has been obscured, however, as Florida landscapes have become drastically altered by modern enterprise. Although I was eager to learn more of the historical context of these gourds, I understood the old adage that "a lot of water had already passed under the bridge" as far as Florida's native cultures and plants were concerned. If I were to find any gourds at all in Florida, I would have to search the tropical shores of Lake Okeechobee.

As I returned to the car and began my journey to one of the largest lakes in the southern United States, I realized that I might not find on Okeechobee the shady tranquility of the forests along the St. John's shoreline. I would discover, two days later, that my premonition was correct. Lake Okeechobee was a combat zone, where environmental degradation and cultural disruption occur at rates seldom experienced in other parts of the United States. Although the Okeechobee gourd was still considered part of the flora of the lake's perimeter, its presence had not been reported in six years. Viable seeds of the gourd itself had not been collected by botanists for a decade. Had this little gourd become a casualty on the battlefield between man and wilderness? I went to find out.

II.

After coming through the Brighton Reservation of the Seminoles, then crossing Fish-Eating Creek, I felt at first as though I were entering another country. The levees and dikes loomed large, while canals and drainage ditches seemed to flow in every direction. The Lake Okeechobee region is just as historian Nelson Blake has described it, "an extreme example of . . . human command over nature. Although this body of water covers almost 700 square miles . . . it is almost impossible to get a glimpse of it from nearby highways. Surrounded by a huge wall of earth and masonry, the vast expanse of water can be viewed only by driving to the top of this barrier."

My guide, Jono Miller, had spent fifteen years investigating the ecological changes in wetlands and islands around the Florida peninsula. I first met him in 1973 when we were both students of island biogeography in the Galapagos. Since then, he and his wife, Julie Morris, had become coordinators of the Environmental Studies Program at New College of the University of South Florida. For our trip, he was furnishing his canoe and pickup, his fine sense of humor, and a long-held curiosity about gourds. For my part, I brought beer, hummus, hot sauce, notes with a few vague directions to where gourds had been seen in the past, and the inherent clumsiness of someone who had not been around a lot of water for quite a while.

After choosing a shoreline campground for our point of departure the following morning, Jono offered the marina attendant there a "wanted" poster he had made for *Cucurbita okeechobeensis*. The yellow flier pictured the Okeechobee gourd, asked for "leads" on its whereabouts, and requested that instead of disturbing the plant, those familiar with it should call Jono's answering service. But before we could get it fastened to the bulletin board, the picture elicited a response from the lady at the desk.

"Oh, people bring those things in here now'n then. They must grow right around here some place! Let's see now . . . who could you talk to?"

We were finally introduced to Margaret LePelley, who had been coming to the lake for years.

"That plant . . . oh, so it's a gourd! It's on a vine, a very tough vine. I know, because I tried to pick one when we were out boating one time along the islands. I saw this thing hanging out over the water. I tried to reach it by leaning out over the edge of the boat so's I could pull it off. I thought it would come off like an orange—you know, just like that—but it stayed on the vine and pulled me over the edge into the water. I'll never forget that!"

So here were a couple of elderly women casually talking about a plant that botanists hadn't seen in six years, one that had been proposed (and postponed) for listing as a federally endangered species the Thanksgiving before! "Is the plant locally common?" we asked.

"Well, it's been a couple of years since I seen it, and then it was just here and there. But where it was, it would kind of take over and crawl on everything. It would be along the shore where there would be dry ground. I suppose it would always be there, but for the fact that the water rises and lowers. Seems like it's been high ever since last summer. Well, I do hope you boys find something!"

Those elderly women with their homespun candor convinced us that we had a chance of finding the gourd, a hope that a dozen calls to botanists had failed to convey. We put up the wanted poster, and did some "wilderness camping," as they call it at the marina, on mowed grass beneath a streetlight, with airplanes overhead spraying insecticides for mosquitoes. Our tent's lack of hookups for electricity, water, and sewer qualified us as wilderness trailblazers in a jungle of travel trailers, motorhomes, and vans. The concrete lid of the RV's pumpout station made a level, if somewhat fragrant, table for our night's repast. That night, I dreamed of squashes as big as Winnebagos, dying of powdery mildew, while tiny wild gourds survived nearby.

III.

A coot chuckled, a tree duck whistled, a limpkin cried. Jono repeated back the sounds unconsciously as he paddled along in the stern of the canoe, eyeing the nearest strands of vegetation. While still a boy, Jono had learned the sights and sounds of waterfowl under his father's guidance. Equipped with an anachronistic long-billed swordfishing cap, Jono guided me out among his web-footed friends. It was hard for me to keep my mind on gourds and paddles with all the birdlife around us: rails, purple gallinules, anhingas, glossy ibises, egrets, wood storks, and several herons.

The wind kicked up white caps and made for slow going on open water. Canoeing took less effort once we found a few narrow channels between dikes and island shoals, and our botanizing began. Water lettuce, cattails, hyacinths, waterlilies, and pennyworts edged the canals. Where Everglades-style airboats had blasted through this floating cover, narrow paths could be navigated by boats with small outboards, or by our motorless canoe. On the south side of the lake, aquatic plants rimmed both the shoreline and four sizable islands nearby.

Even the South Florida Water Management District's bureaucrats have recognized the plants of this littoral zone as "the lifeblood of the lake." During two thirds of its 6,300 year history, Lake Okeechobee has provided nutrient supplies and depth profiles adequate to support sizable masses of aquatic vegetation. These plants, in turn, support both the fisheries and waterfowl. The saw grasses, the floating islands of cattails and willows, and the diverse land plants along the channel banks all have enriched the organic soils over the centuries. When Jono and I canoed up through a cut in a levee, we could see more than four feet of deep, black, friable earth.

"It looks like the milorganite they sell you in bags, doesn't it?" Jono commented.

Just then, we came upon a fisherman. He offered us the Floridian phrase that has virtually replaced "hello" in the local vocabulary.

"Catch anything?"

"No, we're rotten fishermen," I said apologetically. "We didn't even bring our poles. We're looking for plants."

"Well," the man laughed heartily, "If all of the fishermen who were unlucky resorted to plant hunting, there wouldn't be any plants left in the whole world! What kind of plants are you aiming to catch?"

Jono handed me a poster to pass from canoe to motorized skiff. "It's a little gourd that hangs on vines covering trees."

"Well, now," he said, uncapping his head and scratching his thinning hair. "That may be what my daughter has wanted me to get her for making into some kind of decoration. She keeps on describing this gourd, and I keep on bringing her those lotus seedstalks, and she keeps on saying that they aren't what she wants. Maybe this is what she's talking about!"

Women, we discovered, have been the ones who have noticed the gourds in the past. Most men are singularly preoccupied by fish.

As we pulled away, this man was still scratching his head, looking at the poster, his line bobbing without any indication that even one fish cared in the least about it. We drifted down a channel along a high dike that once encircled the island, keeping it dry enough for settlers to grow corn there. Though both the farmers and the corn are now gone, other plants that the farmers brought with them remain: castor beans, papayas, bananas, casaurinas, and sow thistles.

We passed another steep-sided dike, and I thought about the amount of buried lake bottom soil that had been dredged up and placed in contact with air. That exposed dike was a microcosm of the entire Kissimmee River–Lake Okeechobee–Everglades watershed, for the history there has been one of separating water from land. European-Americans decided a century ago that the lake's periphery offered the largest reclaimable mass of organic soils left unexploited on the continent. Since then, reclamation projects have drained thousands of square miles adjacent to the lake and channelized rivers into straight canals. These projects have shaped the entire watershed from Disney World to Everglades National Park into a highly controlled agricultural water supply and delivery system. As a result, the rich littoral zone of diverse island and shoreline vegetation has been diminished. The artificial enrichment of the lake by agricultural waste has increased ten to twenty fold, thereby aging the lake through a process of chemical overloading called eutrophication. And as the *Water Resources Atlas of Florida* candidly puts it, "the ability of the system to store and release excess waters to Lake Okeechobee and its ability to purify the runoff it receives has largely been destroyed. . . . A hydrological yo-yo situation [now exists] in southern Florida . . . [and its] effects on their natural plants and animals . . . are ghastly and tragic."

Jono and I had canoed up to a place where the channel was clogged with water hyacinths and water lettuce. What we would see once we portaged this impasse gave us a glimpse of the lake's tragedy, among other things.

We came around a bend, and there, on the lakeward side of us, we spotted a drowned remnant stand of custard apples, *Annona glabra*. The trees stood nearly leafless, in about a foot and a half of water.

They are capable of enduring water over their roots for a long "hydro-period" each year, but may tolerate or even require unflooded soils for brief periods. Formerly, this particular stand of one hundred or so trees had been much more extensive, but it had been permanently flooded when the Water Management District raised the lake levels several years ago.

Jono and I decided to hop out of the canoe, wade over, and investigate the trees to see if they held any custard apples, a popular edible fruit in the tropics. About fifty yards past a muddy clearing where three baby gators were resting, we found a break in the floating smartweed. There, we safely moored the canoe and waded toward the trees.

As Jono sloshed up to the first custard apple tree, I noticed something floating beneath it. I did a double take. There was a single floating gourd.

We picked it up. It was a slightly punctured, waterlogged, hard-shelled fruit with fermented pulp and seeds oozing out the side. What a battered, soggy piece of evidence that a species still existed!

We scoured the vicinity, looking for leaves, tendrils, vines, or their remnants. We dodged floating fire ant colonies, and retreated from spots where snakes swam out in front of us. Each custard apple and willow was checked for evidence that it had served as a trellis for climbing plants other than the ubiquitous moon vine. But no such clues could be found. Perhaps the gourd had floated in from somewhere nearby.

We returned to our canoe, paddled past the wallow where the baby gators had been sunning themselves, and then we floated around a bend. Jono spotted the last few trees in the custard apple stand, and we decided to spot-check them. We waded through more hyacinths, water lettuce, and smartweed toward the outlying trees.

"Is that one dangling under the tree?" I asked Jono. Just then, he spotted another gourd floating under the custard apple. We investigated further. Both of these gourds were still attached to their skeletonized vines, and were not waterlogged like the one we had seen earlier. One, in fact, was dry as a bone, dangling a foot or so above the water's surface. Although we could not trace their vines back to the main stem or root of a withered annual plant, it was clear that they had grown up under this isolated custard apple. In a "land" where water levels could rise at any time, this tree-climbing vine had advantages over those that only sprawled over the ground.

Still, the sight of two gourds ornamenting a dwarf custard apple was a meager discovery compared to the vision of custard apple forests that Florida Cracker Lawrence Will had seen more than a half century before: "When these woods were in their prime, exploring their shadowy domain was an experience you'd not forget. . . . [Y]ou might walk for miles and scarcely glimpse the sky. . . . Gourd vines with their green pendant fruit, looping and lacing from branch to branch, were less a barrier than those yellow strands, tough as piano wire, spun by enormous brown and yellow spiders."

Ethnobotanist John Harshberger added that the lake's custard apple forests formed such dense shade that at any hour "a twilight pervades the solitudes."

From the descriptions of Will and Harshberger, I could imagine the custard apple forests as they had been when they covered 32,000 acres on the lake shoreline and the islands. They consisted of thirty- to forty-foot-tall trees with overlapping canopies, woven shut by a tangle of gourd vines and lianas. This created an understory microenvironment distinct from anything else near the lake. Jono and I could see no such forest now, only a scattering of ten- to fourteen-foot trees, and a couple of gourds hanging on for dear life.

Realizing that the demise of this useful fruit had happened within his own lifetime, pioneer Lawrence Will lamented the changes his contemporaries had made on the southern rim of the lake: "And so now today, of all those millions [of custard apple trees] that once ringed the lake, how many do you suppose there are left? On the marshy western shore of Torrey Island, lonesome, scraggly, and discouraged, you may find a dozen stunted trees, sorry examples of the former forest, and Sherlock Holmes himself couldn't find a dozen more."

Neither Jono nor I compare well to the world's most famous sleuth, but we did encounter upwards of two hundred custard apple trees in various remnant habitats. Regardless of their height, most appeared to be approaching senility. They were usually bare of leaves. Many branches appeared dead. Water stood to such a height on their trunks that a dry gourd could not seed itself in unsaturated soil beneath their shadows, at least not under present water management practices. The chances for their reproduction were low. If the custard apples themselves were not reproducing to any extent, one could bet that the Okeechobee gourds would have trouble reproducing. Their fates seemed intertwined.

Upon returning to the canoe, Jono was somber. He was pondering this dilemma, as if trying to paddle through a choked, disrupted land-scape: "There ought to be just one place," he opined, "where people could still go to see custard apples and gourds and moon vines to-gether, the way the whole south rim of Okeechobee used to be. I think that's the least they could do, to try to keep one custard apple swamp alive somewhere."

IV.

"The least they could do." By "they," Jono meant the South Florida Water Management District, because he spoke with them on the phone soon after we returned to our "wilderness campsite." The District owned the islands where the gourds were found, having purchased the land after establishing high water level policies that threatened to flood the farmers who had cleared the island interiors. Despite the fact that the District engages more natural scientists in work around the lake than any other agency, its personnel had never systematically sought out the gourd, nor done any review of its rarity in relation to their management practices. We decided to make the gourd's presence known. We hightailed it to West Palm Beach the next day.

Once we had found our way through the bureaucratic labyrinth, we were introduced to a couple of the District's environmental scien-tists in a back office.

"We were looking for the Okeechobee gourd and custard apples on the west side of the islands," Jono began, "and wonder if you have aerial photos so that we can pinpoint where we went."

"Oh, you were looking for them from an airboat," one of the scientists commented.

"No, we canoed," Jono replied.

"Oh, then you never reached the custard apple stands up there, that's too bad. The channels are really choked with hyacinths, aren't they?"

"No, we got there all right," Jono said.

"We just had to drag the canoe for eighty or ninety yards through the hyacinths," I added.

"These boys are not candy-asses!" the senior scientist interjected, bemused.

"Well, it's great that you reached the custard apples," the other scientist said apologetically. "But I suppose you didn't see any gourds . . ."

After confirming that we had found the gourds, we changed the subject to water levels. The District's policy is to maintain the lake's level between fifteen feet and seventeen and a half feet above sea level, in order to provide storage of water supplies for agricultural irrigation and municipal needs. During infrequent drought periods, the lake level drops several feet below the fifteen foot minimum, as it did the last time the gourd vines had been seen in 1981. During our visit, however, the lake level was just above the minimum, at 15.2 to 15.3. Given the amount of water already in the gourd's habitat, this meant that the lake level would have to drop no less than fifteen inches below the District's minimum if the gourd seeds were to find unflooded ground for germination. Drought years were thus more helpful to the gourd's survival than the Districts' own water policies.

I knew that the State of Florida listed the Okeechobee gourd as endangered, but I assumed that there were other rare species that were just as much affected by artificial lake level fluctuations. I was curious to know if the District had to take into account the effects of water management on any other animals or plants rare enough to be protected by federal or state agencies.

"In terms of your water management policy, are there any threatened species that concern you more than the gourd?" My question apparently touched a nerve.

"*Any* other resource is more important to us than that gourd!" one of the scientists quipped. "We try to take into account the wood storks and the Everglades kites. But no, no one has ever thrown an endangered plant at us!"

We left some of Jono's posters behind, to stimulate further interest in the gourd. One of the men incidentally offered us directions to other custard apple swamps of which he had heard. Though the meeting was cordial, it was clear that the District's environmental scientists had worries other than the fates of hard-shelled gourds and soft-fleshed custard apples.

V.

On the way back to the lake to search for more custard apple swamps, I was struck by the omnipresence of smoke in the sky. The Everglades region oftentimes has a pale, powder blue sky, carrying vague wisps and puffs of clouds during the dry season. But as common as the clouds are the dirty gray smoke plumes rising over sugarcane fields.

Along the highway, we stopped where one old cane field had just been lit. The fire crashed and cut through the stubble with a cracking sound not unlike that of the machetes we had heard in another field nearby. The flames crested ten to twenty feet above the ground, and we were enveloped in billows of smoke. After the first rush of fire across the field, the cane debris and even the saw grass peat soil beneath it would smolder for hours.

This burning reminded me of what had happened to most of the custard apples that once grew around the lake. While the remaining custard apple swamps face too much flooding today, the historic threats were draining and burning. The reason, as Lawrence Will told it, was simple: "The custard apples made one bad mistake. They picked for a place to grow the finest soil in all the world, and when farmers found this out, then it was good-bye to the custard apples."

The soil of which Will spoke is technically called Custard Apple Muck. It once formed a natural levee on the southern shores of the lake, allowing a diffuse spillover into the Everglades during the rainy season. This earthen bank is a complex layering of rich, dense, black granular mucks derived directly from the custard apple swamps, and fibrous, brown-gray peats from poorly decomposed Everglades saw grass. When farmers originally burned the swampy forest after draining it, some say that the exposed peats caught fire and smoldered for weeks.

John Small, the botanist who named the Okeechobee gourd, observed that "it will not withstand fire." He surmised that "it is less resistant to fire than the cultivated pumpkins, for the flesh of the fruit is much thinner, and when dry, together with the woody shell, readily burns and destroys the seeds." This, Small added, posed a significant problem, since "at least 95 percent of its former geographic area has been reduced by fire to ashes and smoke."

The torching of vegetation to clear it is only one kind of burning. A more insidious kind of burning has occurred on the southern rim of the lake, without a match being struck or tinder being kindled. This is the slow oxidation, followed by drying and shrinking, of organic soils.

The biochemical burning or oxidation of peat and mulch south of Okeechobee has affected about 1,760 square miles of Everglades soils. About 25 percent of these were so shallow that it did not take too many years of plowing and burning to completely dissipate them. The remaining 1,100 square miles in agricultural use may not survive another two decades given the current rates of soil depletion. Lake Okeechobee, then, has not only lost most of its gourds and its custard apple swamps, but also the organic soils that once supported these plants. During the last seventy-five years, agricultural experiment station staff have kept a benchmark by which to measure this loss of soils in the Everglades region. South of the lake a few miles, ground levels have dropped seven feet below this benchmark since 1912. Soils that were once at least eleven feet deep are less than four feet deep today.

What forces have worn away the soil, and exacerbated the extirpation of the gourd, a symbol of the earth for many peoples around the world? While the last century of exploitation has fully exposed the land to this suffering, I sense that a series of cultural disruptions over several previous centuries set the stage. If there had been any significant cultural stability in the Okeechobee region, it is unlikely that devastation of this scope would have been tolerated.

GARY PAUL NABHAN

How long this instability has been pervasive is not known. We do know, however, that between 500 B.C. and A.D. 1545, prehistoric cultures in southern Florida gradually developed considerable knowledge about native plants and animal resources, managed some of the wetlands near the lake, and carried on far-reaching cross-cultural trade. One of these cultures, the Calusa, built permanent homes, temples, and burial grounds on raised earthen mounds near Lake Okeechobee, and adjusted their food-gathering habits to fluxes in the lake's levels. Fish, shellfish, turtles, alligators, deer, birds, cabbage palms, tubers of the coonti, fronds, and wild grains were among their local foods, and others were no doubt traded in from neighbors. One neighboring group was called *Tocobaga* for their home ground, meaning "place where gourds grow."

The Calusa burned to manage patches of cabbage palms and other edible plants, but used other methods for producing food as well. By excavating shallow marshes to build up long earthen beds, they created new environments on which to intensively grow crops. These farm plots, sixty to six hundred yards long, were not unlike the raised fields of the lowland Maya, who shared numerous other cultural traits with the Calusa. The Mayan region of southeast Mexico is also home of the *Martínez* gourd, the other subspecies of the Okeechobee gourd. Geneticists Robinson and Puchalski have suggested that the Okeechobee gourd must have been carried from Mexican cultures during prehistoric times, perhaps by boats that travelled considerable distances along the Gulf coast, or that hopped from island to island across the Caribbean. They note that the gourd's "hard rind and good keeping ability would make it possible for the fruit to be transported from Mexico to Florida, even with the very long time such a trip must have taken. . . . The extremely bitter flesh of the species precludes it from being used as food, but the seeds are edible and nutritious and the fruit could also have been used for its detergent quality."

Calusa settlements may have received the gourd through their extensive trade networks, but these networks may have also hastened their downfall. Once European diseases arrived and infected one Florida Indian settlement, they rapidly spread to others. It is likely

that these diseases, more than battles, slavery, or food shortages, reduced the Calusa down to a few thousand survivors. Then, the surviv-
ing Calusa dispersed, some settling in the Keys and perhaps even in
Cuba. Others at first fought with, and then became aligned with, the
southward-moving Creeks in the early 1700s. Some historians suggest
that as Creeks from Alabama and Georgia readapted to the Everglades
environment, the remnants of Calusa knowledge helped them make
the transition. Along with the Hitchitee-speaking Mikasukees, these
people became known as the Seminole, from the Creek term, Iste
Semole, meaning "free being" or "runaways."

As Creeks, Mikasukees, and Blacks continued to run away from
Anglo-American soldiers and settlers intent on enslaving them and
seizing their land, the Seminole amalgamation retreated further in the
Lake Okeechobee glades and Big Cypress Swamp. There, they raised
small patches of corn, bananas, root crops, squashes, and gourds.
Around Indian Town and other Seminole camps, early observers
reported the large butternut-like Seminole pumpkin and a diminutive gourd. Both of these had vines that would climb into surrounding trees, where their fruits would sometimes hang beyond reach of
the gardeners who had planted them. These hard-to-reach ones, a
Seminole quipped, "were for the 'coons."

The Okeechobee gourd and the Seminole pumpkin species,
Cucurbita moschata, can produce partially fertile hybrids if cross-
pollinated by bees or by plant breeders. Florida's economic botanist,
Julia Morton, has commented to me that she "can't help wondering if the Seminole pumpkin may not be a hybrid between *Cucurbita
moschata* and the wild Okeechobee gourd, or at least . . . accidentally
crossed with it. [G]rowing the vine on trees seems a practice peculiar to
the Florida Indians. . . . [I]ts sturdiness and self-perpetuation, together
with the great variation in hardness of rind, size, form and color [make
it unique]."

Morton has observed that Seminole pumpkins cultivated in Florida
infrequently carry wild traits: extremely hard rinds, green and white
striping, and a strange unpleasant aftertaste, perhaps from low doses of
bitter cucurbitacins. These are all characteristics that the gourd could

have passed on to *moschata* pumpkins after the latter were introduced from Mexico or from the Caribbean in early historic times. Still locally popular in Florida, the fine-tasting Seminole pumpkin may owe some of its distinctive qualities to the gourds.

It was fortunate that both the gourd and the pumpkin had the capacity to persist in a feral state around Indian camps for a time after the camps were abandoned. Warfare frequently forced the Seminole to temporarily abandon favorite camps. Between 1818 and 1856, the United States government attempted either to remove or to kill all Indians remaining in Florida.

Like the guerrilla fighters of modern times, the Seminoles of the nineteenth century would resist, attack, and then retreat into the roadless swamps of southern Florida. From the first territorial governor of the state, General Andrew Jackson, to business-oriented Governor Brown, who thought he could buy them out of the Everglades, the Seminole were considered obstructions to progress. In 1852, Brown bluntly stated that "the most interesting and valuable part of our state . . . is cut off from any benefit to the citizens and sealed to the knowledge of the world, to be used as a hunting ground for a few roving savages."

Despite the implication that the Seminoles were merely savage hunters, the whites on occasion incited conflict by demolishing Seminole plantings of food crops. In 1855, a surveying expedition "raided Billy Bowlegs' garden . . . and tore down his highly prized banana plants. . . . On Bowlegs' return to his garden he flew into rage when he saw the damage done. . . ." The next morning, he killed two whites.

The end of the battle was near, however. Within a year, all but one hundred Seminoles agreed to move out of Florida for money and for the promise of land. Tiger Tail, an old Seminole resister, committed suicide on the way to New Orleans, and within a year and a half, Billy Bowlegs himself was dead. Some of the transplanted Seminoles later rejoined their kin who remained hidden in the Everglades, but their battles with the whites were over by the time the Civil War began.

At the conclusion of the war, the Seminoles and southern whites around Lake Okeechobee were living as neighbors without major conflicts. But northern carpetbaggers quickly saw that the undeveloped land around the lake might make them millions. In 1881, a northern industrialist, Hamilton Disston, was granted the rights to drain overflowed land adjacent to Lake Okeechobee in return for half the area reclaimed. He soon became the largest landowner in the United States, and began the environmental disruption of the lake's watershed that has spelled doom for wild gourds and sustainable agriculture alike. By 1884, his companies had drained over two million acres near the lake.

Although Disston died before his project was completed, his schemes brought in land speculators and cash-croppers from all over the eastern states. By 1910, the government was involved in opening new agricultural lands by building new canals, roads, railroads, and towns.

Destined to be a fertile vegetable growing area, the southern rim of Lake Okeechobee was drained, plowed, and planted. At first not all the vegetable crops survived; the mucks were rich in organic matter, but deficient in certain essential minerals. "Reclamation disease," also known as "muck sickness," continued to ruin certain crops until agricultural scientists determined which fertilizers should be applied to offset nutrient deficiencies in the soil.

Once artificial fertilization was accepted, then Everglades agribusinessmen were quick to accept other modern technologies: drainage techniques, pesticide applications, and vegetable processing for canning. Lake Okeechobee's fringe became one of the first vegetable growing areas in the country where airplanes were routinely used for spraying and dusting. Aerial seeding and even low-flight air stirring to protect crops from frosts were also attempted. With few immediate social or environmental constraints working to slow or offset modernization, one Everglades county adjacent to the lake soon led all counties in the U.S. in the cash value of its crops.

The variety of crops grown, for a while at least, was great. Snap beans, celery, potatoes, lettuce, peanuts, dates, citrus, and cane consistently provided the highest cash returns, and until the sixties, a fifth of all production was spread through a diversity of other minor vegetables. A few diversified family farms became known as "thousand acre salad bowls." Squashes and gourds, however, were never among the significant crops.

By World War II, corporate farming was developing on such a scale that "native labor"—local blacks and Seminoles—could not meet the demand. Migrant workers were brought in from as far away as the West Indies and Mexico. The conditions of the barracks and bathrooms that companies provided were notorious nationally, yet workers had to pay a significant portion of their wages to use these facilities. Everglades agriculture had begun to degrade people, much as it degraded the Florida soil and watershed.

When Castro took over Cuba, sugarcane, an Everglades crop since Disston's time, became a strategic resource that the muck and peat of Florida's custard apple swamps could provide to the entire United States. However, farmers soon learned that as they burnt the cane stubble, the peat soils would burn as well. The old paved roads through canefields now dip and buckle due to the resulting subsidence of the soils adjacent to the roadbeds. The switch to cane monoculture has simply hastened the drop in soil levels.

Profitable cane production does not necessarily go hand in hand with social welfare, either. Today, the run-down company-owned barracks and buses for Cubans, Haitians, and Puerto Ricans are not much improved over those that sparked federal investigations in decades past. Though sugar may be sweet and white when packaged, it leaves puddles stained and stinking with cane char and diesel oil in its wake.

Where the smell of cane smoke is in the air, there is often the feel of cultural disruption on the ground. Cheap alcohol and prostitution may not be more common on Okeechobee's southern shores than elsewhere in the United States, but they are still a blatant reminder of the ripped fabric of life there. In recent years, however, AIDS has become the local indicator of social distress. Belle Glade, on the lake's southeast shore, is reputed to have the highest density of AIDS victims in the U.S., outstripping San Francisco and New York. It is but one of the many common afflictions that white Crackers, Southern blacks, Haitians, Cubans, Seminoles, and Puerto Ricans now fear.

VI

Jono and I finally left the lake's southern shoreline to search roadsides and canal banks leading away from the lake. Within the last decade, gourd "escapes" had been sighted on ditchbanks some distance from the lake. These out-of-place plants must not have persisted. We spent hours looking for other stray gourds, to no avail.

I guessed that weed control along ditches and fields away from the lake would be severe enough to terminate the growth of any new gourd vines. This guess was reinforced by a talk with the grounds manager of a local recreation park adjacent to canals and cane fields.

"Sure, there used to be vines like them here in your picture," she said, examining Jono's poster. "They were over on that edge at one time," she said, pointing.

"I suppose there's a lot of different kinds of vines here," I replied. "This kind has hard-shelled fruit that get to be the size of baseballs. Seen anything like that?"

"No, we don't let anything get that big before we cut it out. If we can't cut 'em, we use diesel oil or Doomsday. We try to get them out as fast as we can spray 'em."

With that, Jono and I left to drive westward, back past the signs that joked, "It never hurts to raise a little cane." As we veered away from the lake, Jono pointed out where more native vegetation was being cleared away. Small patches of prairie wetlands, overlooked during earlier boom periods, were being drained for pasture or for cropland.

"Well, I suppose they'll tell us they can't live on scenery alone," Jono sighed sadly.

Jono Miller had put his finger on an attitude that affects thousands of rare plants and animals. Most modern farmers assume an inalienable right to convert wildland habitats to "productive space." If they are cognizant of the wildlife they displace, they presume it will survive elsewhere. They are in the business of production, not scenery appreciation.

A cane farmer, from this strictly economic orientation, should not be constrained from clearing a custard apple forest full of hanging gourds. After all, even if custard apples and gourds were useful to someone else, he gains no financial benefit from them. He has been encouraged to think of his value to society not in terms of land stewardship, but in terms of the crop production for which he is paid.

Following the logic of self-interest, a farmer can rationalize away any sense of community responsibility. What if his land maintains a gene pool of a crop relative, potentially valuable to those who grow that crop in some other corner of the world? Will those farmers pay him to keep part of his lands wild enough for the gourd or some other rare plant, to offset the loss of income otherwise gained from growing crops? Even if he lets a plant breeder come and collect some gourd seeds, then the breeder and farmers elsewhere, not the farmer near Okeechobee, benefit economically from subsequent advances in crop improvement.

The Okeechobee gourd may in fact have value to other farmers worldwide. It is a source of genetic resistance to powdery mildew, bean yellow mosaic, cucumber mosaic, and tobacco ringspot virus. Its seed oils are admirably high in linoleic acid, a polyunsaturated fatty acid. Of all the *Cucurbita* tested so far, it has the highest content of bitter cucurbitacins, which naturally attract corn rootworms and cucumber beetles. This makes it an excellent candidate as a trap crop or a supplier of beetle larvae attractants for integrated pest management schemes. Such schemes may save farmers millions of dollars in yield losses and pesticide costs for crop plants more vulnerable to these larvae than are the gourds.

The qualities of Florida's remaining Okeechobee gourds are all of *potential* value. Their closest relatives, the *Martínez* gourds of Mexico, have already proved the point. Genes for powdery mildew and cucumber mosaic virus resistance—comparable if not identical to the genes of the Okeechobee gourd—have already been transferred from them to commercial squash cultivars. This powdery mildew resistance is now protecting butternut squash crops around the world. In addition, it is being bred into the most widely grown squash and pumpkin species, *Cucurbita pepo*.

Still, should this convince cane farmers to manage the lake's irrigation system differently, so that gourd habitats will not be inundated every month of the year? Should farmers feel obliged to protect wildlands on their own properties, wildlands that are potential habitat for gourds? If squashes are no big piece of the Okeechobee pie economically, why should cane farmers concern themselves with a few gourds?

In a stable cultural community of local farmers, perhaps such questions are never asked; wildlands are maintained, because worship of the dollar does not drive every farmer toward plowing up all of his available land. But for Florida's sugarcane farmers, involved in an international economy, a global responsibility is warranted, for they themselves are dependent upon genetic resources from other lands on this planet. Ask sugarcane farmers and mill owners around Lake Okeechobee where their industry would be today if gene transfer had not rescued it from the mosaic virus that spread through the region after 1914. Before plant breeders could find sources of resistance to sugarcane mosaic, the virus had devastated three-quarters of the crop. Over $100 million was lost to this disease in the southern states during the epidemic.

Fortunately, genes for resistance were found in wild sugarcanes from Indonesia and other countries of tropical Asia. Three disease-resistant varieties were bred at the Canal Point Breeding Station not far from the lake. They helped revive the sugarcane industry in South Florida, which went on to gain cane yield records for the United States.

Today, modern agriculture is expanding in Malaysia, Papua New Guinea, and Indonesia, where it is wiping out smaller-scale traditional farming as well as the valuable gene pools of wild cane still found in the rural landscapes there. Wild *Saccharum* species such as those now being lost have been used for developing resistance to bacteria, rats, and fungal root rot in recent decades. As geneticist J. D. Miller told Robert and Christine Prescott-Allen, "If no germplasm from wild relatives had been used, there would probably not be a viable sugarcane industry any place in the world."

Since Florida sugarcane was revived through the use of Indonesian sugarcane gene pools, it is equitable for Everglades cane farmers to consider the value of the gourds in their watershed for the rest of the world. The global economy is now dependent upon such humble plants, which will survive only if their value is recognized in their homelands.

VII.

My preoccupation with lost gourds and spent soils subsided as we passed one last time through the Brighton Indian Reservation of the Seminoles. Traditional chickees or ramadas topped with cabbage palm fronds were a refreshing sight after too many smoke-stained sugar mills. Seminole grocery stores and craft shops were loaded with Indian drums and tomahawks for the tourists, but the few Seminoles I encountered still seemed to carry a distinctive identity with them. As Jono and I pulled into tribal headquaters to leave a gourd poster, we saw a woman leaving there wearing "traditional" dress—a blouse and full skirt made from strips of brightly colored cloth, stitched together into a dazzling collage.

We walked into the receptionist's office at tribal headquaters.

"Is it okay to leave this poster here?" Jono asked.

"Sure, go 'head."

"We were wondering if there's anyone around here who grows squashes or gourds," I asked.

"No, I can't think of anyone who would be able to tell you anything about something like that," the Seminole woman replied. Case closed.

"Thanks."

We walked back to the pickup. Jono was grinning from ear to ear.

"Gary, did you see what that woman had on the table next to her desk?"

"Nope, what?"

"A gourd . . . or a small pumpkin . . . It was striped with a slight neck."

We couldn't be sure what kind of cucurbit it was. Perhaps it doesn't matter. But as I left Seminole country, I felt there was still a chance that someone near Lake Okeechobee had a soft spot in her heart for gourds.

(Postscript: Since the rediscovery of the gourd and follow-up research, U.S. Fish and Wildlife Services botanists in Florida have vacillated over federal listing of the Okeechobee gourd as an endangered species. This action has been vigorously supported by many gourd enthusiasts and genetic conservation specialists. However, its ultimate effects on the management of water levels, and the probability of gourd survival in custard apple swamps, have not yet been determined.)

GARY PAUL NABHAN *is cofounder of Native Seeds/SEARCH, and director of science at the Arizona-Sonora Desert Museum. His books include* The Forgotten Pollinators; Songbirds, Truffles, and Wolves; The Desert Smells Like Rain; Enduring Seeds; Gathering the Desert; *and* Cultures of Habitat. *He has been awarded a MacArthur Fellowship, a Pew Scholarship for conservation research, and a John Burroughs Medal for nature writing. He lives in Arizona.*

THE SWEET HEREAFTER

OUR CRAVING FOR SUGAR STARVES THE EVERGLADES
AND FATTENS POLITICIANS

Paul Roberts

Like any modern farming town, Clewiston, Florida, de facto capital of the American sugar industry and, by its own estimate, "America's Sweetest Town," reveals itself to visitors well beyond the city limits. Thirty miles out, the famous sugarcane crop begins—tall, genetically tailored, and emerald green—stretching out like nappy AstroTurf as far as the eye can see. Next come the thick, mile-high smoke clouds as the freshly cut cane fields are burned off. And then comes the smell: the funky, earthy, sickly-sweet odor of cane juice being boiled down into coarse blond crystals of raw sugar. Six months a year, twenty-four hours a day, in Clewiston or anywhere else in the Rhode Island–size piece of drained swamp known as the Everglades Agricultural Area (EAA), the scent is inescapable and unmistakable, a territorial marker that makes newcomers grimace and reminds everyone else what money smells like.

On this particular October afternoon, one week before Election Day, 1998, the lucrative bouquet is especially sharp in downtown Clewiston. Not only has the cane harvest begun but U.S. Sugar Corporation, headquartered here since 1931, is planning a huge bash for the opening of its new sugar refinery. Located on the south side of town, the refinery towers twelve stories over the flat former swamp-lands, a colossal monument to prosperity in the age of consolidated agribusiness. After today, U.S. Sugar will no longer need East Coast refiners to turn its raw crystals into white table sugar but will sell directly to the customer, in everything from 2-pound bags for home-makers to 100-ton railcar loads for industrial users. This is the kind of vertical integration that already defines most of the food industry, and its arrival in Clewiston is being treated like the discovery of oil, or the acquisition of a pro football team, or something less earthly altogether: for indeed, J. Nelson Fairbanks, CEO of U.S. Sugar, is a fiercely religious man who believes his company is on a mission from God and who is, in any case, throwing a party of biblical proportions. Already, workers are unfolding a circus-size tent that, when erected, will boast stadium-caliber air-conditioning, a magnificent stereo sound system, a full-size catering kitchen, and seating for 750. The guest list reads like a who's who of sugar: lobbyists and industrial sugar users, analysts and report-ers, local lawmakers, top state politicians, and congressmen—even Fairbanks's arch rivals, Alfonso "Alfy" Fanjul and his brother, Jose "Pepe," authentic sugar barons whose neighboring cane holdings are the biggest in America and whose political connections in Tallahassee and Washington are so famous that Hollywood has based movie vil-lains on them.

The political tone of the festivities is no accident. Sugar has always been on intimate terms with government, for without it the indus-try could not enjoy its current size and wealth. For example, until recently, growers like Fairbanks and the Fanjuls relied on a federal "guest" worker program for a steady supply of cheap, docile Caribbean cane cutters. And although that particular embarrassment is gone, cane producers remain absolutely beholden to other forms of govern-mental intervention. Nearly every acre of sugarcane in South Florida is irrigated and drained via a costly, tax-supported system of pumps, dikes, and canals that effectively prevents the Everglades Agricultural Area from reverting to swamp while keeping Lake Okeechobee, to the north, from flooding. Unfortunately, this system, in combina-tion with the heavy fertilizers sugar farmers apply to their fields, has degraded the remaining "pristine" Everglades downstream, yielding years of litigation and an environmental catastrophe that will cost taxpayers $8 billion to fix. But not sugar. Although Florida cane farmers are footing part of the cleanup cost, their small share is all but buried under another, more pervasive government handout: a federal sugar program that keeps the domestic price of sugar some 50 percent above the world market price. This sweet protectionist deal not only adds a nickel profit to every pound of sugar produced by large U.S. cane farmers but has abetted the Everglades' decline by encouraging farming in marginal swamplands that could not be profitably planted otherwise.

Sugar is, in effect, getting paid to do some serious ecological damage, an argument made by environmentalists, free-traders, and other critics each time Congress reauthorizes the sugar program, but to little avail. Each time, the industry prevails with an impressive blend of political skill and resources. Between 1990 and 1998, American cane farmers and their sometime allies—sugar-beet farmers, sugar refiners, and the makers of high-fructose corn syrup (HFCS)—poured some $13 million into presidential and congressional campaigns and tens of millions more into local races, especially in Florida, where sugar has spent at least $26 million on everything from referendums to supporting Jeb Bush for governor in 1998.

That's a lot of money, especially from an industry less than one tenth the size of automobiles or oil, and it has forged a chain of political obligations and alliances that is immune to even the most vigorous good-government crazes. Three years ago, for example, the sugar lobby not only throttled a congressional attempt to phase out sugar price supports (persuading six of the bill's co-sponsors to switch sides) but dished out some $23 million to stop a Florida proposal to tax growers for Everglades restoration. And just this April, sugar lobbyists in Tallahassee pushed through a last-minute bill weakening federal authority over Everglades cleanup, then convinced newly elected Governor Bush to sign the law immediately, before incensed environmentalists could mount a veto campaign.

Nor is the White House immune to sugar's charms. In 1996, just hours after Al Gore proposed his own sugar tax and vowed to make the Everglades the centerpiece of the administration's environmental policy, Alfy Fanjul called Clinton, interrupting the President's meeting with Monica Lewinsky, to remind him of the vast sums the Fanjuls had pumped into Clinton's presidential campaigns. (Lewinsky would later remember the caller's name as "something like 'Fanuli.'") Gore's tax proposal vanished, as did the administration's interest in genuine restoration. In July of 1999, Gore presented Congress with an $8 billion, twenty-year Everglades restoration plan, which calls for ripping out hundreds of miles of dikes and claims to let the swamp flow free and wild again. What Gore failed to mention, however, is that the plan is crippled because, at the behest of sugar lobbyists, it leaves virtually untouched the cane farms that helped to create the mess in the first place. If anything, the new refinery in Clewiston is really a colossal monument to a relatively small industry's success in utterly dominating an entire segment of American policy.

With two days till the opening, Clewiston is abuzz with a homecoming-game excitement. Dignitaries have begun to arrive and the hotels are full. The *Clewiston News*'s "Special Clewiston Sugar Refinery Grand Opening Issue" has hit the stands, and a small army of U.S. Sugar publicists has prepared a paralyzing concoction of press releases, backgrounders, tours, and free food for the coming media hordes. Arriving in Clewiston, I'm greeted by Laura Jamieson, a cordial, businesslike flack assigned to me by U.S. Sugar's public relations firm in Miami. Over a small table in the dimly lit Everglades Lounge, Jamieson thanks me profusely for my interest in sugar, passes me several pounds of press material, then outlines my itinerary for the next two days—a nonstop series of refinery visits, executive interviews, and aerial tours, culminating in a front-row seat at the refinery opening, with side options for a fishing trip or a tour of Miami Beach, if the journalistic need arises. It's a blend of Southern hospitality and sophisticated "communications strategy," a full-court press designed to keep me exhaustively informed, thoroughly occupied, and completely out of mischief while I'm in Clewiston.

In contrast, U.S. Sugar's main competition, the Fanjuls, and their company, Florida Crystals, seem altogether indifferent to the press. Neither Alfy nor Pepe will consent to speak to me even by phone, and requests to visit the company's vast offshore cane holdings in the Dominican Republic are steadfastly ignored. The brothers' reclusiveness isn't surprising. Whereas Fairbanks and U.S. Sugar have continued to bank on their image as sugar pioneers with close ties to the land, the Fanjuls have no such cachet. Rich, controversial, and Cuban-born, with Palm Beach mansions and a $500 million fortune, the brothers are easy targets for muckrakers from *60 Minutes* to the *National Enquirer,* most of whom portray the Fanjuls, in not so subtle racist undertones, as symbols of why America is going down the toilet. The unkindest cut was *Striptease,* a satirical 1996 film featuring two cutthroat Cuban-American sugar barons, their toadying congressman, and the dancer that brings them all down. *Miami Herald* columnist Carl Hiaasen, on whose novel the movie was based, called his barons Joaquin and Wilberto Rojo. But any reader of the South Florida society pages had no difficulty recognizing Alfy and Pepe, their collection of yachts and politicians, or their family's elitist disregard for those who work their lands. "Christopher had never been to the farm, but he'd seen photographs," writes Hiaasen of Joaquin Rojo's womanizing, barhopping son. "The cane fields looked like a stinking hellhole; he was astounded at the fortune they produced. There was so much money that one couldn't possibly spend it all."

Begging off a dinner invitation from Jamieson and her P.R. colleagues, I spend my first night exploring America's Sweetest Town, a task that takes all of about ten minutes. Clewiston's 6,348 residents live in a narrow crescent, bounded on the north by the huge earthen levee that keeps Lake Okeechobee from overflowing its banks and in every other direction by cane—a sea of green that laps up against backyards and parking lots, playgrounds and curbs, and fundamentally shapes every aspect of life within. In fact, although cane is grown in some eighty tropical and semitropical nations and states—and sugar beets nearly everywhere else—few spots on earth render the bizarre spectacle of the modern sugar industry quite so visible as South Florida. Three counties south of Lake Okeechobee account for more than half the country's cane production, a focus on sugar so intense and deeply entrenched that, depending on the time of year, a visitor will find not only the U.S. Sugar Corporation and the Sugarland Highway but also Sugar Industry Appreciation Week, the Sugar Festival, the Taste of Sugar Country Dessert Contest, the "Miss Sugar" Beauty Pageant, and even, in the small black town of Harlem, a Miss Brown Sugar contest. Driving slowly down Clewiston's main street, hunting for something other than political ads and Christian rock on the radio, I nearly rear-end a green Ford pickup making a left turn. The driver, wearing the customary straw planter's hat, stares searchingly at me in his rearview mirror, then smiles warmly and makes his turn. His bumper sticker reads: WE RAISE CANE.

Factory and farming towns have always found quaint ways to celebrate their economic mainstays, but there is more to sugar's pull than mere dollars. Sugar has power because almost no one who has once tasted sugar ever wants to do without it. We love sugar, and our affection is physical, an involuntary, evolutionary adaptation that guided our ancestors to fruits and other crucial carbohydrates and that seems to involve the same pleasure-producing neural chemistry associated with opiates. That may or may not explain why people kicking heroin crave sugary snacks, or why, in lab tests, even healthy subjects eat significantly more food when it's sweetened. But it certainly does make clear why the food industry now adds sucrose and other sweeteners— notably HFCS—to nearly all processed foods, from ketchup and sandwich bread to frozen entrées and baby food. Like Elvis or sex, sugar is everywhere and in everything—our economy and politics, our language and demographic makeup, our physiology and mass psychology, and, of course, our diet. Sweeteners now make up a fifth of America's caloric intake: the average American consumes a pound of sweetener, or 117 teaspoons, every sixty hours.

All green plants create sucrose from sunlight, air, and water via photosynthesis. But the most proficient species are the sugar maple, the sugar beet, and sugarcane. And although beets are now the nation's greatest source of sucrose, it was cane, or *Saccharum*, that launched the sugar business and that has, for better or worse, provided most of the industry's visible character. A massive, bamboo-like grass that can grow twenty feet tall, *Saccharum* was discovered in southern Asia 10,000 years ago and by 300 B.C. was being processed into sweet syrups. Crusaders brought a crude crystalline sugar back to Europe, where demand soon outstripped supply. By the fifteenth century, when European explorers sailed south to the African coast and west to the New World, they were driven as much as anything by the need to find more suitable sugar-growing regions.

At a boat ramp just off the Sugarland Highway, on the eastern edge of the Everglades, Freddy Fisikelli slides a battered aluminum airboat into the tepid waters of an irrigation canal and beckons to me. Sixty-nine years old and rail thin, tanned to the color of shoe leather, Fisikelli grew up on the swamp, hunting and fishing until the game and fish disappeared, and is said to know the Everglades better than anyone alive. I've ditched my sugar publicists for the morning to take a ride in his boat, a sixteen-foot-long flat-bottom barge with a huge rear-mounted propeller and a gargantuan 500-cubic-inch V-8 engine pulled from a Cadillac, sans muffler. Fisikelli hands me ear protectors, hits the ignition, and casts off. We motor slowly down the canal until he finds an opening into the swamp. Tugging on the rudder, he nudges the boat through a curtain of reeds and drops the throttle.

From the air, the Everglades look pretty much like what you'd expect from a huge swamp—miles and miles of soggy grasslands sprinkled here and there with trees. But down low, racing along a narrow canal at 45 mph, the effect is much more like being in a jeep on a savanna, with head-high, brownish-green grass stretching off to a flat horizon and a huge, pale blue sky. For half an hour we roar down the watery track, gathering a gossamer sheath of spider webs on our hands and faces and startling the native fauna. Blackbirds rocket skyward, while the larger, wading varieties—blue herons and cattle egrets— heave up and flap along ahead of us for a dozen yards before veering off. Reeds whip by; a dragonfly creases my hair. The canal widens momentarily, and to one side something large and shiny rolls beneath the water. Fisikelli taps my shoulder: "Alligator."

The engine's roar drowns out any real conversation, encouraging a bizarre, vibrating introspection as the landscape flies by. At irregular intervals the boat jogs from side to side as Fisikelli, navigating by invisible landmarks, turns into secluded side canals—right, right, left, right, left—winding deeper and deeper into the marsh. The place is a maze, and I begin to understand why hunters and surveyors who go astray here might spend days looking for a way out—and why drug dealers and other thugs use the place to hide problematic objects. Fisikelli himself has walked out twice after his boat broke down. Once he was just five miles from a road, but it took him six hours to slog through the knee-deep water and muck, and when he reached terra firma, his trousers had been ripped to shreds by the razor-sharp native saw grass. That time, Fisikelli was lucky: he got out before nightfall, when mosquitoes come on so thick that marooned hunters paint themselves with engine oil to ward off bites. I'm about to ask, half-jokingly, whether Fisikelli knows where we are when the track widens, the engine goes silent, and we start to drift across a pond-size space of open water dotted with lily pads and purple gallinules. I pull off my earmuffs. The humid air is surprisingly fresh, filled with the sweetish smells of hay and peat and the sound of crickets and frogs. Waves slap rhythmically against the boat's metal sides. I peer down: the water is still and clear, revealing a few tiny minnows above a copper-colored algae bottom. Looking more closely, I realize that the water is actually moving, barely, from north to south—the slowest river in the world.

The Everglades were created more than 6,000 years ago, when a receding ocean exposed the vast limestone plain of southern Florida. Inundated by heavy rainfall, invaded by subtropical plants that favored the low-nutrient limestone soil, the landscape gradually gave rise to a forty-mile-wide "river of grass" that began at the southern shore of Lake Okeechobee and flowed in a gentle curve all the way to Florida Bay, 100 miles to the south. Actually, "river" is a misleading term. Between lake and bay, the land slopes less than a quarter of an inch a mile; before 1900, water moved so slowly that a droplet leaving Okeechobee would have evaporated and returned to the marsh as rain perhaps a dozen times before reaching the bay six months to a year later. Nor did the river always flow. In the dry winters the river would drop, its waters receding into millions of shallow pools that teemed with trapped fish and were a haven for wading birds, which nested on the temporarily dry ground. In the wet summers the Everglades would again be waterlogged, soaking up trillions of gallons of rainwater like a natural reservoir, filtering it, and slowly discharging to Florida Bay. Oscillating on the extreme hydrological cycle, the Everglades offered a particular environment, amenable to a narrow band of plants and animals and utterly contemptuous of nearly all other life forms.

Especially sugar. For all its association with the swampy Everglades, sugarcane is actually a *dry* land crop requiring constant irrigation yet intolerant of flooding, growing best when the water table lies two feet below the soil surface. In the Everglades the water table is two feet *above* the soil. Or was, before the mid-nineteenth century. That's when Congress handed twenty million wet inland acres to Florida lawmakers, who saw the Everglades as the main obstacle holding their new state back from a rightful, prosperous destiny. "Reclamation" became the rallying cry, a righteous crusade complete with glorious visions of an evil swamp giving way to vast orderly rectangles of cotton, rice, oranges, and, of course, sugarcane. "The statesman whose exertions shall cause the millions of acres they contain, now worse than worthless, to teem with the products of agriculture industry," warbled one booster, "will merit a high place in public favor, not only with his own generation, but with posterity."

Slowly, expensively, crews dredged the muck, and by 1920 four massive canals had been carved from Okeechobee to the Atlantic Ocean, draining the swamp just south of the lake and raising in its place a fertile crescent of new farmland. The floodgates were now literally open. Between 1900 and 1930, southeastern Florida's coastal population jumped tenfold, and with postwar sugar prices sky-high, sugar wasn't far behind. Even as realtors were selling northerners swampland "by the gallon," backers of sugar ventures were promoting the Everglades as a cane-growers' paradise. By one consultant's reckoning, the black saw-grass peat, or "muck" soil, was so rich in nutrients that, properly drained, the region's "fertility will be established, practically *forever*"—without costly fertilizers. Investors came running like children to sweets, among them Charles Stewart Mott, the former General Motors magnate and philanthropist.[1] Civic hopes were stratospheric. In Clewiston, city fathers laid out plans for a sprawling lakeside metropolis of 20,000 souls, complete with a massive street grid and a new moniker—"the Chicago of the Everglades."

They were a little ahead of themselves. Even after drainage the only thing to grow on the unfertilized saw grass peat turned out to be . . . more saw grass. Not only was the soil less fertile than advertised but the climate of South Florida lacked the warmth that cane is accustomed to. By the time sugar farmers solved that small problem— by breeding new strains of cane and, more to the point, by massive applications of phosphorus and nitrogen—the inevitable oversupply of sugar, followed by the global Depression, pushed prices to a few pennies a pound. Many ventures, including Mott's, were driven into the muck. Even after Congress came to the rescue, stabilizing prices by limiting imports and controlling domestic production—and even after Mott relaunched his venture as U.S. Sugar Corporation—the Florida sugar industry remained tiny.

Then came the 1959 Cuban revolution, and overnight the state's fortunes were made. Having embargoed all Cuban sugar, U.S. trade officials filled the gap by encouraging domestic production of sugar through massive incentives. The results were swift and predictable. U.S. Sugar Corporation and its smaller rivals expanded as fast as they could acquire land and get it planted, while engineers drained more swamp. By the mid-1960s, Florida's cane acreage had jumped tenfold; the state's sugar industry now was a real player, with big money and an absolute stranglehold on Florida politics, especially in matters of water and drainage.

The post-Castro opportunities also drew outsiders, among them Alfonso Fanjul, heir to the Fanjul-Gomez-Mena sugar empire in Cuba, a sprawling enterprise that, before Castro "stole" it, included 150,000 acres of sugarcane and ten mills. Forced to flee Cuba, Fanjul had no intention of quitting sugar. Moving to Palm Beach in 1960, he and some fellow exiles raised $640,000 to buy Osceola Farms, which boasted a 4,000-acre parcel of drained farmland in the EAA. By the time of

Alfonso's death, in 1980, the eldest of his four sons, Alfy and Pepe, were doing $30 million in annual sales. Five years later, in a move that confirmed Alfy's strategic touch, the company leveraged $240 million for the sugar holdings of an ailing rival, netting the Fanjuls 90,000 new sugar acres in Florida plus 110,000 acres of sugar in the Dominican Republic. By 1990, the company, now known as Florida Crystals, had not only surpassed U.S. Sugar as America's biggest cane grower but had become the dominant force in sugar politics, pouring money into election campaigns, flying lawmakers around in company jets, even hosting a Bush Administration official at its posh Dominican resort, Casa de Campo. In nearly every way, the Gomez-Mena empire had been reborn.

But by then the thirty-year post-Castro bubble was ready to burst. Health experts were again denouncing sugar. Alternative sweeteners, such as HFCS, were eroding the sugar market while Congress was threatening the sugar program. Labor lawyers, meanwhile, claimed that Florida cane growers routinely, and profitably, abused the thousands of cane cutters brought in each year from the Caribbean—claims that resulted in multimillion-dollar lawsuits and forced the U.S. industry to convert to mechanical harvesting. But the most serious threat came from environmentalists, who argued that phosphorus runoff from cane farms was slowly poisoning the Everglades and that the government's system of canals and dikes had destroyed the swamp's crucial flooding cycle—all as state officials looked the other way. In 1988, the U.S. Attorney in Miami filed suit against Florida for failing to enforce its own water-quality standards. For the sugar industry, it was a systemic shock that would, in the parlance of B movies, either kill it or make it much, much stronger.

"We're talking *phosphorus* here, not mercury or heavy metals." In the small conference room at Florida Crystals' packing plant, Jorge Dominicis, the Fanjuls' spokesman, is tutoring me on the finer points of environmental science. Through a cooperative P.R. deal with U.S. Sugar, Dominicis has joined my media tour and for the last hour has used maps, charts, and a steady stream of gee-whiz comparisons to demonstrate just how overblown the pollution issue really is. "We're talking parts per *billion*," says Dominicis. "It'd be like taking ten drops and putting them into a backyard *swimming* pool." Across the room, Malcolm S. "Bubba" Wade, Dominicis's counterpart at U.S. Sugar, reminds me that phosphorus is necessary for all life; why, the bottled water you buy in the store has more phosphorus than is allowed under federal water standards in parks and refuges. Adds Dominicis: "You'd have to drink 1,400 *gallons* of the stuff to get your daily recommended allowance."

Like much else with sugar, the issue isn't so clear-cut, nor is it simply about the toxicity of a single chemical. When engineers turned the upper third of the Everglades into farms, they effectively severed Lake Okeechobee from the swamp and reversed its natural water cycle. Where the Everglades had been too dry for farming in the winter and so flood-prone in summer that hurricanes wiped out entire towns, engineers could now irrigate farms in winter and drain them in the wet season. City dwellers benefited, too. Engineers built a massive north-south levee to keep Everglades water out of the narrow coastal strip that runs from West Palm Beach down to Miami, home today to 5 million people. And to supply those thirsty urbanites, engineers sealed off huge tracts of Everglades just south of the farms—essentially, the middle third of the swamp—as million-acre reservoirs, or Water Conservation Areas. Almost as an afterthought, in 1947 the bottom third of the swamp was reserved as a national park.

From the window of U.S. Sugar's corporate aircraft, five thousand feet up, the signs of so much alteration are unmistakable. South from Okeechobee, the Everglades Agricultural Area unfolds like an enormous emerald checkerboard, its fields perfectly rectangular, neatly scribed by dikes, roads, and rails. Just below the farms lie the water-control structures—huge floodgates and some of the world's biggest diesel-powered pumping stations, each of which can move 2 million gallons a minute from the farms into the highway-size canals that run south and southeast, toward the coast.

From this height, it's also clear why the orderly layout doesn't work. In the dry season, the EAA essentially dams up Lake

Okeechobee, diverting water that once flowed into the swamp and sending it instead to sugar farmers or urban users. But in the wet season, to keep farms and suburbs dry, canals in and around the EAA carry away the rainwater as fast as it falls. Some is pumped into the Water Conservation Areas, often faster than the swamp can absorb it, drowning out bird and wildlife populations there. The rest—several hundred billion gallons a year—is simply sent down the main canals "to tide" (where this unnatural flood of fresh water is destroying Florida's delicate saltwater estuaries). Not enough water remains to filter down to the last pristine sections of swamp in Everglades National Park. In other words, while the lower glades are starved of water, the upper glades are drowning—a bizarre and ugly situation that has nonetheless allowed sugar officials to insist that the *real* Everglades problem isn't water *quality* as much as water *quantity.*

In fact, the sugar industry knows good and well that water quality and water quantity are inseparable. By draining the saw-grass muck, engineers exposed underwater soils to the air, allowing fertilizers and natural nutrients to oxidize, thus freeing them up to blow away as dust or float off in rainstorms. Over time, up to six feet of phosphorus-laden topsoil has washed from the farms into the Everglades. Granted, phosphorus isn't particularly toxic, and farm runoff concentrations were relatively tiny—200 to 500 parts per billion. But keep in mind that the original Everglades vegetation developed in the nutrient-poor limestone soils, and that even a little phosphorus goes a long way. In the pristine parts of the park, water contains only a few parts per billion (ppb) of phosphorus. But research shows that as concentrations rise even slightly, native plants, such as saw grass, react—first by growing to monstrously unnatural sizes, then by dying off and giving way to phosphorus-loving species, such as cattails.

Exactly how much phosphorus the swamp can tolerate before changes occur is, naturally, a subject of ferocious debate. Ron Jones, a microbiologist at Florida International University and a veteran of the Everglades controversy, claims that 5 ppb to 7 ppb is the natural level, with a maximum of 10 ppb. Sugar scientists say it's higher—as much as 50 ppb. Regardless, changes are occurring. In the national park, for example, cattails are almost nonexistent. But move north and cattail density rises, until, in the upper parts of the Water Conservation Areas, where farm water discharges, cattails have completely replaced saw grass and caused a ripple effect through the Everglades' ecosystem. Cattails grow so thickly that wading birds—the wood storks, white ibises, great egrets, and others—have no place to land. They also have nothing to eat, since all this new plant life sucks oxygen from the water as it dies and decomposes, killing algae and the fish that feed on it. The process is known as eutrophication, and the numerical impacts are staggering. As feeding and nesting sites have dwindled, the annual breeding population of wood storks in South Florida, for example, dropped from twenty-five hundred in 1960 to only several hundred today. The Cape Sable seaside sparrow, dubbed by ecologists an indicator species for the swamp, has dwindled from the tens of thousands to roughly 3,500. Similarly severe declines are reported for American crocodiles, snail kites, and other birds and animals—declines that usually presage outright extinction. "Cattails are the grave marker," says Jones. "But the first sign that things are amiss is saw grass that has had too many nutrients and is fifteen feet high. Wading birds don't care if it's fifteen-foot saw grass or fifteen-foot cattails; they can't land. It's a mess."

Nearly everyone involved in this debate agrees that saving the Everglades requires two basic actions: reducing phosphorus and restoring some or most of the swamp's historic water flow. Both are far easier said than done. It costs many millions of dollars to remove each additional part per billion of phosphorus, and the preferred method—building huge, artificial filtration swamps just downstream from the farms to cleanse the runoff—has had mixed results in tests. Similarly, the only feasible means of restoring water flow is to tear out all the dikes and canals, elevate the bisecting highways, and, above all, convert a sizable chunk of sugar's precious acreage back into swamp in order to reconnect Okeechobee with the Everglades. Not surprisingly, neither approach has much appeal to an industry accustomed to guaranteed profits and an ever-expanding landbase. So for the last decade, sugar makers and their political allies—including a sizable congressional contingent, dozens of Florida officials, nearly the entire state legislature, and, with depressing regularity, the Clinton Administration—have done all they could to ensure that the Everglades problem remains unsolved.

The U.S. Attorney's suit offers a dramatic case in point. After failing to get it dismissed, sugar companies and state officials, including then-governor Bob Martinez, lobbied the Justice Department to remove the U.S. Attorney, a Republican named Dexter Lehtinen, from the case. Justice refused, so sugar spent millions of dollars on private research to discredit Ron Jones, Lehtinen's star expert. (During discovery, the state's lawyers were forced to produce a folder labeled "More Dirt on Jones.") Then, after the state broke with the industry in 1991 and agreed to cut phosphorus levels by building expensive filtration marshes, sugar lawyers filed three dozen lawsuits to keep the deal from being implemented. One Justice Department attorney called it "the most aggressive and skilled stonewalling I have ever seen."

Sugar hadn't even begun to fight. Stymied in court, the industry wooed friends in higher places, pouring millions of dollars into the 1992 campaigns. The traditionally Republican Fanjuls, for example, played both sides: Pepe vice-chaired the Bush-Quayle Finance Committee, while Alfy joined the Clinton-Gore team, hosting a $120,000 fund-raiser and smoothing Clinton's way into the staunchly Republican Cuban-American community. "Alfy Fanjul became a Democrat because he has an empire to protect," one state Democratic activist told Miami's *Daily Business Review*. "He's developing his own way to be heard."

And heard he was. In March 1993, Alfy Fanjul met privately with Bruce Babbitt, Clinton's new interior secretary, presenting him with an Everglades restoration plan drawn up by Florida Crystals' scientists. And lo! When Babbitt unveiled the administration's restoration plan at a July ceremony, it bore an uncanny resemblance to Fanjul's plan— stipulating, among other things, that state taxpayers would pick up more than half the estimated $700 million for the filtration marshes. Babbitt denied any link between Fanjul campaign dollars and the administration's plan, but Alfy Fanjul himself made no such protestations. Speaking directly after Babbitt at the ceremony, Fanjul held up the new plan as proof that "the Clinton Administration delivers."

Clinton would keep delivering. In 1994, Florida Crystals persuaded Babbitt to turn the Everglades matter back over to the state legislature, thus bypassing the federal courts in favor of a political body over which sugar had enormous sway. Exploiting the homecourt advantage, sugar recruited an all-star lobbying team, including two former state house speakers and Governor Lawton Chiles's former chief of staff, then launched a media blitz to downplay the phosphorus problem. "We're talking parts per billion," and "drops in a swimming pool" became standard industry tropes, as did dark hints that development might replace sugar if regulations forced growers out of the EAA.

Victory was never in doubt. At a May 1994 ceremony in Everglades National Park, with Babbitt looking on, Chiles signed the Everglades Forever Act.[2]

Written mainly by sugar lobbyists, the new state law capped industry cleanup costs at $320 million, obligated taxpayers for the remainder, and suspended state water standards until 2003, at which point state officials, not federal scientists, would determine an allowable phosphorus level. Efforts to restore water flow met a similar fate. When federal scientists suggested reconnecting Okeechobee to the remaining Everglades by buying and converting nearly a third of the EAA into a massive flow way, sugar interests went ballistic. The administration publicly denounced the scientists and their proposal, effectively signaling that the sugar farms were off-limits for any future restoration efforts. Indeed, by 1996, when administration officials began talking boldly about ripping out dikes and restoring natural water flows—a plan known as the Army Corps Restudy—it was understood that restoration would occur *south* of the sugar farms, even though most technical staff knew that such an exclusion effectively undermined genuine restoration. Editorialists and some environmentalists complained bitterly. But, as he had done with nearly all his liberal constituencies, Clinton exploited divisions within the green community, scolding critics and stroking supporters. By 1996, big groups like World Wildlife

Fund and National Audubon Society were not only backing the White House plan but actively criticizing any greens who opposed it.

For many critics, sugar prevailed because it bought lawmakers. Yet the industry's main advantage was to have grasped, earlier than most, how badly Clinton needed Republican-leaning Florida for his reelection bid—and how perfectly the Everglades fit into that strategy. In a trademark Clinton move, the president's team calculated that even a weak restoration plan would still let Clinton look green to urban voters without enraging key contributors, such as sugar and real estate interests, and without undercutting state Democrats—among them U.S. Senator Bob Graham, a Clinton ally and the main architect of Clinton's Everglades policy.

Sugar's presidential aspirations almost backfired. Florida was a GOP prize as well, and by mid-1995 candidates Richard Lugar and Bob Dole had promised hefty restoration packages; Lugar went so far as to propose that they be partly funded through a mechanism sugar abhorred: a growers' tax. To sugar's horror, the White House joined the chorus, dispatching Gore to Everglades National Park to propose a "polluters' tax" and, worse, to promise to convert at least 100,000 acres of sugar farms back into swamp. When Alfy Fanjul made his infamous call to the White House on President's Day, he was apoplectic. "Alfy felt betrayed," says a lobbyist who asked not to be identified. "He'd campaigned for Clinton, delivered a lot of votes, and here was Gore paying him back with a tax. Alfy was actually bitching [Clinton] out. Just yelling." Too late. Although the White House dropped the "polluters' tax," the idea had already gained enough momentum to appear on a statewide ballot initiative in 1996. With $13 million in funds, much of it from wealthy donors, a group called Save Our Everglades (SOE) campaigned on the theme of sugar's greed: surely an industry with subsidized profits of a nickel a pound could spare a penny to fix its own mess. The Fanjuls made especially plump targets, with their sumptuous Palm Beach lifestyle, their crass campaign spending, and their foreignness. With months to go till the election, polls showed the industry twenty-five points down and headed for a slaughter.

But again, opponents had misjudged sugar's adaptive powers. In *Striptease*, when the Rojo sugar empire is threatened by a blackmailer, the brothers simply hire hit men and have the body thrown into Lake Okeechobee. In real life, sugar's hired guns were strictly political, but they attacked the environmentalists with the same single-minded intensity. Armed with $23 million in PAC money, sugar companies launched a sophisticated media campaign that painted the initiative as a radical move that would kill jobs and raise everyone's taxes. Latino newspapers and radio were filled with ads comparing one of the initiative's wealthy backers with Castro. Jesse Jackson was brought in to tell black voters that the tax was "a showdown between alligators and people." Seniors and condo dwellers were bused to the cane fields for "informational" tours and a free lunch. Voters heard how the measure would raise property taxes throughout the state, even though the sugar tax applied only to sugar farmers within the EAA. But no blow was too low. When sugar executives learned of a $1,000-a-plate SOE fund-raiser at Miami's Fairchild Tropical Garden, U.S. Sugar announced plans to bus in a thousand workers for a $1-a-plate hot-dog dinner on an adjacent lot, forcing environmentalists to cancel. In the final three weeks, sugar outspent its opponents seven to one with a $5.2 million ad blitz. On Election Day, voters crushed the initiative in what a *Fort Lauderdale Sun Sentinel* editorial called "a triumph of disinformation" and "voter confusion, most of it deliberately created by the two largest sugar growers."

In Florida, it's the same story. In 1998, sugar lobbyists hammered through a variety of pro-sugar bills, including one to give state lawmakers line-item control over all future restoration efforts—in essence, handing the issue once again to the one legislative body most in sugar's pocket. In the end, Governor Chiles vetoed the bills, but only after weathering yet another phony grass-roots call-in campaign. At the time, Chiles's office reported receiving hundreds of calls from people "who sounded confused or uncertain, and [our operators could hear] people in the background coaching them." When questioned, callers admitted that they were cane-field workers, adding that "they had been told by their employer they would lose their jobs" if the bills were vetoed.

Whether newly elected governor Jeb Bush will continue the tradition of sugar toady is yet to be seen. This summer, Bush surprised environmentalists by arguing for a phosphorus standard of 10 ppb—lower than industry had asked for. At the same time, however, Bush has fought to keep all enforcement of that standard at the state level. And as for the sugar growers themselves, although the new refinery signals that U.S. Sugar is here for a while, Florida Crystals' long-term strategy has never been as certain. The topsoil on its farms was thinner to begin with and thus far more vulnerable to subsidence. That, say critics, makes it far more likely that the family will farm until the land no longer supports sugar; then they will sell their acreage to developers and move off shore, a threat the Fanjuls have been making for years.

The swamp itself has no such escape clause. Although a federal judge is expected to rule sometime this year on a deadline for the state to issue a phosphorus standard, it's not clear how such a standard will be met. In tests small filtration marshes have cut phosphorus levels in outflow water down to 20 ppb—still twice the recommended level—but federal and state scientists expect the effectiveness to drop sharply as the superexpensive filters saturate with phosphorus.

Even gloomier are prospects for a restoration of historic water flows. Despite all the bravado Gore displayed as he presented the administration's plan to Congress in July—"after three years of work, we now have a final plan that is terrific for the environment, terrific for communities, terrific for business, and saves a world and national treasure"—the plan gets poor marks from Everglades scientists. Researchers praise the goal of removing some 240 of the 1,800 miles of levees and canals. But because the plan would convert just 50,000 acres (rather than the recommended 150,000 to 200,000 acres) of sugar farms into rain reservoirs, scientists say it fails to reconnect Lake Okeechobee and the Everglades, or reverse the cycle of drought and flood that have pushed the swamp into a coma. As a result, the various chunks of the remaining pristine Everglades—the national park, several state preserves, and the lands owned by the Miccosukee tribe—now exist in a kind of eco-competition, fighting to get enough water in the dry season and avoid it in the wet season. In a report last year, the science staff at Everglades National Park rejected the plan because it "largely retains the fragmented management and compartmentalization characterizing today's Everglades." The staff found "insufficient evidence" to suggest that the Clinton plan would bring "recovery of a healthy, sustainable ecosystem" and, in fact, found "substantial, credible and compelling evidence to the contrary."

Still, if the plan is not exactly what doctors ordered for a sickly ecosystem, it truly is, as Gore notes, "terrific for business." In a deftly timed move to help the struggling presidential contender woo Florida's politically powerful development lobby, the Clinton plan guarantees the urban southeast coast enough water for roughly twice its current population—even while depriving the Everglades of sufficient water in the dry season. "They've turned 'restoration' into a huge water-supply project," gripes Joe Browder, Washington environmental consultant and a longtime Everglades advocate. And, of course, sugar companies just love the Clinton plan, since it won't cost them a dime, doesn't interrupt their irrigation or drainage regimens, takes only a small chunk of farmland, and, best of all, makes it considerably easier to sell the public at large on the concept that the Everglades "problem" is being taken care of. In the summer of 1999, less than two weeks after Gore sent his $8 billion restoration plan to Congress, President Clinton wrapped up his inner-city tour by jetting down to tony Coral Gables for a $25,000-per-couple Democratic fund-raiser. The host was none other than Alfy Fanjul, who was probably in a cackling good mood, knowing that all the talk of a substantial change in the Everglades status quo had been just that—talk—and that, at least for America's sugar barons, it would be business as usual for the foreseeable future. During a newspaper interview, Fanjul opined that Bill Clinton had been "a great president."

Out in the swamp Freddy Fisikelli points his airboat northward. We pass an old fishing camp—essentially, a mobile home on stilts, with two airboats tied out front and four men sitting on the deck, drinking beer and staring at us. No one is fishing. Fisikelli waves and cruises by, moving slowly, keeping the big V-8 quiet enough for conversation. He tells me how he used to want to be a cowboy, back in the 1930s and '40s, when cattle, not cane, was king in the Everglades. He talks about hunting for duck and deer and boar, and how he first began to notice the changes—the dwindling numbers of birds and animals, the bizarrely huge vegetation, even the way the swamp had begun to smell. Fisikelli falls silent for a moment. Up ahead, still out of sight, is a massive floodgate known as S-10, which lets out water from the farms into the Water Conservation Areas. Phosphorus around S-10 has been measured as high as 500 ppb, and the closer we come to the floodgate, the more the saw grass gives way to cattails, many of them incredibly tall from the overly fertilized soils below. Fisikelli eases back on the throttle and lets the boat drift on the molasses-slow current. I peer over the edge of the airboat. The water is murkier here, and the minnows are gone. "Smell that?" he asks. The once-fresh breeze is now tainted with the slightly sulfuric scent of rot, as the overabundant cattails die and decompose. Fisikelli shakes his head, then slowly turns the boat around, and heads back south, toward cleaner water and away from the smell of money.

NOTES

1. *U.S. Sugar is still partly owned by the Mott Foundation, whose devotion to environmental causes has yet to reach Florida. In the 1990s, the foundation spent $800,000 saving a South American wetland; in 1996 alone, U.S. Sugar spent $3 million to defeat efforts to protect the United States' largest wetland.*

2. *Asked by one environmentalist how he could support the deal, a grim Babbitt replied, "It's my job."*

PAUL ROBERTS *is a contributing editor of* Harper's *magazine.*

LOSING GROUND

SOIL SUBSIDENCE IN THE EVERGLADES

Juanita Greene

Over the half-million acres of drained Everglades south of Lake Okeechobee hangs a long-established but persistently ignored truth: the soil is disappearing. Sometime this century the Everglades Agricultural Area (EAA) will be down to bare rock, unless it is reflooded.

Historically, this is a fact that people in the Glades knew, but didn't know. They could see the evidence of soil subsidence, but they refused to believe it. Even today, the vanishing land, most of it in sugarcane, is a subject seldom discussed. There are no plans to put the water back on the land now while there still is some soil left. Nor are plans being made to protect the EAA from urban development once the soil becomes so thin it no longer can be farmed.

The EAA sits in the heart of the Everglades, extending south and southeast of Lake Okeechobee. It is about fifty miles wide and twenty-five to forty miles deep. Its eastern edge presses against the urban palm beaches, and its southern boundary meets publicly owned water conservation areas. Its total size is about 700,000 acres, of which about 550,000 acres are under cultivation, 90 percent of which is in sugarcane.

It was here that Lake Okeechobee periodically overflowed its banks and added water to the slow-moving river of grass, life source of the Everglades, but most of the EAA was drained about fifty years ago with the first entry of the Army Corps of Engineers into the Everglades. Here saw grass once grew tallest—ten feet or more. The peat and muck were thickest, and the water levels were among the highest in the Everglades, providing an abundance of natural storage for the ecosystem. Today, the drained EAA acts as a huge dam, blocking the shallow sheet flow of water that once began north of Lake Okeechobee and ended at the tip of the Florida peninsula, in Florida Bay, 140 miles to the south.

Current plans to restore the Everglades devote scant attention to the EAA and none at all to the prospect of restoring it to its former function as headwaters of the river of grass. Government's only significant move has been to purchase from the Talisman Sugar Corporation about sixty thousand acres of sugar land at the south end of the EAA, where the soil is thinnest, to be used as a water reservoir.

Knowledge that the drained Everglades soil would subside was available even before the first dredge arrived south of Lake Okeechobee around the turn of the twentieth century. It was ignored long after the time that extra doorsteps routinely had to be added to Everglades houses so occupants could reach the ground, and well past the time when backyard septic tanks took on the appearance of solitary graves as the dirt around them disappeared. In 1924 a post driven into the bedrock showed that the soil was nine feet deep at Belle Glade. Now the depth is only about three feet at the same spot.

Organic soils are found around the globe, but one of the largest areas of peat and muck to be converted to agriculture is the Everglades, particularly south and east of Lake Okeechobee. It is one of the world's richest farming areas. Most soils are mineral based and contain sand, silt, clay, and other materials that come from rock. Muck soils contain 25 to 65 percent organic matter; peat contains 65 percent or more. Peat and muck are created when organic matter, such as saw grass and other plants, amasses in lush, sometimes submerged areas like the Everglades faster than it can decompose. When the plants are submerged, water shuts off the oxygen that causes matter to rot. When the water drains, the rotting resumes. "The process keeps us from being up to our ears in plant material," said Dr. George Snyder, professor of soil chemistry at the University of Florida's Belle Glade research center.

Drained organic soil dries, shrinks, compacts, and turns powdery. Wind carries it away. Fires burn it up. Most damaging of all, biochemical oxidation and subsidence begin as invisible bugs satisfy ravenous appetites.

In the early days, before sugarcane farming came to dominate the EAA, subsidence was less of a problem. But in the early sixties, after the Castro revolution in Cuba, sugar imports from the island were cut off and exiles from Cuba moved their sugar operations to the Everglades, into extensive lands that were uncultivated or in cattle. Sugarcane took over the Everglades Agricultural Area.

Subsidence in the sugarcane fields is hastened by the manner in which the South Florida Water Management District controls the water on them, with the help of some of the world's largest pumps, owned by the taxpayers. Sugarcane can't tolerate groundwater too near the surface, so the water table is kept lower than it is beneath fallow land or pasture land.

Draining the organic soil also increases the amount of pollution sent from the EAA into Lake Okeechobee to the north and the Everglades to the south. Peat and muck contain phosphorus, which is released when the soil is dried. The natural Everglades can take only a very small amount of phosphorus, no more than ten parts per billion, and maybe even less. With more than that, exotic plants take over and crowd out natural flora, such as saw grass.

It took many centuries for nature to create the three thousand square miles of organic land that lay at the bottom of the Everglades floodway. The shallow channel was fertile ground for aquatic plants, growing and dying and dropping under the hot sun. When the first adventurers began to explore the Everglades in the early nineteenth century, they moved through sharp, triple-edged saw grass that was more than head high. They poked long rods in the muck and peat and learned it was eight to fifteen feet deep.

Out there on the steaming, smothered plain, a dream was born. People would drain the Everglades, create an agricultural Eden, and get rich. The dream invaded the public psyche as early as 1837, when the Second Seminole Indian War gave the country a flashing glimpse of the awesome land. The Everglades might be drained, wrote one John Lee Williams, Esq., by deepening its natural outlets. By the time Florida became a state in 1845, many of its officials were convinced that drainage was possible. A survey headed by Buckingham Smith, an aristocrat and state leader from St. Augustine, agreed with them. Here was fertile land in a somewhat tropical setting, where crops should be able to grow the year around. All that was needed was to get the water off the land. There surely was great bounty to be reaped with little labor. Just scratch the ground and plants will grow. Or so it seemed.

Before the end of the nineteenth century, Floridians were beginning to learn about subsidence. The first great wetlands drainer in South Florida, Hamilton Disston, was growing sugarcane in the Upper Kissimmee River valley north of Lake Okeechobee in 1890. One of his scientific advisers urged him to move to the Everglades, describing it as ideally suited for sugar plantations. In 1909, results of official studies stated that if the organic soil was drained, it would soon begin to disappear, that even careful handling would only slow the process. The report was delayed and, essentially, buried. By this time, too, Governor Napoleon Bonaparte Broward had launched his big drainage project in the Glades.

The subsiding soil was mentioned again in a 1913 publication that minimized the problem. Loss rates from subsidence, it said, were exaggerated. The author predicted that no more than about eight inches eventually would disappear. So the populace believed, although reality proved otherwise. Not until the 1920s, when visible signs of subsidence were all over the Everglades, did engineers begin to consider subsidence in their designs, taking into account that canal depths would diminish as the banks eroded.

In 1926, a hurricane ripped through Miami, proceeded to the Everglades, and blew the water out of Lake Okeechobee, drowning people and farms on the southern rim. Because of subsidence, the drained land had receded over the years, forming a bowl to draw the high water from the lake. A 1927 report from the Everglades Drainage District, based on fifteen years of data, found that up to 4.6 feet of soil had been lost. Still, the authors predicted that at some point the subsidence would slow and eventually cease.

"How such a conclusion could be reached by such eminent engineers is difficult to understand," wrote engineer Lamar Johnson, who held important posts in both the old and new Everglades water districts. "The conclusion did reflect the hope of the farmers of the organic soil in the Everglades," he added.

Later, Johnson himself and J. C. "Jake" Stephens, research project supervisor for the U.S. Soil Conservation Service's Everglades Project, gathered up all available data on subsidence, did some research of their own, and came out with a report. It found that the soil was disappearing at the rate of about one foot every ten years. The future held little chance for continued farming in the Everglades, they said. The Everglades Drainage District, Johnson's agency, would not release the report. It became public in 1951 when Johnson and Stephens were invited to speak before a private group, the Soil Science Society of Florida. The audience included many Everglades farmers.

Johnson told the group that the rapid rate of subsidence "means, of course, that we must develop these Glades lands as rapidly as possible, to mine them for everything they are worth if we are to get out of them their total value as a natural resource so long as they last." At about the same time the Army Corps of Engineers was preparing to drain hundreds of thousands of additional acres in the EAA as part of its project.

Some of the farmers at the 1951 meeting dismissed the predictions in the Johnson-Stephens report. Others expressed hope a solution to the subsidence could be found, or complained that none had been offered. "They haven't given me an answer to prevention or cure," said George Wedgeworth, whose family had longtime holdings in the Glades. Others felt a little contrite. "We didn't come in to make our money quick and then get out. We didn't come to mine this good land," said Harrison Raoul, manager of a large plantation in the middle of the Glades. His land was disappearing, he said, "because I just didn't know what I was doing." Like many, he refused to believe nothing could be done. He said his farm would experiment with growing aquatic crops. One man wanted to know what he could tell all the wealthy northerners he had talked into investing in the Everglades. A county agent said he was getting a lot of requests for information, but was left with nothing to do but "listen to land speculators."

Forty years later, in 1993, Stephens acknowledged that he and Johnson "had had a little trouble getting published.

"Behind the scenes," Stephens said, "I perceived that the Corps didn't want this published until they got their plan. I expect, but I can't prove it—wouldn't want to prove it—but there was a little objection up there to this until they got a little further along." The corps project for draining the EAA, he said, would need a long life to justify its favorable cost-benefit ratio. Predictions that the land eventually would disappear did not do much to support the claim that benefits would outweigh costs, he said. Stephens and Johnson decided to write their report, he said, because "there were so many people jumping up and down and saying their land was not subsiding. We had to try to convince the farmers they had a problem."

About twenty years after the two men finished their subsidence report, Johnson wrote of his Everglades experience in *Beyond the Fourth Generation,* a book published in 1974 by the University of Florida. He reported subsidence still was being ignored.

"Subsidence has never been a popular subject in the Everglades," he said.

PREDICTIONS COMING TRUE

In their report, Johnson and Stephens had predicted the end of agriculture would come about the year 2000. Stephens revised his estimate in 1993, putting it off until around 2005. In 1994, Snyder, the soil scientist at the Belle Glade station, reported that "today, some farmers are in fact growing sugarcane on soil somewhat less than one foot in thickness over bedrock, but already areas have been abandoned, and only a few years of conventional production can be expected from such soil.

"The shallower the soil, the higher the cost of production. I could grow sugarcane on the tile floor of my office, but the cost would be very high," he said.

Despite the predictions of vanishing agriculture, government currently is spending more than $800 million to build treatment areas for polluted water that comes principally from EAA farms. This is the Everglades Construction Project, which will not be completed until 2006. Suggestions that government purchase EAA land as it goes out of sugar production are meeting opposition and even hostility from official sources. Yet the need for space to store water is one of the most urgent concerns of the long range, costly Everglades Restoration Plan, which would return the remaining half of the Everglades to a semblance of its natural condition. Unfortunately, the plan, which will take twenty-five years or more to complete, virtually ignores the subsidence problem in the Everglades. Further, it calls for very limited water storage in the EAA, which before drainage was a natural and abundant storage area.

Under the restoration plan, giant reservoirs will dot the Everglades outside the EAA, and water would be stored underground in a process called Aquifer Storage and Recovery, which is not yet guaranteed to work. In the meantime, urban development steadily encroaches on the EAA. Belle Glade is becoming a suburb of West Palm Beach. Speaking of the EAA, sugar executive Don Carson declared, "If it doesn't grow sugar, it's going to grow condos and golf courses." In time, a city could rise in the heart of the Everglades, imperiling the remains of the natural system that sustains South Florida.

Although some experts say higher water tables and better management practices have slowed subsidence, all agree the soil loss will continue unless water is put back on the land. Average soil depth in the northern area of the EAA was a little over three feet the last time measurements were taken four years ago. When the depth is less than two feet, canals must be deepened, at a considerable increase in production cost, to maintain water flow. When down to six inches, soil can't be farmed, say most experts.

Putting the water back on the land is the only feasible solution.

(The cost of buying all the land in the EAA would come to $2 or $3 billion and could be diverted from restoration projects, such as storing water underground, no longer needed because of the buyout.) Finding places to store water that currently is wasted to sea is one of the principal challenges of Everglades restoration. Millions of gallons of freshwater are wasted to sea each year, just to keep the EAA dry. Yet the corps plans only one 60,000-acre water storage area in the EAA. What should happen to the remaining 640,000 acres, the corps does not say. The EAA is the principal disrupter of the Everglades' natural hydrology, yet no attempt is proposed to restore the water flow through the area so Lake Okeechobee again could be connected to the Everglades.

Until the drained-dry heart of the Everglades is reflooded, there can be no effective restoration of South Florida's vast wetland system. The impending demise of farming in the EAA due to soil subsidence is about to hand government an unmatched opportunity to save the Everglades. But whether government will do so in the face of tremendous development pressure remains to be seen.

———————

JUANITA GREENE *is a journalist who spent thirty-one years with the* Miami Herald, *much of that time as their environmental writer. She retired from the* Herald *in 1978 but continues to write about and participate in environmental matters. She is active in Friends of the Everglades, a grassroots organization founded by Marjory Stoneman Douglas.*

Part Two

RIVER OF GRASS

The truth of the river is the grass. . . . They call it saw grass. Yet in the botanical sense it is not grass at all so much as a fierce, ancient cutting sedge. It is one of the oldest of the green growing forms in this world. There are many places in the South where this saw grass, with its sharp central fold and edges set with fine saw teeth like points of glass, this sedge called Cladium jamaicensis, *exists. But this is the greatest concentration of saw grass in the world. . . . When the original grass thrust up its spear into the sun, the fierce sun, lord and power and first cause over the Everglades as of all the green world, then the Everglades began.*

THE EVERGLADES: RIVER OF GRASS, MARJORY STONEMAN DOUGLAS

After leaving the lake and its ancient rich sill-lands, the freshwaters gathered in the Kissimmee Valley continued south down the long, nearly imperceptible tilt of the Floridan plateau, spreading wide through an island-studded marsh. This was the emergent marshland made famous by the great conservationist and writer Marjory Stoneman Douglas.

Hundreds of small tree islands rode the saw grass, marching like ships adrift in the south-flowing waters. A complex tangle of tropical plants on the islets offered sanctuary to rare panthers and tree snails, zebra butterflies and white-crowned pigeons. As the Everglades waters bore south in shallow sheet flow toward the tip of the peninsula and Florida Bay, some evaporated, and some filtered down into the underground aquifers. Water also flowed east or west to estuaries of the Atlantic Ocean (via the St. Lucie River) or the Gulf of Mexico (by way of the Caloosahatchee River).

In 1947, after hurricanes flooded thousands of acres in the Kissimmee Valley and on the east coast near Ft. Lauderdale, Congress approved a huge public works project to control the flow of the Everglades. Ironically, Harry Truman dedicated Everglades National Park that same year, saying, "We have permanently safeguarded an irreplaceable primitive area." The park encompasses about one-fifth of the greater river of grass portion of the Everglades and holds three international designations: International Biosphere Reserve, World Heritage Site, and Wetland of International Significance. At the same time it is one of America's most endangered national parks, severed from its source of sheet flow upstream and polluted with pesticides and mercury.

The central core of the river of grass north of the park proved exceptionally difficult to drain and was unsuited for agriculture, so engineers compartmentalized this interior portion into three water conservation areas. The northernmost conservation area is Loxahatchee National Wildlife Refuge, established in 1951 just downstream of Everglades Agricultural Area. Levees and canals now enclose about 1,860 square miles of saw grass marsh within the three water conservation areas, providing flood protection in the wet season by storing water, and irrigation and municipal water supply in dry times.

EVERGLADES NATIONAL PARK
FIFTIETH ANNIVERSARY

HOMAGE TO A MAGICAL PLACE

Carl Hiaasen

OCTOBER 19, 1997

The cabin hung on wooden stilts in a marsh pond, the stilts rising up through lily pads as big as hubcaps.

Getting there was tricky but my friends Andy and Matt knew the way—gunning a johnboat down subtle and sinuous trails, the sawgrass whisking against the hull. If you were foolish enough to stick out your hand, it came back bleeding.

The stalks were so high and thick that they parted like a curtain when we plowed through. The boat's bow acted as a scoop, picking up gem-green chameleons and ribbon snakes and leopard frogs. By the time we reached the cabin, we'd usually have spider webs on our heads, and sometimes the spiders themselves.

We were kids, and it was fantastic. It was the Everglades.

One night we stood on the canted porch and watched tiny star-bursts of color in the distant sky. At first we couldn't figure out what they were, and then we remembered: It was the Fourth of July. Those were fireworks over the city of Fort Lauderdale.

But we were so far away that all we could hear was the peeping of frogs and the hum of mosquitoes and the occasional trill of an owl. We didn't need to be told it was a magical place. We didn't need to be reminded how lucky we were.

I don't know if the old shack is still standing in Conservation Area 2B, but the eastward view certainly isn't the same. Instead of starlight you now get the glow from the Saw Grass Mills mall, a humongous Ford dealership and, absurdly, the crown of a new pro hockey arena.

We wouldn't have thought it possible, three teenagers gazing across wild country that swept to all horizons. Ice hockey on the doorstep of the Everglades! We couldn't have imagined such soulless incongruity and blithering greed.

Fortunately, somebody was smarter than we were. Somebody 30 years earlier had realized that the most imposing of natural wonders, even a river of grass, could be destroyed if enough well-financed intruders set their minds to it.

And somebody also understood that Dade, Broward and Palm Beach counties would inevitably grow westward as haphazardly as fungus, and with even less regard for their mother host.

So that, politically, the only part of the Everglades that could be set aside for true preservation was its remote southernmost spur, and not without a battle. As impenetrable as the area appeared, speculators nonetheless mulled ways to log it, plow it, mine it or subdivide it.

That the U.S. Congress and state legislature ever went along with the idea of an Everglades National Park remains astounding, 50 years after its dedication.

Nature helped its own cause. Hurricanes hammered South Florida in the 1930s and 1940s, so most land grabbers weren't in the market for more submerged acreage. It was hard enough hawking the soggy, stamp-sized lots they already had.

Seasonal flooding and fires had become such a threat to coastal development that extravagant technology was being directed toward a radical solution: containing and controlling all water near the farms and newly sprouted towns.

Thus preoccupied, most entrepreneurs remained wary of the buggy, moccasin-infested wetlands below the Tamiami Trail. That particular wilderness was, if not unconquerable, presumed not worth the high cost of conquering.

So in 1947 there came to be a spectacular national park, 1.3 million acres and destined to grow.

Ironically, it wasn't long afterwards that the rest of the Everglades, an area five times the size of the park, came under attack from the dredge and the bulldozer—a methodical and arrogant replumbing. Hundreds of miles of canals and dikes were gouged through the saw grass meadows, pond apple sloughs and cypress heads.

Once the big "water management" project got under way, not enough people considered what might happen to the park itself, to the south. Too few understood its vascular, life-or-death connection to the sugarcane fields of Clewiston, the limerock mines of Medley or the tomato farms of Homestead.

As a consequence, hundreds of millions of dollars are today being requisitioned to undo the damage and "restore" both the flow and purity of the Everglades. Nowhere in the world has such a massive, complex hydrological repair been attempted. If by some miracle it succeeds, your children and their children probably will never run out of clean water.

And, as a fine bonus, they might get to see a healthier Everglades National Park.

As vulnerable and anemic as it is, the park remains impressive and occasionally awesome; still rightfully mentioned in the same breath with Yellowstone and Grand Canyon.

Visually, its beauty is of an inverse dimension, for the Glades are as flat as a skillet, the trees mostly tangled and scrubby, the waters slow and dark. The monotony of its landscape can be a deception, as endless and uninviting as arctic tundra.

But for anyone finding themselves on that long two-lane road to Flamingo when the sun comes up, there's no place comparable in the universe.

True, the Everglades have no regal herds of elk or buffalo to halt tourist traffic—you might briefly be delayed by a box turtle plodding across the blacktop, or by a homely opossum. Yet for the matchless diversity of its inhabitants, the park is truly unique.

That's because it is essentially the tailing-out of a great temperate river, transformed on its southerly glide from freshwater prairies to an immense salty estuary, Florida Bay.

Entering by canoe at Shark River, you would be among woodpeckers and mockingbirds, alligators and bullfrogs, garfish and bass, white-tailed deer and possibly otters. Most of them you wouldn't see, but they'd be there.

And by the time you finished paddling—at Cape Sable or Snake Bight or the Ten Thousand Islands—you would have also been among roseate spoonbills and white pelicans, eels and mangrove snakes, sawfish and redfish and crusty loggerhead turtles.

Buffaloes are grand, but name another park that harbors panthers at one end and hammerhead sharks at the other. Name another park where, on a spring morning, it's possible to encounter bald eagles, manatees, a jewfish the size of a wine cask, an indigo snake as rare as sapphire, and even a wild pink flamingo.

I feel blessed because the park's southern boundary reaches practically to my back door. One June evening, I walked the shore of a mangrove bay and counted four crocodile nests; in a whole lifetime most Floridians will never lay eyes on one. Another afternoon, in July, I helped tag and release a young green turtle, a seldom-seen species that once teetered toward extinction.

And only weeks ago, near Sandy Key, I saw a pod of bottle-nosed dolphins doing spectacular back-flips for no other reason but the joy of it. Nobody was there to applaud or snap pictures; the dolphins were their own best audience, exactly as it ought to have been.

Such moments are remarkable if you consider what has happened to the rest of South Florida in the past half a century. It seems miraculous that the Everglades haven't been completely parched, poached or poisoned to stagnation by the six million people who've moved in around them.

The more who come, the more important the national park becomes—not only as a refuge for imperiled wildlife but as a symbolic monument for future human generations; one consecrated place that shows somebody down here cared, somebody understood, somebody appreciated.

CARL HIAASEN

A fantastic place from which your children and their children will, if they're lucky, never see the lights of an outlet mall or a car lot or a ridiculous hockey stadium. Just starburst glimpses of birds and baby gators and high-flying dolphins.

CARL HIAASEN *is a syndicated columnist with the* Miami Herald *and author of several novels, including* Lucky You, Tourist Season, Stormy Weather, Skintight, Double Whammy, *and* Striptease.

THE CORN LADY

Betty Mae Jumper

There once was a family living at the edge of the Big Forest, a wonderful place with swamps full of meat and fish. The family had places to grow vegetables, pumpkins, potatoes, beans and tomatoes. They also raised pigs and cows. These were happy people with no worries—they had everything!

The children could be seen running about everywhere, playing around and swimming in the ponds nearby. But sometimes, when the older children were playing really hard, they would forget to keep an eye on the younger children.

One day an older sister put her baby brother down to play with the little children while she played with the older ones. They played a long, long time and she forgot about her baby brother. When she finally went to check on him, he could not be found anywhere. She called and called and called his name but could not find him anywhere.

The big sister ran home to tell her mother. Soon, all of the women in the village were out looking for him. They kept looking until sundown but were unable to find the baby. When the men of the village returned from their Big Forest hunting trip, they all looked for the child well into the night. But no baby was found.

A few days later, the men returned to hunting and fishing. The father of the baby sent for the wise medicine man. Since he lived quite a distance from the village, it took the medicine man two days to get to the village at the edge of the Big Forest. When he finally arrived, he asked everyone to sit down. He told them about the "unseen people" that lived on small islands deep in the swamps.

The medicine man believed that one of these "unseen people" had picked up the baby and run off with him. He told the village people that they could not find these "unseen people." But, the wise medicine man believed that the baby was still alive someplace in the Glades. The family was very sad at this news and gave up looking for the baby and all hopes of ever seeing him again.

Years went by. The missing boy's family still lived in the same village. The brothers and sisters had grown up and some were married. Then one day a strange thing happened out in the jungle in the heart of the Everglades on a little island. No one had ever been there before, nor had anyone ever seen the place.

On the island was a beautiful camp with three chickees: one for the campfire, one for sleeping and one for eating. An old witch lived there and she had a young boy living with her. Every day she would prepare corn sofkee and vegetables for the boy. He soon grew to be a strong teenager.

The old witch was so ugly that it made you wonder where she came from. But her love for the boy was great and she raised him well. She knew that someday she would have to tell him the truth about himself. This made her very sad because she knew this day was very near.

The boy noticed that the chickees were old and falling apart and often asked why he was not allowed to repair them. The witch would never give him a reason. The boy questioned where she got the corn she prepared for him but she would never tell him. All he knew was that there was always plenty of corn to eat.

The day came when the boy decided it was time for him to follow the old witch. She would always get up very early, check to make sure the boy was asleep, pick up her basket and walk toward the swamps. One day the boy pretended to be asleep until she had gone, and then he followed her. She walked quite a distance to a cool running stream where she stepped in and scrubbed her legs until they were very clean. A little further away, she sat on a log, dried her legs and started rubbing them from the knees to the ankles until beautiful yellow corn fell and filled her basket. She continued doing this until her basket was full.

On the way back, she stopped and filled up another basket with white sand. The boy was watching her all this time. He ran back in front of her and quickly jumped in his bed and pretended to be asleep when she returned. She built a fire and parched the corn in the sand in an iron pot. She then placed the corn in a log which was about two feet from the ground. The log was about seven feet long and 12 inches around. She pounded it up and down until it was ground into cornmeal.

When breakfast was ready, the old witch called the boy to come to eat. But he refused. The old witch went to where he lay and said, "You know, don't you?" The boy didn't answer and she asked again. Finally he told her that he had followed her that morning and saw everything.

"I knew this day would come," the old woman told the boy. She began to cry. "Yes, my son, you have given me much happiness all these years, but it is now time you returned to your people."

She then told him the story of how she had taken him years ago when he was just a baby. She gave him the name of his family and told him where they lived. She also told him it would take at least two and a half days to reach his home. She then gave him the necklace he was wearing at the time she stole him away.

"I am an old woman and my time is drawing near," she told him. "You must do as I say: Leave and don't turn or look back. Just keep going! Tonight when the sun goes down, you must go to bed and sleep. When you wake up past midnight, you must get up and get ready to go.

"Go east toward the sun, and go past two big forests on the other side of the Big Lake. This is where your people live and you will find them there. Now, sleep, my boy, you have a lot of walking to do. When you get up, pick up the fire and throw it all over the chickees and run.

BETTY MAE JUMPER

"Follow the trail we have walked many times and go. Run! Run! Run! Don't cry! We have had many wonderful years together and I have enjoyed seeing you grow into a fine boy. Get yourself a pretty girl and marry among your own people."

Somehow, the boy knew she meant well for him. She had been good to him and taught him everything he knew, including how to hunt. Past midnight, the boy got up, sadness in his heart. But he did as the old woman had requested. He threw the fire on the chickees and started running. He ran until he was very tired and started walking. He walked all through the night.

At daybreak, he passed the first big forest and continued walking until that evening, nearing the second big forest. He was very tired and wanted to rest because he knew he was near his village. He wanted to be rested before he saw his people.

The boy found a large oak tree and climbed up about midway to a large branch that looked like a saddle. He could sleep here without falling out of the tree. He awoke at sunrise with the birds singing all around. Feeling hungry, he climbed down from the tree to look for berries to eat. After eating the berries, he found fresh water to drink.

He continued walking until he reached the Big Lake the old woman told him about. The men from the village were on their way hunting and he quickly jumped out of sight as he didn't want to meet them yet. He knew the village was very near.

The boy continued walking until he saw many chickees. He climbed up in a large tree and watched the people until almost sun-down. He wondered what he would say to the people about where he had lived for the past years. After a while he climbed down from the tree and started walking to the edge of the village.

The children saw him and started yelling, "New man. New man. Visitor." The older men of the village came out to shake his hand and talk to him. When he told the old men about himself, the old men remembered the story of the little boy who was lost long, long ago.

The boy then gave an old man the necklace he was wearing when he disappeared. "Yes, yes!" cried the old man. "I know your family." They slowly walked to the other side of the village, where a man and woman sat talking.

THE CORN LADY

The old man placed the necklace in the old woman's hand. She stared at the beadwork for a long time and then looked up to say she knew the work. The old man then told her that this was her son, returned from being lost a long time ago.

The story was told over and over to everyone that joined the happy family around the campfire. They sat and listened all night long to the boy's stories. After many months, the village men decided to go and see where the boy was raised.

They left early one morning and were gone for about a week. When they returned, they told of finding the place where the boy was raised. Only now it was a patch of beautiful green corn that stretched all over the island. Soon, everyone went to see the corn, which was so yellow and pretty. The men gathered all the corn they could carry and took it back to the village with them. They saved the seeds and planted them year after year.

After the boy returned home and the corn was discovered, a Green Corn Dance was held every year to thank the Great Spirit for his blessing. And this is where the Indians got their first corn.

BETTY MAE JUMPER is currently director of communications for the Seminole Tribe of Florida. She was the first Seminole Indian to graduate from high school, and has spent most of her career in tribal government positions, including tribal chairman and editor of the Seminole Tribune.

A CULTURE ENDANGERED

Jeff Klinkenberg

At the Miccosukee Indian Reservation, at South Florida's Tamiami Trail, I see garfish roasting over a fire. I see sturdy men building the huts called chickees as an alligator grunts from the high weeds next to a slough and a great blue heron stalks minnows on the bank of a clear creek. The saw grass in the endless marsh bends with the wind as gray clouds scud across the Everglades sky.

Life can look so beautifully simple here, so innocent, so unchanged. But looks deceive. Things have changed, and times never have been less innocent. Consider those gar, roasting on a chickee fire on a breezy fall afternoon.

"Would you like something to eat?" asks a Miccosukee man, and I am ashamed to decline his friendly offer. I no longer eat fish from the Everglades.

Nobody should be eating them now, but at least some of the 550 Miccosukees who live here are eating them, sometimes every day. Consuming gar and other Everglades fish, turtles and alligators, could make them sick and even kill them.

There's mercury in the food chain.

Mercury—a toxic metal that can accumulate in the body, affect the brain and nervous system and cause birth defects and childhood learning disabilities—has come to the wild heart of Florida, the Everglades.

No human has been harmed so far. But already it has killed at least one of North America's rarest mammals, a Florida panther, symbol of Everglades wilderness. And it has prompted the state to issue health warnings and begin a series of studies to learn why it's happened and what can be done about it. Answers may be years and millions of dollars away.

"We will not be able to eat the fish in the Everglades in our lifetime," says Forrest Ware, chief researcher for the Florida Game and Fresh Water Fish Commission.

For well-heeled city anglers who trailer boats into the Everglades, going without an occasional fish dinner is an inconvenience. Most Everglades anglers release their catch as a matter of sportsmanship. For the city poor who drive into the Everglades with their cane poles and dreams of a fish supper, it's a hardship.

For the Miccosukees, traditional hunters and fishers who were able to subsist on what they caught and killed for almost three centuries, poisoned fish is another matter. Some might even call it a tragedy.

They have already endured much. Over the years they have watched their homelands shrink because of warfare, encroachment by settlers, development, agriculture, major highways, the institution of a national park and million-dollar flood control measures.

And now mercury, a byproduct of the incineration of garbage and medical wastes, the burning of fossil fuels by power plants, escaped paint fumes, forest fires and mercury vapors leaching through soil, threatens their food. Fishing and eating fish—living a natural life—takes on religious implications within the traditions of their culture. Giving it up may prove difficult for some of them.

I ask a Miccosukee man called Ronnie Jimmie why he and his family eat gar that could make them ill.

He answers without hesitation.

"They are the food of my people," he says. "It's the fish our parents ate, and our grandparents. It's the food of our ancestors. We have no choice."

THEIR HOME

Jimmie, 33, was born in the western Everglades known as the Big Cypress. His great-great-grandfather fought the white soldiers who tried to expel the Seminole and Miccosukee people from Florida during the last century. And when wars ended they refused to go to reservations in Oklahoma. Instead, they hid in the Everglades.

He grew up eating the fish, turtles, deer and alligator killed by his father and grandfather in the woods and swamps. He ate the delicate buds of cabbage palms. His mother pounded coontie plants into flour and baked bread. In the spring, he accompanied his parents and grandparents to the Green Corn Dance and thanked the Great Mystery for the Everglades that sustained all life.

He lives in a camp along the Tamiami Trail with his wife's people, the Miccosukee custom. He has gone to school and learned English, and for a while worked at the Miccosukee Cultural Center explaining to visitors his people's traditions.

These days for a living he builds the traditional cypress and cabbage palm huts called chickees. Sometimes he is hired by white city people to build chickees next to their backyard swimming pools and barbecue pits. Occasionally he's invited to Miami community colleges to talk about his culture.

"White people are interested in Indians now," he says. "Why is that? I think there is something missing in their lives. They own a lot of things already. They read the Bible and go to church on Sunday morning and Wednesday night. But there is still something missing. They don't know their place in the universe."

He is an athletic man who wears his long black hair in a ponytail. Jewelry dangles from his ears. He is dressed in jeans, a T-shirt, running shoes and sunglasses. He drives a Chevrolet Blazer, listens to the radio and reads the *Miami Herald*.

Still, he tries to live a traditional way of life, at least as traditionally as a young Miccosukee man can live an hour west of Miami in the waning years of the twentieth century.

He and his wife, Mary, and their two children, Gemini and Sylvester, live in a chickee made with his own hands with cypress poles and the fronds from cabbage palms. Mary cooks over an open fire. They attend the Green Corn Dance in the spring and consult with powerful medicine men about important matters. Friends believe Jimmie has the makings of a future medicine man. He shrugs.

"What I do is sit and listen to my elders tell their stories. I listened when I was a boy, but what they were telling me didn't sink in then. Now I know they are trying to keep our culture alive. They haven't given up the natural world. For the Miccosukee people to give up the natural world would make us like the outsiders. And then there is no hope."

His older son, Gemini, 11, attends the reservation school, where there are IBM computers and teachers who instruct in English, math and American history. Sylvester, 5, speaks only Miccosukee. He attends no school. He accompanies his father when he builds chickees. His toys range from homemade spears to a train from a toy store.

"One day he will learn the American ways," Ronnie Jimmie says. "But right now, the first and foremost thing in his life is the Miccosukee religion, which is about nature. He will learn the songs and the dances that praise Mother Earth. Singing and dancing have kept the Everglades alive."

As I listen to this eloquent man, I think only of mercury, fish and the future of people who eat them.

Mercury poisoning can be so deadly. In 1956, 700 people died and 9,000 were crippled after eating fish poisoned by mercury dumped into Japan's Minamata Bay by a chemical company. In Florida, mercury is coming from both natural and unnatural sources. Experts say Florida industry is releasing 42,000 pounds of mercury annually into the atmosphere. Some of it is landing in the Everglades, the world's largest wetlands.

"All the water that comes to us makes many stops along the way," Ronnie Jimmie tells me. "It stops at ranches. It stops at farms. It stops at industries. It stops at roads. It stops at cities.

"It is because of this trip we are told we shouldn't eat the fish and the turtles. All I know is that it started out as good water and comes to us as a deadly material. Yet it's our way to eat fish even if it kills us. We ate garfish last night. But I am afraid for the Everglades."

A COMMON ENEMY

Miccosukee people came to the Everglades from Alabama and Georgia and North Florida in the 1700s. They were part of what is sometimes called the Creek Confederacy, a group that included Creek, Choctaw, Oconee, Yuchi, Yamassee, Apalachee, Talasis and other Indian people. When they came to Florida, white settlers lumped them together and called them "Seminoles," a corruption of the Muskogee word *siminoli*, which meant "people of distant fires." They had come a long way.

The Muskogee-speaking people, who became the Seminoles as we know them today, were good farmers and ranchers. The Hitchiti-speaking Miccosukees were talented hunters and fishers. "Until they fought the same war, under their own leaders, against the common enemy, the Miccosukees and the Seminoles always hated each other," wrote Marjory Stoneman Douglas in her Everglades history.

They get along today. Some Seminoles live with the Miccosukees and some Miccosukees live with Seminoles. More Seminoles speak the Miccosukee language than the Seminoles' traditional Muskogee dialect. There are mixed marriages. After Hurricane Andrew reared across the Everglades, toppling chickees and crushing mobile homes, the Seminoles were the first to arrive with help.

There are about 2,500 registered Seminoles, who have reservations in the Big Cypress, Hollywood, Brighton and Tampa. The Miccosukees, who number fewer than 550, live for the most part along the Tamiami Trail just north of Everglades National Park.

The Miccosukees especially have seen a lot of changes over the years. Three long wars with federal troops drove them, bloody but unbowed, into the deep Everglades to live in peace. But peace was short-lived.

There were endless campaigns to drain the Everglades, their hunting grounds, by ambitious politicians and developers. Once there was even a state campaign to eradicate deer, another important food source, because deer harbored ticks that weakened cattle and upset wealthy ranchers.

In 1928, the first road across the Everglades, the Tamiami Trail, was completed. It brought white settlers and hunters into Miccosukee territory. In 1947, when Everglades National Park was born, the Miccosukee people had to move. And they lost their hunting rights.

That same year, following a hurricane and a tropical storm, the state asked the federal government to build a series of canals to drain the parts of the Everglades that had refused to be tamed. Some people say the new flood control measures marked the end of the Everglades.

So mercury is only the latest threat to the river of grass and the Miccosukee.

I call up Tom Atkeson, mercury specialist with the Florida Department of Environmental Regulation, and tell him I've seen Miccosukee people eating fish that are on the state list to avoid.

"We've issued warnings," he says, sounding distressed. "Keeping the word out there is very difficult. We mean those warnings and think people should abide by them."

JUNK FOOD AND ALCOHOL

The Miccosukee people once were considered among the most traditional and healthy Indians remaining in North America. "Geography saved us," says Stephen Tiger, the tribal spokesman. "We lived out here in relative isolation. It saved us first from the federal troops and then from total assimilation. We kept our ways."

But assimilation is happening. Tiger, 43, was among the first Miccosukee to leave the reservation and attend a public school. He lives in Miami and commutes 40 miles to the reservation. He and his brother have a rock band, Tiger and Tiger, and they are working on an album called *Space Age Indian*.

"Our influences are the Beatles and the Stones," he says.

His father, Buffalo Tiger, now in his 70s, was the tribal chairman for 25 years. He worked to get the federal government to recognize the Miccosukee as a tribe independent from the Seminoles. Today the reservation has its own school, police and a health department. It has 266,163 acres that stretch from the Tamiami Trail north to beyond Alligator Alley in Broward County.

The Miccosukees run the only gas station and service plaza on Alligator Alley, the new Interstate 75. They have a 2,000-seat bingo parlor in western Dade County. On the reservation, on the Tamiami Trail, they have a gas station, a restaurant and the Cultural Center where tourists watch young men wrestle alligators and later buy jewelry and clothing from shy Miccosukee women.

Other Miccosukees earn money taking tourists on airboat rides and gigging frogs for Miami restaurants. Some build chickees for a living. Some go to Miami and work as house painters, carpenters and plumbers. Still, about 40 percent are unemployed. And some are unhealthy.

Alcoholism is a growing problem. So are diabetes and hypertension, aggravated by obesity. "Over the years some of the people have changed their eating habits," says Jann Kenyon, a reservation nurse. "They've gone from a very natural diet to eating a lot of high fat junk food. Their bodies don't seem to tolerate the new diet very well."

Cheryl Shechter, a nutritionist, visits Miccosukee camps daily with tips about healthier eating. She encourages people to eat natural food like fruit and vegetables and fewer fats and sweets. Jennifer Showers, reservation health specialist, has plans to start an aerobics class. "We talk about the value of exercise," she says.

Gato, an Aztec who married a Miccosukee and lives on the reservation, is the tribal environmental health specialist. He tells people to avoid eating fish because of the mercury, but he is unsure whether his words are being heard.

"I don't know how many are eating fish," Gato says. "I think most everybody knows about the dangers by now, but I suspect some of the older and traditional people are eating the fish."

"I eat the fish, and I'm alive," says Terry Willie, a 26-year-old alligator wrestler. "I don't worry about it. I eat bass, gar and mudfish a couple times a week."

"I eat less fish than I used to," says Mary Jane Billie, a 26-year-old health clinic assistant whose great-great-grandfather was the late Ingraham Billie, the famous medicine man. "I eat a garfish once in a while. Maybe some bream. But mostly I buy seafood. It's safer."

The Environmental Protection Agency and the Indian Health Service are negotiating with the Miccosukee government about testing its people for mercury poisoning. Gato knows that approaching some of the people, especially the traditional ones, about submitting to tests may be a delicate process.

"They are very, very conservative," he says. "Dealing with them can be a definite challenge. If you want to test their water or something, they are offended. They think it's the white man's way."

A MICCOSUKEE HEART

"I was born right here in the Everglades," says Buffalo Tiger. "Maybe two and a half miles down the road. Except there wasn't a road."

Now a Miami resident, he's tall and fit with dark skin and gray hair. He wears slacks and loafers from city department stores, and a vest and necklace made by Miccosukee women on the reservation. When his tribal chairmanship ended in 1985, he started offering airboat rides into the Everglades he has known well for seven decades.

"There was no Tamiami Trail," he says. He looks at me hard. He wants me to understand that Miccosukees lived out here—alone. "I remember when they built the road. I was a boy and hid behind the bushes to watch. The elders said never to talk to white-skinned people like you. White people would kill you or send you to Oklahoma to the reservations."

The water was clear and full of good fish to eat. There were plenty of birds. Bird feathers were used in ceremonies and the flesh of their bodies consumed. Miccosukee men poled dugout canoes through the saw grass all the way to Miami to trade alligator skins for butter and cloth from whites. Young people honored their elders with respect.

"The old people would have the last say on everything," he says. He has to pause for a moment as a huge truck rumbles down the highway toward Miami. "It's not always that way now. Too much of a white man's way has come here. The young people don't listen to the older people.

"Most of the older people, the people my age, they hold on to the old ways. I worry about the younger ones. I don't think they understand how easy we could lose our language and our culture. I think TV, it seems to be overtaking everything.

"In our culture, we have clans. I'm from the bird clan. You are not supposed to have a wife or a girlfriend from the same clan. We remind the young people of that, but they don't always listen.

"I think a lot of the younger people are lost. Sometimes they feel hateful. Some of them drink. They're bored. They think there's nothing to do. They think of money. In the old days, you didn't need money.

"I feel lucky. I grew up in my culture. I got away from it, it is true. I moved to the city and played around. But I never thought I was a white man. I have a Miccosukee heart."

I visit Tommie Tiger's camp in the afternoon. He is Buffalo's brother, a chickee builder and Ronnie Jimmie's father-in-law. He and Ronnie are grilling meat on the chickee fire. The burning logs seem to be arranged so each points at one of the four directions—north, south, east and west. It's the Miccosukee way, I've read. They talk about their Everglades.

"More and more the city of Miami is creeping toward us," Jimmie says. "At night we can see the glow."

Tommie Tiger, like his older brother Buffalo, was born before any roads were built. He is 69, though he looks more like an athletic man of 50. "He has tried to avoid white foods and stayed active and kept the old ways," says Ronnie Jimmie. Even now Tommie Tiger can shimmy up a cypress pole while hammering the nails that attach the palm fronds to a chickee roof.

He was born in a hammock near Krome Avenue, the two-lane road that skirts the Everglades in western Dade. A hammock is an island, shaded by trees, out in the saw grass marsh. Tommie's hammock, where he was a boy, is gone.

"They're mining limerock there now," Ronnie says.

"They dig, dig, dig. Hammock no more," Tommie says quietly. "Everything has changed."

He and his son-in-law talk about fishing. It used to be better. There were more bass. There were snook. There were plenty of gar and mudfish. A good man with a spear could feed his family.

Now there are strange fish, from other countries, inhabiting the Everglades. There are catfish from Asia that can walk out of the water and breathe air. There are smaller fish, oscars from Africa, that over the years have escaped Miami tropical fish owners, moved into the Everglades and crowded out native fish. They don't belong. Anyway, they are poisoned from the mercury.

A little before dark I say my farewells. On the way to my truck I pass Ronnie Jimmie's 5-year-old son on the footbridge that spans the creek. The boy holds a small stick tied to his wrist with a string. It's a toy spear.

I watch little Sylvester. He throws his stick into the creek again and again.

He's pretending to spear a gar, the fish of his father, the fish of his grandfather.

The fish of the Miccosukee people.

JEFF KLINKENBERG *is a columnist for the* St. Petersburg Times *and the author of two collections of essays about the state:* Real Florida: Key Lime Pies, Worm Fiddlers, a Man Called Frog, and Other Endangered Species *and* Dispatches from the Land of Flowers.

THIS PATH DON'T LEAD
TO MIAMI

EVERGLADES TREKS OF THE 1800s

Jan Godown

I tried some Indian words out of Longfellow's Hiawatha, *but could not make them understand, so concluded that my accent was not correct.*

FROM A LOGBOOK OF A SAILING TRIP INTO THE OLD EVERGLADES,
NOVEMBER 1891–FEBRUARY 1892

One of the most powerful things I know to do is to begin to learn the history of a place. Without a sense of history we arrive in new regions with a childlike, self-centered gaze. As I visit a favorite archaeology collection for families in South Florida, my daughter Anna hugs its giant display crystal that, Smithsonian-like, is a three-and-a-half-ton speck of glitter the size of a coffee table. This moment feels good. We don't think about the fact that for the Graves Museum of Archaeology and Natural History to be here today, next to busy U.S. Highway 1 in the town of Dania, an entire region with people, animals, and plants was made to disappear.

Not far from the Graves, my newspaper colleague Betty Mae Tiger Jumper puts it another way. She sits in a glistening, multistory building one afternoon, the Seminole Tribe of Florida headquarters, in nearby Hollywood. There is a toothy alligator head on her office desk and a helipad with a shining 'copter atop the tribe's office roof. She sweeps her arm to the window where, outside, traffic jockeys for position on a divided highway.

"This was the Everglades in the beginning," she tells me. "We used to ride around in canoes here where the tribal building is now. We used to have guava and other kinds of trees. All that is gone now."

All that is gone now. The Everglades once stretched from today's Everglades National Park of Travel Channel fame, north to the Kissimmee River of U.S. Army Corps of Engineers infamy. The story of this Old Everglades, a region of flood-season Seminole Indian sailors who climbed out of cypress canoes to hike the Glades in the dry times, a region of Seminole families who tended islands of sweet potato patches, scratched charcoal images on palm tree trunks and dug with great interest in ancient Indian mounds, is a largely unheard testimony of a place and time forever beyond our grasp. The story of the native sailors' pursuers has a more available record, so it is better known. The pursuers, and also others who fancied themselves explorers, trudged through the inscrutable Old Everglades, somehow keeping journals. Within 1800s diaries, maps, photographs, and expedition reports, I find glimpses of the Old Everglades. The reports, often written up to satisfy a federal government sponsor, are flecked with natural history notes from a wilderness that in places flashed with "immense flocks of cranes, pink spoonbills, curlew and wild turkey in plenty"; with instances of federal-Seminole combat, such as "accidentally wounded a squaw, who was endeavoring to escape with her child on her back. In another direction, they overhauled a squaw with a girl about 12 years old and two small children"; and also, I read of a pause in camp for a memorable moment of "an inquisitive moccasin snake attempting to crawl up his left shoulder."

It is the uncommon tour company operating in Florida that hires guides who share these stories with Everglades travelers. These visitors—more than a million each year to the park alone—deplane from around the world, lured by literature and images limning a belief that this is a region of wild orchids, quiet Edens, and thick bird roosts. As I look at two imaginatively colored green toy alligators on my Tallahassee desk—alligators are grey black, baby alligators are black with zigzag yellow stripes—I think of the perfectly named Bunnie Bloom and of our shared affection for both history and nature. She leads a travel company founded in Miami about twenty years ago by a fellow retiree, a South Florida biochemist named Al Rosenberg, who called his venture All Florida Adventure Tours. This small and quiet tour business makes it a point of pride to unfold to school children and other groups the story of the flora, fauna, hydrology, and people of the Old Everglades. They'll have you touch a blade of saw grass to feel the cutting power, and they'll share a trick of Old Everglades survival known to the Seminoles: there's an edible pulpy bulb filled with moisture at the root of the saw grass blade.

Were I ever to be Queen for a Day in Florida, I would change quite a few things. But in the area of travel culture I would wave my sabal palm wand at least twice. Then, with every new Florida driver's license issued, the driving citizenry would receive a primer, in choice of format—CD-ROM, video, print—of hand-tinted old postcard views of a dredge chewing a section of the Old Everglades, of a coastal Everglades mangrove island rookery flecked with plume birds, of a Seminole family gliding with white sail hoisted in their cypress tree-trunk canoe, or of a smiling pioneer girl about age thirteen who is holding up by the tail a four-foot alligator and clutching in her other hand her rifle. The images would accompany excerpts of Old Everglades travel and life. I don't expect residents and visitors to be aware that the ice cream shop selling coconut milkshakes, the book store selling nature guides, or the miniature golf course selling fun in South Florida were all once part of a clear fish-filled stream. Until Florida better educates its visitors and residents, few will know that the nature-named housing developments of the South Florida interior were once teeming with aquatic and bird life, were once lush areas of a sustainable natural system where native green, yellow, and orange Carolina parakeets the size of crows flashed in the skies.

The second magic palm frond wave would ensure that every

guide operating through South Florida complete a course of field trips conducted by Bunnie Bloom, with her sign-off required, indicating that the guide now demonstrates a grasp of the history, flora, fauna, and hydrology of the Old Everglades. Without it, there's no guide van fill-up. It will be a novel experiment for the region to experience more taxpayers and residents who begin to understand the workings of a crucial aspect of the region. And also, as luck would have it, this history stuff is riveting.

THE END OF A SEMINOLE WAR LEADER

One early recorded Everglades crossing was of a twelve-day sailing trip in December 1840. A man identified only as John, an African-American slave, guided more than ninety U.S. Navy sailors. The flotilla took sixteen thirty-foot cypress canoes west from the young Miami settlement and Fort Dallas outpost. Soon the men felt disoriented in the sea of tall saw grass. They spent an uncomfortable night crammed unexpectedly in the boats; there wasn't land on which to camp. The men doubted John's guidance until "sure enough, contrary to the expectations of us all, he in a short time halted at a low tuft of bushes, about half a mile in circumference, which seemed to all to be entirely flooded with water, but after penetrating about 300 yeards [sic] we came to a magnificent little spot in its centre." John expertly guided them to a deserted Seminole camp, shaded by a circle of pawpaw bushes, two fig trees, and a clutch of cabbage palms, a fine specimen of the many islands of refuge in the Everglades' saw grass stream.

Repeatedly on this journey, the big sky of the Everglades' vista above and the big saw grass of the watery land below, plus innumerable water trails that abruptly stopped at saw grass walls, made for confusing reference points, especially for sailors who brought their own restricted views of northern stream and river travel with them into the Everglades. Disregarding John's advice, one group of Navy men struck out away from John "and continued to wander to every point of the compass until late in the evening," when John found them and brought them in to camp. During the expedition John led them to several island farms, all deserted by residents who had noted the expedition's approach. The camps yielded a tidy acre of cultivated corn, another with a garden of pumpkin, beans, and corn, and an island with banana trees, plantains, and "a great number of palmetto huts, very well-thatched." The Everglades islands bore names John knew—to the best of the expedition diarist's ability recorded as *Ho-co-mo-thlocco, Efa-noc-co-chee, Cochokeynchajo,* and *Intaska.* These elevations of tended land in the wilderness, named for a fig tree that grew there, or a pet Seminole dog that was buried there, sustained family life. They sheltered people with an oral history that included older tales of war; now the families evaded these very pursuers. In fact, the "campers" John guided weren't on basic maneuvers; they were soldiers with orders to hunt the native men and their families who lived in the saw grass secrecy of the Old Everglades. This expedition sought the ones who made a stand with Seminole leaders, including Chakika, also spelled Chekika, who himself had piled up an estimable record of victory scalps, especially along the Caloosahatchee River.

In the early 1800s, the U.S. Government nearly cleared the Florida peninsula of four thousand natives to prepare for pioneer settlement, almost exterminating a people. Soon afterward, and just as ignorantly, in 1848, with U.S. Senate Bill No. 338, "to authorize the drainage of the Ever Glades," the federal government would try to clear the Old Everglades of its pure, clear water, exterminating a universe of flora and fauna. Eventually, some of the December 1840 expeditioners painted their skin dark and dressed in turbans and long shirts like Seminole men, so their far-off profiles would look in place. They traveled at night, and these crackerjack guerrillas achieved deadly results. The military diarist noted: "Our tent or shed was pitched last night within a short distance of the tree on which Chakika was suspended. The night was beautiful and the bright moon displayed to my view as I lay on my bed, the gigantic proportions of this once great and much dreaded warrior. He is said to have been the largest Indian in Florida, and the sound of his very name to have been a terror to his Tribe. We have among the captives, his mother, sister, and wife." Today, former Seminole Tribe of Florida Chairman James Billie is persistent in saying there are fewer Seminole people left in Florida (about 2,500 Seminoles and about 600 Miccosukees, a related tribe) than there are of some endangered species. The proud Seminoles were among Florida's first endangered species.

GREEN PARROQUETS, CRANE LIVERS, AND A BRUIN, CHASED

Two years after Chakika's manhunt, a military diarist kept track of a fifty-eight-day quest in 1842, departing north of Miami. Rather than kill Seminoles, the men expected to bring them in alive, for removal to the West. The expedition paddled up the south fork of the New River at Ft. Lauderdale to plunge into the Old Everglades. It began as a hunter's dream trip, the stuff that good travel stories are spun from. The eighty-six men and one woman—wife of a native guide—dined well on what they bagged: wild hogs, immature heron taken from the nest, blackbird, woodpecker, turkey, fish, and rattlesnake. Many alligators were taken for the tail meat, along with turtle, and a "fry of some little fish that foolishly jumped into one of the canoes." Delicacies were snatched from trees: "Robbed the nests of over thirty young birds, and had a famous stew of crane's livers." The group paddled into a wildlife abundance: "Captured forty white cranes, and might have taken a thousand had I wanted, and hats full of eggs." They glided past "fields of water lilies." From their front row seats in a subtropical wilderness they witnessed the sights and sounds of "immense flocks of curlew flying in two irregular columns, each apparently miles in length." They didn't realize that they also perched below one species' flight path to extinction. "Saw ten parroquets," and "saw large flocks of green parroquets," the diarist noted. These American avians, the size of a crow, once nested north from Florida into Virginia. Today nearly five million people live in what was once the Old Everglades, but there are no large, green, orange, and yellow "parroquets" to be seen. Not even one in the child magnet that is the Miami Metrozoo. A verified glimpse of one occurred in 1904 in a long-drained Old Everglades region near the village of Kissimmee, and the last sightings were possibly in the 1920s.

The hunters on this 1842 trip lucked into an Everglades black bear, but they were forbidden to discharge guns because they were close to some Seminoles whom they hoped to surprise. They chased the bear into a palmetto thicket, "surrounded and closed in upon it with the men and endeavored to beat him up, but our shaggy-coated gent managed to elope unseen."

Despite the provisions bagged, the journey was a physical ordeal—the downside to hunters' paradise. Water trails disappeared, requiring men to walk beside the canoes and push, day after day. The saw grass cut raggedly into skin, making healing difficult. At the end of the journey the diarist's ulcerated and festering legs and feet prompted a surgeon in Miami to suggest double amputation, although the limbs were finally saved.

The diarist concluded, "For years after, I felt the effects of those sixty days in a dug-out canoe in Florida." His statement was bad news for the Old Everglades. Such hardship reports from the wilderness only fueled desire to drain the saw grass sea and tame it. Tales of travel woe—moccasin snakes that climbed up arms, alligators that clambered into boats, expeditioners who became lost on water trails that vanished at saw grass walls—these travails were not a help in keeping people away. No, instead, they undergirded the government and developers' desire to remake the region into something familiar—a resolve that strengthened to eliminate all the unpleasantness.

No Seminoles were met on that trek; they had kept silent and, I like to think, bemused track of the expeditioners, despite the group's quiet restraint in not shooting at the Everglades bear. Soon after, the U.S. Government said the equivalent of "never mind"; this "Florida War" to remove Seminoles was over. That sentiment lasted until the final, 1855-58 war, at the end of which it was no surprise that remaining Seminole families—perhaps two hundred people—made it taboo to have contact with the settlers whose desire for land since the 1700s had pushed the Seminoles from North Florida cabins in the woods south to Central Florida fields and, finally, into the extreme land's end. In exchange for leaving settlers alone—no ambushes allowed—the Seminoles could fish, hunt, and farm knowing they would no longer be hunted and brought in, man, woman, or child, for bounties of two hundred to five hundred dollars. The families poled canoes, cultivated island farms, remembered relatives killed or relocated to Indian Territory (Oklahoma), and tried to keep isolated. It lasted about forty years.

LEECHES, EXPEDITIONERS TREED, AND SEETHING FLAMES

In 1882, the *New Orleans Times-Democrat,* vocal champion of development, announced that it would help find the way to "civilize" the Everglades. It sponsored two expeditions, each led in successive years by Civil War veteran Major Archie P. Williams. The first trip, of two weeks, began at the Kissimmee River. By the close of the second expedition, launched from the pioneer settlement of Fort Myers on the west coast, the reality of the Everglades as a primarily wet and unchangeable landscape had rooted with Major Williams. He declared, "Drainage is utterly impractible and even if it were practible the reward for such an undertaking would be lands that could be utilized for no other purpose than as a grazing ground for stock. They are nothing more or less than a vast and useless marsh, and such they will remain for all time to come, in all probability." Sadly—for the Old Everglades, for the Seminoles, and, ultimately, the U.S. taxpayer—Williams wasn't a clairvoyant.

On the *Times-Democrat's* first trip, the men found an Indian burial mound created by native dwellers from a time before the Seminole people. They poked in it, unearthing beads and a small amount of silver. The official expedition report noted that "some gentlemen from the Smithsonian Institution visited this mound last year, and dug into it for about eight feet, their search being rewarded by quite a number of relics." On one especially memorable camp night, the men rushed from their tents to scramble up the trees they had camped under, as a "peculiar snarling, snapping and grunting is going on, together with a general overturning of everything." It was a slew of Everglades alligators barging across the almost water-level, twenty-five-foot-long island, overturning camp pots and blundering into expedition gear.

On the second *Times-Democrat* trek, in addition to the jagged saw grass cuts, the men dealt with leeches, worms, and the absence of most game to kill and eat. (This group killed alligators but didn't have the stomach to cook the reptiles.) While areas of the Everglades fed hordes of terrestrial and airborne animals, the vast and shallow saw grass sea itself was not much of a home for deer, otter, rabbit, bear, or other creatures. To make matters worse, this group torched the saw grass, creating "for tens and tens of miles, . . . one mass of seething flames" in hopes of making an easier path. But burned to the waterline, the saw grass remained stubbornly, stuck in the muck. "A deathlike, oppressive stillness prevailed everywhere. There were no fish in the water, no birds in the air." Spirits crumbled. The situation of the men deteriorated day by day. They toiled, at times waist deep in the mud and water. Leeches sucked nourishment from their legs until the water around them was dyed a deep red. With thousands of bugs pestering them, with prickly plants bruising them, they slogged along in water employed as a highway by snakes, including moccasins. Near the end, Major Williams's men were "ragged, barefooted and broken down." One moaned, "There is hardly a man in the party that is not sorry he's living, or at least, life has no attraction for him at present." Some struggled on to the Everglades coast near the not-reassuringly named Shark River and a prearranged pickup that became a rescue. The sobered newspaper leadership opined, "In 1848 when the United States Senate investigated this question, a committee reported that the swamp could be drained. Major Williams reports adversely. He can see no hope or possibility of redeeming the greater portion of this region, which must remain a swamp forever." Of all the editorials the *Times-Democrat* published through the 1800s, this was an unusually informed warning that should have wielded the force of an alligator's crushing jaw instead of the ineffectual flick of a crane feather.

The first *Times-Democrat* trek inspired a memorable trip in 1995 by Sean Dougherty and Robert McClure of the *Fort Lauderdale Sun-Sentinel*. The men paddled in engineered canals, and the changes they observed included portage over a giant levee, the Hoover Dike, and a night's camp at pumping station S-5A, once the largest pumping station in the world.

In contrast to the lush world of the 1800s, the modern-day newspaper expeditioners found an Everglades in retreat and travel hardships very different from those of one hundred years earlier.

IN THE SPRING, NAVIGATION CLOSES

An Everglades-smitten expeditioner, Kentucky medical doctor James A. Henshall, published an 1884 book, *Camping and Cruising in Florida,* based on his several travels. A normally reclusive Seminole family welcomed him into camp. He learned from them that, following the summer rains, the Seminoles expected about four to six feet of water to provide easy canoe sailboating. "But in the spring, navigation closes," Henshall advised would-be travelers. By then, the seasonal winter drought would have reached its natural low of a few inches deep, except in normally deep pools. The doctor found delight in the wilderness.

"It is a hard matter to convey a correct or even an approximate idea of the region called the 'Everglades'; it is unique, there is nothing like it anywhere else. As far as the eye can reach stretches a broad, level expanse, clothed in verdure of a particularly fresh and vivid green, a rich and intense color seen nowhere but here." He wrote of the thousands of islands from a few yards wide to many acres in size and listed the flora: mangrove, coco-plum, swamp maple, sweet bay, mastic, water poplar, gumbo-limbo, satinwood, water oak, palmetto, and, twining all around, "in their exuberance, are innumerable vines and creepers bearing flowers of gorgeous dyes." As enlightened as his admiration was, the good doctor—and a legion of subsequent writers and photographers, myself included—in sharing irresistible images, helped love a place to death.

TRYING OUT SOME *HIAWATHA*

From November of 1891 through February of 1892, four responsible young men from pioneer citrus families put a wood stove on the deck of a thirty-foot sloop, the *Minnehaha,* and towed a dinghy. They took a trip into the Old Everglades, down the Kissimmee River to the

Caloosahatchee River and Fort Myers and points farther south before retracing their path home safely. The boys—light-hearted young adults in their early twenties and at least one teenager—fished and hunted with glee, noting ducks in the thousands around them. They braved occasional stiff winter winds, cold weather, and storms, but delighted in the freedom of their camping trip. With the seasonal high water they enjoyed a comfortable journey, especially compared to other earlier travelers. The enthusiastic sailors recited Native American words from Longfellow's *Hiawatha* to a Seminole family they met, without response, and concluded that their accent was off. They conducted the silent family on a brief tour of the *Minnehaha,* showing off their equipment and quarters. We'll never know what that family thought.

ON STRICT RATIONS, IN NEED OF RESCUE

One of the more contemporaneously commented-upon expeditions took railroad executive James E. Ingraham into the Old Everglades in 1892 to prove that passage between the two coasts was possible and to encourage a railroad or telegraph line. As the twenty-three men with him collected in the Fort Myers frontier village, other men who had already dredged for the draining project told Everglades horror stories. One veteran assured the men they would become lost "in the maze, wandering around, trying to find a path or channel and would starve before we could get out."

The usual torments hit. Three days into the trek, on March 21, one expeditioner noted mildly, "My first experience with saw grass was not very encouraging." His severely cut right hand was soon "greased with mutton suet." At seven days into the expedition, this diarist was ready to faint from fatigue. Everglades water levels were low, the canoes couldn't be paddled, and dragging them was the work of Hercules. He spied open mud and slumped into its coolness, resting for two hours while men passed him by, their feet working like suction pumps in the muck. Clothes were in shreds. With supplies nearly gone, the men were put on daily rations of only hominy and coffee. Daily they trudged, realizing the predictions heard in Fort Myers were true. The saw grass had destroyed their idea of distance and height. When the men saw two young blue herons on a nest, opening their mouths and crying, the diarist moaned, "We were great idiots to come into such a place when we had no wings with which to fly out." But, on April 3, fish jumped into a boat and the men stumbled upon an island with edible berries and deer tracks on it. Then the men were even more elated to see another island in the distance, this one with a native-built palm-thatched hut. The home owner, a Seminole, became their reluctant savior, guiding four somewhat-able men to nearby Miami so that provisions and a rescue party could save the others, some of whom had been pulled along in boats because they could no longer walk. By April 7, the Ingraham expedition across the Old Everglades was pronounced a success in Miami, barely snatched from the fruition of the Fort Myers' prediction. Feet festering, all men reunited in Miami, where pioneer booster Julia Tuttle sheltered them. In their honor she exploded some festive dynamite, an element soon to be a key instrument of Everglades' destruction, used to blast limerock underlying the saw grass muck. Boom! Cheers all around.

INDIANS GONE WITHOUT A MURMUR

Longtime Florida visitor Hugh L. Willoughby followed the techniques of the experts—the Seminoles. His Old Everglades trip notes, published in 1898 from travel with a rugged pal in 1897, brimmed with appreciation for a magnificent place about to be forever altered within just thirty years. On his journey from the west coast to the east, he used a Seminole canoe carved with a small platform at the back, the aft, to stand on while poling through the shallow saw grass sea. He packed a canoe sail and used it Seminole-style. His trek required arduous backtracks caused by water trails that ended at saw grass walls, nights spent in the canoe for lack of dry land, unceasing jabs from nighttime mosquitoes, and the torture of the raggedly cutting saw grass. Still, it also rippled with exquisite moments of discovery of the natural order of things. Unlike expeditioners whose low moments focused on their own difficulties, this man's most depressing time occurred when he reached outside himself to contemplate someone else. He was near his expedition's end, arriving at the island camp of his friend, a Seminole man. Instead of finding Miami Jimmie, he met a gruff settler who had commandeered the island, driven the family off, destroyed their carefully crafted palm-thatched, open-air, elevated homes, and told them that the island no longer belonged to the Seminoles. "The Indians had gone without a murmur, but through no spirit of cowardice; . . . loyalty to their pledge makes them submit to many an outrage," Willoughby wrote. The next day, his journey across the Old Everglades ended via a swift descent along the Miami River into the Miami frontier village, where the outdoorsman was welcomed back to civilized society.

When I look at a 1855 Florida map of the famed region that these expeditioners crossed, labeled Indian Hunting Grounds, I wonder what we have buried under our highways and schools, playgrounds and parking lots, and where rich muck remains, I wonder what is buried under the muck. The Old Everglades evolved as an unacknowledged district of archaeological, cultural, historic, and natural treasures long before laws against the ruin of such estimable places landed on the books. The Old Everglades held mounds in which Seminole and, later, nonnative travelers found breastplates and beads from a long-ago native people. Islands of higher-elevation cabbage palms in the shallow saw grass sea hid charcoal drawings of deer, people, and inscrutable symbols, messages sketched on scraped areas of palm tree trunks. Who knows what sort of silent evidence of people past—such as the Miami Circle, carbon-dated to nineteen-hundred years ago, a mysterious limestone carving hastily granted protection from development only in 1999—fell to dynamite or became entombed in pavement for our pleasure? If Florida, the fourth most-populous state with about 16 million souls (contrasted with only 140,000 in 1860), is to have more visitors and more residents, I wish for the state to receive the ones who are curious. And when one of them crosses the Everglades on the Alligator Alley or Tamiami Trail I hope it's not difficult from inside the tour van to gaze at the saw grass and momentarily make a time past reappear. That narrow water course over there could be the very spot where once, in the middle of nowhere, a horribly cut, half-starved, lost expeditionist sunk into the mud, unable to any longer drag a canoe. Or, on the same hidden water trail, there might have once easily glided a native cypress-log canoe with sail puffed, taking a silent Seminole family past pond lilies, apple snails, and a limpkin, feeding. For our gaze across the saw grass sea to be more generous than self-centered, we need only to seek out the stories of its natural and human history. And we'll collect citizens, armored with history, who can make enlightened decisions that may just sustain the Everglades.

The author thanks her helpers, including Dr. Joe Knetsch, Florida historian and friend, who provided some materials and offered his always careful read. The author absolves him of responsibility for any errors of fact. She also thanks the Florida Historical Society *and the State of Florida Archives, especially its Florida Room and able staff. Several sources are invaluable, especially the* Florida Historical Quarterly, *the Florida Historical Society;* Tequesta: The Journal of the Historical Association of South Florida; "South Florida's Amazing Everglades," *by John O'Reilly,* National Geographic, *January 1940;* Camping and Cruising in Florida, *by James A. Henshall, Robert Clarke and Company, 1884;* Journey Through the Old Everglades, *edited by Pat Dodson, Trend House, 1973;* Across the Everglades: A Canoe Journey of Exploration, *by Hugh L. Willoughby, J. B. Lippincott Company, 1898; and* The Everglades: An Environmental History, *by David McCally, University Press of Florida, 1999.*

After graduating in journalism from the University of Florida, JAN GODOWN *lived in Fort Myers on an ancient Calusa Indian trade route, the Caloosahatchee River, also a travel route into the Old Everglades for many an 1800s expeditioner. She was a 1999 Atlantic Center for the Arts associate artist in residence for literary journalism, and has been a director in the Florida Folklore Society and Florida Historical Society. Her next Florida book is for the National Geographic Society. Falcon Publishing debuted her* Scenic Driving Florida *(1998) and* Family Fun in Florida *(2000). Although Florida is her muse, she has hiked Mt. Katahdin in Maine and Mt. LeConte in the Great Smoky Mountains, and has reported from Costa Rica during a three-month sabbatical. Jan lives with her husband, Paolo Annino, Florida State University College of Law clinical instructor, and their daughter in Tallahassee, where she finds it easy to indulge her interest in history.*

THE STORK AND THE SPARROW

Don Stap

Driving south out of Orlando in late April, I follow Highway 441 through the cattle ranches of south-central Florida past Yeehaw Junction and Fort Drum and on down to the north edge of Lake Okeechobee. There the old state highway follows the eastern rim of this big bathtub of a lake (730 square miles of water that is twelve feet deep on the average) to its southeastern shore before breaking due east toward Palm Beach. I turn off, continuing south, and enter what once was the northern edge of the Everglades. From this watershed, all of fifteen feet above sea level, a shallow, fifty-mile-wide sheet of water once flowed unobstructed more than a hundred miles to Florida Bay. Now, the "river of grass," as Marjory Stoneman Douglas called it, is only a memory here. For an hour I drive through dusty cane fields and sod farms, then past a series of nurseries, and finally I turn west just south of Homestead, where the fields are planted with tomatoes— more tomatoes than I've ever seen or could imagine, tens of thousands of which appear to be rotting on the vine. In one field the plants have been removed, but the ground is completely covered with the putrefy-ing tomatoes left behind.

Moments later, at the entrance to Everglades National Park, the agricultural fields end abruptly at a line of trees. Decades ago, the bulldozers stopped here, leaving what remains of the native pines of Everglades National Park. Nowhere could a boundary between a

natural landscape and an unnatural one be more distinct. Nowhere
could it be a greater illusion.

The truth of the matter—noisy, homely, begging for attention—is
stirring shortly after sunrise the following morning in a clump of mangroves: a couple dozen bawling wood stork chicks. Once, thousands
of young wood storks fledged each year in the Everglades. This large,
long-legged wading bird with a bare head and neck and a heavy, decurved bill is North America's only member of the stork family. Despite
the protection that Everglades National Park provides, the wood stork
population within the park's boundaries has been declining since the
national park was established in 1947. Now, a small rookery such as
this is all a visitor is likely to find—a clear indication that the environment is anything but natural. In the 1930s, before the Everglades had
been extensively drained and subjected to a complex water control
system, there were an estimated 4,000 nesting pairs of wood storks in
the park. In 1960, a census revealed that the number had dropped to
roughly 2,500. By the mid 1980s, the population began a precipitous
descent that has left the park with only several hundred nesting pairs
in recent years.

As sunlight warms the rookery, the chicks' cries increase until the
mangroves are throbbing like a frog pond. On the edges of the nests
and in the uppermost branches the adult wood storks stand silently.
By the time the chicks have reached adulthood, they too will have
fallen into a silence that will last the remainder of their lives. Wood
storks are one of the few birds in the world that (with the exception of occasional hisses and bill clacking) make no sound. Edward
Forbush, in his classic *Natural History of the Birds of Eastern and Central
North America*, quotes an early naturalist's account of the wood stork's
repose: "Often one may find them on the wide marshes, either salt or
fresh water, standing perfectly still for an hour or more at a time, the
long heavy bill pointed downward and resting on the skin of the thick,
naked neck. On such occasions they seem to represent the personifica-
tion of dejection."

Although the twentieth century has given wood storks cause
for dejection, to me these tall, silent dignitaries of the marsh seem

self-possessed and imperturbable. I've always suspected that the settlers who gave them a series of unflattering names—flinthead, hammerhead, gourdhead—held more than a grain of admiration for the homely birds who carried themselves with stoic uprightness in an often inhospitable and unpredictable world. Wood storks rarely take notice of someone standing a short distance away watching them. If they fly off, they go without complaint. I have often watched wood storks feeding in the shallows of a marsh in small groups or singly. Sweeping its long, decurved bill from side to side in the water, its mandibles apart, the bird slowly lifts one foot, extends its leg slightly forward, then dips its toes just below the surface and delicately stirs up a murky mixture of mud, detritus, and bottom-resting fish. ("As soon as they have discovered a place abounding in fish, they dance as it were all through [the water]," John James Audubon wrote.) The stork's slow, deliberate strides belie its quick response to fish that brush against its bill, which snaps shut in less than three-hundredths of a second, one of the fastest reflexes known among vertebrates.

A pair of wood storks and their young (two hatchlings usually) need an estimated 440 pounds of fish over the course of the nesting season, and their specialized feeding technique—locating prey by touch rather than by sight—requires a high concentration of fish in shallow water. Historically, heavy summer rains in South Florida caused seasonal flooding of low-lying areas of the Everglades, which produced an abundance of fish. During the dry winter months that followed, much of the water evaporated, forcing fish into shrinking pools of water—ideal feeding grounds for wood storks. Wood storks will fly up to eighty miles from their rookeries looking for these feeding areas. They ascend on warm air currents and move from one thermal to another, often soaring in groups that turn in great circles like lazy figure skaters on the blue ice of the sky. Locating shallow pools with high concentrations of fish is critical, and the wood stork is so closely linked to this natural cycle of heavy rains followed by drought that the decreasing water level of winter appears to trigger the stork's reproductive instincts. If water levels are not suitable at the right time, wood storks often delay nesting, as they have more and more frequently in the Everglades. Late nesting often results in nests that fail completely, because by the time the young have hatched the summer rains have begun. As a result, the small pools of water that the wood storks depend on disappear as the land is once again flooded.

It has been a long time since summer rains alone have determined water levels in the Everglades, where 1,074 miles of canals, 720 miles of levees, 250 primary control or diversion structures, and 18 major pumping stations control the flow of water in and around the national park. As agriculture became big business in South Florida, the South Florida Water Management District often stockpiled summer rainwater in two large water management districts north of the national park, holding it there in case it was needed to irrigate the farm fields during the dry winter months. Eventually, in early spring, the remaining water had to be released, and since areas to the east were now heavily populated, the water management district dumped the water into the national park. Water levels rose suddenly, sometimes flooding out the wood stork feeding areas overnight. Some years whole colonies of wood storks abandoned their nests.

The effect of these unnatural water fluctuations on a large, conspicuous, tree-nesting bird was not hard to see; it took longer to notice how it affected the Everglades' smallest endangered bird, the reclusive Cape Sable seaside sparrow. Discovered in 1918 on Cape Sable, the wild southwest tip of Florida, this was the last distinctive bird from the continental United States to be described to science (it is now considered a subspecies, one of nine races of seaside sparrows that inhabit coastal marshes from Texas to Massachusetts). But in 1935, when a hurricane ripped through Cape Sable, the discovery seemed a cruel joke, something to tease ornithologists. The saltwater storm surges altered the sparrow's habitat, and the sparrow disappeared, sliding into extinction, it seemed, before it could be properly studied.

In 1942, the Cape Sable seaside sparrow was rediscovered when a biologist came across a small colony of the birds farther inland near Ochopee, but when others searched the area they could not find a single bird. Eventually, researchers turned up a few sparrows at a different site. In 1949, another colony was discovered even farther inland. In the late 1960s, birdwatchers reported seeing the elusive sparrows near the national park headquarters. Their accounts were viewed suspiciously until John Ogden, then a wildlife biologist with the National Park Service, found the remains of two seaside sparrows in the nest of a short-tailed hawk near the same area, and subsequently located about a dozen of the birds nearby in Taylor Slough. It wasn't until 1981, though, when Sonny Bass, another national park wildlife biologist, began conducting aerial surveys of hard-to-reach areas, that a formal Cape Sable seaside sparrow census was established. Bass estimated a total population of sixty-five hundred birds in three major colonies and a few small groups. By 1993, Stuart Pimm, a conservation biologist from the University of Tennessee, was leading the study of the sparrows.

In August of 1997, I met Stuart Pimm at the national park's research center. Pimm was there to participate in a conference on the status of the Cape Sable seaside sparrow, but he'd kindly offered to take me out to see a sparrow firsthand. Under a full moon, an hour before sunrise, we walked into the backcountry of the Everglades, sweating under our mosquito-proof bug shirts and hoods. Slipping and sliding in ankle-deep water on a layer of marl that barely covered the limestone bedrock, I followed Pimm out into the marsh. Growing out of the marl along with the saw grass was a short, coarse grass in the genus *Muhlenbergia*. The presence of *Muhlenbergia* indicated that this area was a foot or two higher than the grounds surrounding it and, therefore, was usually dry during the late winter and early spring. This made it good habitat for the ground-nesting Cape Sable seaside sparrow.

The sparrow builds its nest in clumps of grass, usually about eight inches above the ground. Historically, by the time the summer rains begin to flood the bird's territory, the small, olive-gray sparrow has already raised a brood of young. But the same water management practices that destroy the wood stork's feeding areas also flood the sparrow's nests. From 1993 to 1995, the water conservation areas north of the Everglades were brimming with water from unusually heavy summer rains. The excess water was dumped into Shark River Slough three years in a row. On the western edge of the slough, the Cape Sable seaside sparrow's largest population—two thousand birds—suffered a 90 percent loss. "The water rose sixty inches," Pimm recalled, "and in that area it's only twenty inches from the bottom of the 'hill' to the top." Even when rising water levels don't cover the birds' nests, it affects them. "If the water rises just four inches above ground level in nesting areas, the eggs and young are totally wiped out by predators—possibly snakes, which seem to move about more freely when the water level is higher." By the time I met Pimm in 1997, the total population of Cape Sable seaside sparrows had declined to an estimated three thousand birds, half of what it was in 1991. "If we drop another three thousand birds," Pimm said, "there won't be any left."

As we walked farther into the saw grass and *Muhlenbergia*, we watched the grasses for movement. The small, drab sparrows blend into this landscape perfectly. During his annual census, Pimm hears the birds more often than he sees them, though now and then one will pop out of hiding and perch momentarily on a stalk of saw grass. We stood and scanned the area around us with binoculars as the first rays of sun lit the tips of the saw grass and then poured the day itself into the flat landscape. We were not far from the road, but at the moment it was easy to imagine that there were only miles and miles of silent grasslands.

It reminded me of the spartina grass marshes at Merritt Island National Wildlife Refuge on Florida's Atlantic coast where the last wild dusky seaside sparrow was seen twenty years ago. A near relative of the Cape Sable seaside sparrow, the dusky once could be found throughout the coastal marshes of Merritt Island, but its population, estimated at four thousand birds on Merritt Island, collapsed over a period of several decades, a victim of coastal development, DDT spraying, poor habitat management, bad luck, and a grass fire that devastated what remained of the Merritt Island population in 1975. The last dusky seaside sparrow died in a cage in 1987, where it was the focus of an unsuccessful captive breeding project.

Before the morning was over, we got a good look at a Cape Sable seaside sparrow when it rose out of the *Muhlenbergia* and perched atop a stalk of saw grass. I stared long and hard at the bird. It fidgeted, looked quickly one way, then the other, then back again. For the few moments that I watched it, this one sparrow seemed to be at the center of its world, and mine. Finally, it flew off, diving down into the grass again. On the walk back to the road, Pimm talked of the conference he was to attend later that day, an effort to share information on the sparrow and to discuss how the plans that were being developed for the Everglades restoration project would affect the tiny bird.

Today, three and a half years later, there are small signs that the restoration project is underway. This morning as I drove through the national park on my way to the wood stork rookery, I slowed down where the road crosses Taylor Slough. There, barricades divert traffic around the old roadbed where the Army Corps of Engineers is putting in a new bridge that will allow a greater flow of water through Taylor Slough. On Tamiami Trail, which runs along the north border of the park, the corps plans to build a twenty-mile-long bridge over the larger Shark River Slough. The complexity of the plan to restore the Everglades—a multi-billion-dollar, three-decade-plus project—cannot be exaggerated. It involves thirteen federal and six state agencies, as well as two tribal governments. Canals and levees will be removed. Billions of gallons of freshwater may be pumped underground for storage. Land outside the park boundaries is set to be purchased. Computer-simulated models of different water management practices have been run in the hope that they will predict how best to simulate what once were natural conditions. That we now preside over the rains themselves is one more example of how we control what we do not understand. To this the wood stork brings its inscrutable silence, and the Cape Sable seaside sparrow its ghostly reflection of another sparrow that is lost forever.

––––––––––

DON STAP *is the author of* A Parrot Without a Name, *a firsthand account of an ornithological expedition into an unexplored area of Peru. He is a frequent contributor to* Audubon *and has written as well for* Smithsonian, Orion, International Wildlife, Travel and Leisure, North American Review, Chicago Tribune, *and the* New York Times. *In addition, he is the author of* Letter at the

End of Winter, *a collection of poems, and the recipient of a Florida Individual Artist grant and a fellowship in creative writing from the National Endowment for the Arts. A native of Michigan, Don Stap has taught at the University of Central Florida since 1985, where he is a professor of English.*

Part Three

ATLANTIC COASTAL RIDGE

*East along the curving Everglades borders and west by the farther coast
stood everywhere in their endless ranks the great companies of the pines.
Where they grew the rock was highest—"high pine land," people called it.
Their ranks went off across an open slough in a feathery cliff, a rampart
of trunks red-brown in the setting sun, bearing tops like a long streamer
of green smoke. Their warm piny breaths blew in the sun along the salt
winds. They covered here, as they did everywhere in Florida, interminable
miles.*

THE EVERGLADES: RIVER OF GRASS, MARJORY STONEMAN DOUGLAS

Were it not for the slightly elevated curve of land—the Atlantic
Coastal Ridge—rimming Florida's extreme southeastern tip, Everglades
waters might never reach Florida Bay. And this landscape, essential
as it is to the structural integrity of the greater Everglades ecosystem,
is unique in its own right, ecologically equivalent to the open slash
pine forests of the Bahamas. The limestone formation that underlies
the Atlantic Coastal Ridge consists of a series of rocky outcrops called
Miami oolite, and it extends more than fifty miles, from Ft. Lauderdale
south to Florida City and then westward into Everglades National Park.
The ridge is the highest and oldest land in southern Florida, formed
from deep banks of shells washed ashore during an elevated sea level.
Portions of the ridge have stood just above the surrounding landscape
for tens of thousands of years.

Before white settlement, ramparts of slash pine formed an almost continuous forest the length of the rock ridge, an area about fifty miles from top to bottom and no more than two to six miles wide, from sea to saw grass. A much smaller percentage of upland vegetation on the coastal ridge is its tropical hammocks, which occurred wherever naturally occurring fires had been excluded. Broad-leaved West Indian trees and shrubs—strangler figs, paradise tree, pigeon plums and many more—intermixed extravagantly with the temperate flora of North Florida—live oak, mulberry, and bay. In the mid-1800s, like the rest of predrained South Florida, the coastal ridge abounded with freshwater springs. An abundance of deer, bear, and panther shared the uplands with the small community of human settlers.

The Atlantic Coastal Ridge has arguably been transformed more than any other part of the greater Everglades, into an urban belt crammed with five million people living between the ocean and a buffer strip along the Everglades in Dade, Broward, and Palm Beach counties. The population of Dade County alone has burgeoned in less than one hundred years from just a thousand hardy folk to two million residents of many cultures. Planners estimate that more than six million people will live in South Florida by 2015. The land required for these millions has erased all but 2 percent of the original pinelands and hammocks from the ridge.

STRAWS IN A SWIMMING POOL

Michele Hatton

Homestead, the little town where I grew up, perches at the tail end of the long thin Atlantic Coastal Ridge that stretches from Georgia down to the tip of Florida. The ridge, a mere five to fifteen miles wide, is a natural barrier that prevents rainwater from sliding off into the Atlantic and instead steers it gently inland toward the Everglades. Homestead sits low, approximately ten feet above sea level. Downtown Miami, a forty-minute drive northeast, is almost equally as low and lies on this same ridge. A few miles south of Homestead, the ridge ends and the lower Florida Keys begin.

When nature had sovereignty, the Everglades covered most of South Florida from Lake Okeechobee southward. Seasonal downpours and hurricanes periodically drenched the area, forcing Lake Okeechobee to overflow its banks and replenish this enormous expanse of wet, flat land. Rimmed on the east by the long, narrow, coastal ridge and on the west by a more inland ridge, the greater Everglades terrain forms a large shallow basin that slopes imperceptibly southward and tugs the water toward Florida Bay.

As a child, I wasn't aware that the levees and canals, built just to the west of us, protected the edges of my town from repeated flooding. Specifically, Levee-31N and Canal 111, built in 1948, blocked the southwesterly flow of Everglades water, keeping our home dry—and simultaneously eliminating the natural aquatic communities that had thrived in the region for thousands of years. Before those two thousand miles of flood protection devices and canals were constructed, I could have hiked a short distance from my home and, with my little pink inner tube and some gumption, paddled my way along Taylor Slough to Florida Bay, twenty miles away.

Last spring, I took a trip back to South Florida to see what had changed in the southern half of my state over the past thirty years. My trip was not simply an excursion into nostalgia; I went also to investigate the management of water in the Glades and how the twenty-year plan to restore these waters, now in the beginning stages, might work. I particularly wanted to see one of the aquifer storage and recovery (ASR) wells, which inject and store surface water in the aquifer system. It was easy to find the technological information I was after, but what was unexpected and somewhat unsettling was the difference I found between my childhood impressions of South Florida and present reality. The Florida I saw outside my car window contrasted sharply with the place I remembered; I found myself journeying backward in time as I drove forward.

I prepared for my trip by packing only the bare essentials: tent, sleeping bag, gallon jugs of water, a reliable sun hat, and a stack of reference material on the Everglades. I mapped the route to Boynton Beach, where a functioning ASR well is housed at the city's utility plant. The geologists I had consulted prior to this trip told me that a wellhead wasn't much to look at, just some dials and tubes, but the impulse to see even that urged me on.

ASR wells are an enormous part of the twenty-year Everglades Restoration Plan; in fact, the cost of these wells will consume $2 billion of the $7.8 billion set aside for the plan. Although the technology is not new, the magnitude of the ASR proposal has caused great alarm. Nowhere else in the world have so many wells, in such close proximity to one another, been drilled into an aquifer. Never before has an aquifer system been expected to store so much injected water. Florida is engaging in a colossal experiment.

The Everglades Restoration Plan, however, is a noble effort, led by the Army Corps of Engineers, designed to restore the remnant

Everglades ecosystem to function as it did a hundred years ago. ASR wells are pivotal to that plan, offering a potent, new way to store excess water that will be channeled primarily to the natural areas and secondarily to the cities and farms. John Outland, with the state's Department of Environmental Protection and a key player in the plan, says that the wells will assist with managing the quality, quantity, and flow of water so that it most closely resembles nature's original design.

As I drove south, my mind drifted back to the Everglades of my childhood, pristine and seemingly undisturbed. Then I remembered the simple facts of today. The Everglades are now half their original size. The five- to fifteen-mile-wide ridge on the east coast, which terminates just south of Homestead, now accommodates five million people. Fifteen million are predicted to inhabit the region by 2050. Thousands of truckloads of fill have converted the marshland to solid ground, providing the foundation for unbridled growth. Over two hundred control and diversion structures, twenty-five locks, and two thousand miles of canals and levees have been installed to block, lock, drain, direct, and divert the free-flowing water of this natural system. In short, nearly every last drop of water is managed and pumped to meet the competing needs of agriculture, navigation, urban populations, and natural areas. From a satellite view, South Florida today looks like a poorly made patchwork quilt, sliced, bunched, and padded, put together by sometimes well-intentioned quilters, all of whom have failed nature miserably.

It was an unbearably hot day to begin a trip, but once I cleared Central Florida, the roads became more remote and edged with lush greenery. A few miles north of Yeehaw Junction—a town whose name summoned endless chuckles from my sister, Alexa, and me during our family trips upstate and which, I was surprised to see, is still just one intersection with a rundown gas station on the southeast corner—I accidentally ran over a snake. When I turned back around to check on it, it was gasping for breath. I burst into tears. The snake was dying a senseless death—anyone would be upset about this—but its death, I came to find, was a metaphor that revealed itself to me over the course of the trip.

The dike of Lake Okeechobee reared up into view before long, and I drove straight up the embankment to catch a glimpse of the lake that spreads out like a sea. I circled the east rim of the lake, crossing the L-8 Borrow Canal where a complex of locks and colossal cement blocks that move with the push of a button join the St. Lucie River with Lake Okeechobee.

I turned onto Highway 98, traveling through a vast spread of sugarcane fields. Slender stalks of cane, silky leaves waving in the wind, were beautiful, restful to watch. It was troubling, though, to think how extensively this crop has displaced native saw grass marshes. Sugar requires massive amounts of phosphorus, a nutrient that has dramatically altered the nearby marshland. When we were children, we thought of the sugar processing plants, with their billowing white smoke and jagged scape of chimneys, as Wizard of Oz castles that had somehow dropped anchor in Swampville, Florida. But this time, passing through, I thought how creepy these processing plants looked, coated a dirty brown, an inevitable byproduct of processing cane.

Paralleling Highway 98 was a long, perfectly straight canal, uniform in width and depth. The canals in this region traversed my childhood the same way they crisscross the land. On any family outing, there was usually a canal running along the road we took to get there. I was frightened by their murky depths, for good reason, too: many a car had plummeted to the bottom of these trenches, evidenced by the crosses that appeared alongside the roads. I remember riding in the back seat of the car, hypnotized by the unchanging regularity of these canals, startled into anxiety every twenty miles or so when we'd pass by another lone cross. One more death by drowning.

As kids, however, we had a ball canal diving. Often on a lazy Saturday afternoon, one of my sister's boyfriends would pick us up and drive us out to our favorite bridge. With any luck, he would be the one with the Thunderbird convertible so that we could parade through downtown. We'd drive twenty miles through sunbaked terrain, then cross a bridge over a deep blue trench of water, circle back under it, and park. The boys did jackknives and backflips off the bridge. We girls specialized in swan dives, cannon balls, and forward flips. My sisters considered canal diving one of the more risky adolescent activities, an illegal and closely guarded secret from my parents. But splashing in these cool, deep, artificial ravines was one of the best ways we knew to escape the heat, and we did it as often as we could. A few fishermen caught bass here, but with no shade and nothing but craggy limerock to sit on, fishing conditions were less than ideal.

It was dark before I reached Boynton Beach. The next morning, I made my way to the utility plant, which I assumed would be on the outskirts of town. But the five-acre facility squatted right in the middle of downtown Boynton Beach on a corner lot, adjacent to a convenience store and a gas station. The manager of the ASR well, Dora Formanek, gave me a tour of the plant, showed me the wellhead, and praised the productivity and economic benefits of this particular well. I was secretly thrilled that we were two women discussing wells and other traditionally male topics. Would this have occurred twenty years ago, even ten, I wondered?

ASR wells are designed to manage surplus surface water by using the natural aquifer as large, underground storage tanks. Water may be held for days, months, or even years, and then may be retrieved and channeled to natural, agricultural, or urban areas. The injection and withdrawal of surface water depends largely on weather conditions. When South Florida is experiencing heavy rainfall, water is injected and stored. During the dry season, the aquifer is tapped. The process may be in continuous fluctuation depending on the demand for water.

The Everglades Restoration Plan proposes that approximately three hundred of these wells be placed in clusters around Lake Okeechobee, the Hillsboro Canal, and the Caloosahatchee River basin. (Nationally, the number of functioning ASR wells is fewer than fifty, thirty-four of which are in Florida.) They will be sunk one thousand or more feet into regions of the Floridan aquifer. There, an immense bubble of fresh surface water will displace the native aquifer water. Each of these wells alone can send millions of gallons of water into the aquifer, though the actual quantity is still unknown and will depend on the conditions of the aquifer at each specific injection site. It is anticipated that the three hundred wells cumulatively will be capable of injecting 1.7

billion gallons of water into the aquifer. The sheer scale of this proposal skirts the unfathomable.

An aquifer system, the Floridan, for example, is difficult to visualize. Imagine an enormous underground layer-cake of rock, running the length of the peninsula and extending far out to sea on the west coast. Imagine it pockmarked, brittle, and cracked with winding conduits and hollow caverns, some big enough to drive a truck through, packaged in irregularly shaped boxes wrapped with thick, impermeable, confining clays and silts. Every microscopic pore space in the rock, as well as each mammoth cavern, is saturated with water. Some of the water has been there for eons. Some trickled down during last night's thunderstorm. Though simplistic, this is a birds-eye view of the Floridan aquifer, the dominant aquifer system in the state and the source of drinking water for millions of North Floridians.

Picturing ASR wells at work isn't easy. Where will the native waters go? Will they bubble up to the surface in a whoosh in some unexpected location? Considering how enormous the Floridan is, biologist Richard Deuerling, of the state Department of Environmental Protection, likened the ASR concept to "straws in a swimming pool."

"It doesn't mean diddly-squat if you stick a few straws in a swimming pool and add water," Deuerling told me. "However, we don't know what may happen if the pool is packed with straws and filled to the brink with water. There is a good possibility the foundation will crack." Food for thought.

I stood by this ASR well for a good hour while Dora explained the complexities of the system to me. As she spoke, a kind of primordial cognition took shape in my mind, and I realized why I had felt so compelled to see one of these wellheads. Relatively small contraptions on the surface, they exercise enormous power underground, plunging into a subterranean world we cannot see or touch and can barely envision. There, submerged in darkness, they embark on a task that is appallingly violent, forcing newly fallen rainwater through the pores of ancient rock, displacing brackish waters that have resided in the aquifer system for thousands or millions of years and that may have arrived at that particular spot in time by traveling at a speed of inches per month. A thousand feet was a relatively short distance on the surface, but that same distance straight down through the earth was significant. I could not combine the enormity of this job with the mystery of the dark underworld in which it was being carried out. As I stood there, I almost believed I felt anguished rumblings beneath my feet.

The wellhead itself is a massive jumble of silver tubes with dials and odd steering wheel gismos that stick out on top. I didn't think these contraptions marred the landscape to any great degree, but like tips of icebergs, these few pipes and valves didn't fully indicate how much lay beneath. Many of the areas predestined for ASR wells are in rural Florida, where life is slow. People go about things leisurely. I had to wonder how such a technologically intensive strategy wound up here, and indeed, if this is the best way to restore a natural system.

I lunched at a small Greek restaurant, patronized by gray-haired snowbirds who were obviously accustomed to the fine ethnic cuisines of the northeast. The food was out of this world. I considered this a good omen since the restaurant was located in a seedy strip mall and I wound up there by sheer chance. I hoped to reach Everglades National Park by midafternoon for two and a half days of wilderness camping.

I drove through the heart of the east coast development. It was worse than I had imagined. Sprawling cookie cutter houses on sandy, treeless lots stretched endlessly, black tarmac roads twisting among them like monstrous snakes on the sandy fill. As a child, I may have very easily gazed upon this spot and enjoyed a vista of undefiled marshland. I tried to imagine fifteen million people living here in fifty years, on counterfeit land. The shortsightedness of the idea struck me as monumentally reckless.

I exited the interstate and headed onto Saw Grass Expressway, hoping for a breath of fresh air and a drive through the saw grass marshes I had grown up with. Instead, I bumped into more hideous sprawl. This time the houses crept right up to the base of the east coast levee, a soft mound of muck and rock and sand dredged from adjacent canals, about thirteen feet high, spanning three counties north to south. I wondered when the slow climb up the embankment would begin and which chain restaurant would stake its claim there. It brought to mind a point made by John Outland, back in Tallahassee. "The most important thing we can do is buy the land. But it takes money, a lot of money." He added, "It will be a heck of a fight if the Everglades agricultural lands are converted to residential land. You can make a lot more short term money from subdivisions than you can from agriculture." The idea of further development seemed preposterous to me, but in light of our history, not at all improbable.

Homestead and Miami were smaller, simpler, less complicated in the 1960s. The two towns were connected by Highway 1, which ran next to a train track, some packing houses, a shopping plaza, and some limerock mining pits. My three sisters called Homestead "Deadstead" or "Flatstead," partly because of what they considered monotonous landscape, but mostly because it lacked any form of cultural sophistication. We made periodic trips to Miami to purchase bathing suits and penny loafers. When Miami got a two-story department store with an escalator, we thought we were in heaven.

I was the youngest of the four girls, and although Miami occasionally got my attention, I knew that a home bordering the Everglades, that was in fact in the Everglades, was an unusual and extraordinary place to grow up. The lack of culture in our town was immaterial to me. I sensed even then that the flagrant pink of a roseate spoonbill in a setting sun or the sharpness of crocodile teeth were on a much higher order than the Jordan Marsh department store. My formative years were profiled by these miracles of nature, so close to my home, and the experiences that followed from living there were, at the very least, uncommon.

It was a family tradition to go frogging after a particularly heavy downpour. Frogging was done on hot, steamy, summer nights when the frogs bellowed like a band of discontented tubas and the mosquitoes swarmed, thick as pudding. The six of us would pile into the old Plymouth, find a dirt road on the swampy edge of town, and embark.

We four girls sat in a line on the hood of the car, armed with old brooms scrounged from deep in the garage. It was leopard frog we were after, noted for the tenderness of its meat. My father drove slowly, lights on high beam, in search of the plump, spotted prey. He was also, I found out later, watching for the occasional cottonmouth that slinked across these roads after a rain. My mother kept an eye on her four girls, making sure none slipped off the hood. Enervated by the humidity, the frogs leapt across the road. When their numbers reached in the dozens, my father stopped the car and we girls jumped from the hood and stunned them with a blow from our brooms. One by one, my father gathered up their slack bodies, threw them in the cooler, and the hunt continued. The cooler filled.

Once home, my father had the gruesome task of delegging the critters, then battering and frying them in the skillet. He served them to my beautiful mother as if she were a queen, and she ate with the gusto of a lumberjack. "Prairie chicken," she dubbed them. We girls ran squeamishly into the bedrooms pantomiming puking gestures.

I reached Shark River Slough in Everglades National Park midday, where the wading birds mesmerized me. I watched them pick their way around on stick legs swallowing fish with their smooth tubular necks. The next afternoon, I traveled west to Big Cypress Swamp, which offered the first bit of shade I'd yet found. If you look up toward the sky there, you can see needles from the Florida slash pine mingling with fronds of the royal palms. Sharing this same piece of the heavens may be the feathery leaves of a massive bald cypress. Together, the bottoms of these diverse-looking trees were probably sharing a small mound of muck. For dinner, I feasted on broiled snapper and baked potatoes in Everglades City.

Evenings, I reflected on the wells, and on the wildlife surrounding me. I kept returning to the same thought. "What a grand experiment! What a risk!" For whom were these wells being built? I considered the population growth in South Florida, now skyrocketing. Was this land, barely escaping the sea, meant to be inhabited by people? I wasn't sure. And if so, should it not be by those who know how to maneuver through it and leave little imprint?

Water is Florida's birthright. It is one of the wettest states in the union, its southern half a natural flood zone. The waters here engage in a relentless and dramatic hydrological dance. Seasonal flooding, a natural outcome of abundant rain falling on low, flat terrain, is augmented by the large amounts of water dumped by hurricanes. In lakes, steams, and sloughs, the water pools. In higher land, it spreads out and thins. The rest either evaporates, is transpired by plants, or seeps down through the soil and into the subterranean aquifer.

Cities now prevent the natural system from absorbing these waters. Instead, water is channeled to the coasts and dumped directly into brackish estuaries or held in storage on the surface in large water preservation areas. But storing water on land is problematic—it rapidly evaporates in the Florida sun or seeps underground. Furthermore, land is expensive, scarce, and difficult to acquire. "We have three choices," warns Outland. "We can stack it [in Lake Okeechobee—a threat to the health of the lake], let it rip to tide [slang for dumping it in the ocean], or put it underground. All the easy stuff's been done. Now, we're into the hard stuff." This is where the ASR proposal comes into play.

The challenge of drilling these wells into our ancient limestone subsurface and making them work is more than just technological. The even more difficult issues are political. What, or rather who, will ultimately claim this water? What does it mean to provide supply on such a grandiose scale? What does it mean to restore a natural system with sophisticated technology? Do we have the bucks and skills to keep these wells safe and productive? What if science isn't able to lead the way?

In an official document, the Florida Chapter of the Sierra Club responds to some of these questions. "Engineering alone won't save the Everglades. The Everglades needs space, land, and natural processes. The [restoration] plan creates a system of high-tech underground water storage which would supply twelve to fifteen million people by mid-century. To quote a famous movie, 'If you build it, they will come.'"

The ASR proposal raises technical issues of equal magnitude. The underground world of interior South Florida is neither completely mapped nor well understood. We don't know what will result when surface water takes up residence in ancient limestone. In one study, arsenic and uranium, though in acceptable levels, were found in ASR well water, a result of chemical interplay between the old rock and the new water. In another study, conducted with laboratory models, the interaction between the two waters produced an iron-hydroxide that clogged both the pores in the limestone and the simulated borehole itself. The hope of withdrawing vast amounts of usable water from these wells may be a grave disappointment with a sizeable price tag attached. Problems mount when we consider that much of the water to be stored is gathered from a surface contaminated with pesticides, fertilizer, and runoff.

Because the Floridan aquifer system is not uniform, one injection site may easily receive water, while another may respond by cracking. Geologists refer to this as "fracturing the bucket," a very real concern, especially when wells are clustered close together, creating cumulative pressure. A fractured aquifer system could pose serious risks. Changes could take place in the flow of underground water. Test wells that monitor our drinking water could bear skewed results. Worst-case scenario: contaminated water could migrate into our drinking water. Most scientists working on this project agree that proceeding with caution is imperative, and a quiet war is waging between the cautious and the not-so-cautious in the planning for these wells. The natural Everglades, with its history of engineering disasters, cannot afford another blunder.

Florida spent 145,000 years building its aquifers, putting down layer upon layer of limestone and dolomite in a slow progression upward from the bottom of the sea. These layers were formed mostly from minuscule marine creatures who fashioned homes or skeletons out of calcium carbonate, then lost them to the sea at the time of their death. Countless numbers of these limy shells dropped to the ocean floor where they underwent the age-old process of compaction and lithification to form the aquifers. It would behoove us to know exactly what we are drilling into before we begin tampering.

The last day of my visit, I stayed in a small campground off Tamiami Trail. The right side of the road looked different from the left side, an indication that the road was obstructing moving waters. I noticed that the thatched chickees that had dotted the road in the early 1960s, and the amber-skinned Seminole women selling handmade trinkets in front of them, had disappeared.

The beauty of the region was breathtaking. A roseate spoonbill cast its pink glow and caught my eye with its beak shaped like a big flat spoon.

At dusk, I sat for a long time in front of a small lake in the campground and took in the softness, the sound of water animals, the rustle of fellow campers. Sunset glazed the sky in hot pinks and oranges. Slowly, the sedges and cottontail faded to splintered silhouettes. This indeed was paradise, and seemed as wild as a place could be.

I considered the final recommendation made by the Sierra Club to revamp the restoration plan and base it on a population projection of eight million, rather than fifteen million, by midcentury. This would significantly reduce the number of ASR wells needed. I had to agree. I wondered why putting limits on growth is viewed by so many as a political nonoption.

The animals dipping and paddling in the pond went about their affairs, some preparing to bed down for the night, others just rousing. I wondered if we, as an intelligent species, had the collective courage and foresight to put their needs on a level playing field with our own. I watched a baby turtle plop down into the lake and swim eagerly to the bottom. I pretended we played an insignificant role in its life.

––––––––––

MICHELE HATTON *lives with her husband in Tallahassee, where she is an educational administrator and freelance writer and is currently pursuing a third degree, this one in geology. She has contributed to numerous educational publications and is researcher, writer, editor, and graphic designer of* SDFS Notes, *a quarterly newsletter on school violence and drug prevention. She is a reporter and writer for the* New Leaf News *and is former editor and graphic artist for the monthly newsletter of the Big Bend Chapter of the Sierra Club. She spends her free time camping in the wilderness, reading literature, and dancing.*

PUTTING DOWN ROOTS

EXOTICS IN THE EVERGLADES

Sharon Rauch

Exotic plants get a bad rap. They're called invasive. Noxious. A royal pain in the rear. In some parts of the Everglades, they've gobbled up the landscape so completely they've blotted out native vegetation. Deer and alligators give them a wide berth. Herons and egrets shake their long beaks and move on. They'll build their nest elsewhere, thank you.

To top it off, these invaders are tenacious as hell. Chop down a melaleuca tree, for instance, and the stump will sprout back within weeks. Burn it or douse it with herbicide, and two million seeds no bigger than a pinpoint explode into the air. Use the bark as a fence post, and it'll grow roots. You can't even drown the dang thing—seeds can live up to six months underwater.

"Heeehawww!" these Australian natives must have shouted when they first hit Florida soil around the turn of the century. Plenty of land (they grow in wet and dry soil). No natural controls. Plenty of sunshine. Can you blame them for wanting to stay?

I can't. In fact, I have to confess to possessing a certain sympathy for these colonizers. I, too, am nonnative. Eager for a home, a land to call my own, I have sunk deep roots in Florida soil and refuse to let go. About six hundred of us a day adopt this state. We come. We multiply.

We overwhelm the natural landscape, change it beyond recognition. Yet once we get past our self-serving needs, we have to admit: We're doing this place wrong. It breaks the heart to see the natural land dissolve quicker than a video on fast rewind. It's got to stop.

Weirdly enough, I look to the exotics for inspiration. People who deal with these opportunists are quick to say that not all nonnative species are bad. These plants and trees—azaleas, mimosas, Japanese magnolias, elephant ears, water hyacinths, the list goes on—are found everywhere. Some hark back to the day Spaniards first landed in St. Augustine. For the most part, they have led quiet lives alongside the native species. Only a few cross the line. These bad boys jump the fence, spread across the field, chase others out of their homes. Out of thousands of exotics in Florida, only about twenty-five fall into this dangerous category, according to Don Schmitz, a biologist with the Florida Department of Environmental Regulation.

As humans, we should take note. We may always be nonnative, but we don't have to be invasive. We just have to figure out how to contain ourselves.

Two people who were born and raised in South Florida—natives, if you will—may hold the key. For years, both men, like valiant knights, have volunteered time every week in the Everglades to wage war on exotic plants. They sweat buckets. Swat buzzing mosquitoes. Mop up blood after blades of saw grass slice their skin. Even some of their best friends ask, "Are you nuts?"

But the rewards are sweet. When Chris Murch gets stressed out, he drives down to the levees where he and other members of the Everglades Restoration Movement have hacked melaleuca to the ground, then squirted the stumps with herbicide. (This double-whammy has become the best method for wiping out the intruders.) He can look out for miles across the saw grass with no exotics in sight. Coming back along the fringes are the native trees: red bay, coco plum, pond apple, fig. He scans the horizon for deer.

The real land—at least part of it—is back. Imagine for a moment standing with him on the levee breathing in the sweet wind. The saw grass sways in the breeze, streaks of green, darker green, black, and gold moving side to side. We can make this land better—all of us—native and nonnative alike. We just have to have the determination. The passion. And the courage, like the lion in the *The Wizard of Oz*, to face down our fears. Are we going to let a few snakes and mosquitoes stop us?

Melaleuca quinquenervia: Also known as cajeput, punk-tree, five-veined paperbark, bottle-brush tree. Characteristics: Fast-growing evergreen reaching heights of fifty to seventy feet. Branches slender and moderately short. Multiple trunks. Bark contains layers of peeling, paperlike material. Blooms white flowers most of year. Broken branches that fall on suitable soil can root and grow. So can felled trees.

I moved to South Florida in 1970 when I was thirteen. Everywhere I looked in my new neighborhood in Plantation, just west of Fort Lauderdale, was gray rock. The land had been bulldozed down to that washed-out color, the only relief being a few new homes with incongruous sod planted around them.

Even after our house was built and some greenery returned to the neighborhood, I longed for something wild. I would take my blue one-speed bike out of the garage and pedal for miles in every direction. Most of it was the same. New. Stripped of native vegetation. Street after street of new homes. At times, I found it hard to breathe. Little did I know that fewer than ten miles west were the Everglades. Miles and miles of saw grass. Flocks of egrets. Apple snails crawling among the reeds. I never made it that far. Instead, when I was nineteen, I escaped to Tallahassee, taking root alongside live oak and pine, breathing in air that would go all the way down to my lungs.

But Chris Murch stayed. In 1970, he was just a toddler living in Coral Springs at the edge of the Everglades. As he grew, he ventured more and more into the watery wilderness. He hunted for snakes. He rode his bike on the levees for miles. He daydreamed and felt the sun on his back, choosing to be surrounded by saw grass on Sunday mornings rather than by church pews.

As he became an adolescent, then a young man, he witnessed the continued erosion of the Everglades. Development progressed nonstop. Water was diverted here, then there. Exotics like melaleuca and the Australian pine were choking parts of the land. To him, the Everglades had lost its magic. He stopped going. Then in 1990, he read an article about a group of volunteers who were cutting down melaleuca in the Big Cypress National Preserve. His interest was piqued.

"I can't alter water flow," he thought. "That's the Army Corps of Engineers' job. But I can cut down melaleuca."

He immediately called Tony Pernas, a botanist at the preserve.

"What's the name of your group?" Pernas wanted to know.

"M-my group?" sputtered Murch. "I'll call you back."

Within a week, he had persuaded a half-dozen friends to join him in the melaleuca-hacking adventure. They called themselves the Everglades Restoration Movement. There they were, a bunch of energetic young guys, driving to the middle of the preserve in a swamp buggy, machetes in hand. They had a blast.

Murch loved it so much he's been back practically every weekend since. (Now that's what I would call one dedicated guy!) He hacks and squirts away, just daring the melaleuca to try and come back. If I were an exotic, I'd be afraid. A half-dozen people donning boots and leather gloves come clomping through the saw grass. Some have chain saws, others have smelly herbicide attached to belts around their waists. They all have that wicked-witch-of-the-east look in their eyes: "I'll get you, my pretty—and your little stumps, too!"

It's enough to make you shrivel on sight.

The best part is that the hackers are winning. Not just the volunteers, of course. What they do is just a small part of the overall picture. But their efforts combined with those of the preserve, Everglades National Park, and the South Florida Water Management District have managed to reduce melaleuca in the Everglades by about a third. If funding continues, they should one day bring melaleuca down to manageable levels. Score one for the good guys.

Melaleuca, of course, is only one exotic. Others, with overactive reproductive organs, lurk in the wings.

Schinus terebinthifolius: Also known as Brazilian pepper, Christmas berry, Florida holly, copal, and chichita. Characteristics: An evergreen shrub growing ten to fifteen feet, with crowns growing in dense, closed stands. Female trees produce red berries between November and February. Seeds spread by native and exotic birds, particularly the American robin. Invades disturbed soil rapidly.

Jorge Perez is another volunteer melaleuca killer. He hates the tree. Ever since he learned about exotics in a plant identification class in the early 1990s, he sees red whenever he spies one of the interlopers. Since 1997, he's hacked and whacked the stubborn trees to the ground, helping to make a dent in the problem. Now he's setting his sights on another exotic: Brazilian pepper.

"I'm dying to get my hands on it," enthused the avid naturalist.

When he was a child at Seminole Elementary School, a huge Brazilian pepper—which had grown to the size of a tree—sat in the middle of the school field. Unaware of what it was, he happily played in its shade. Now he knows better. Owner of his own groundskeeping business, Nativescapes, he sees the exotic everywhere. Seeing one homeowner in Little Havana using it as a hedge, he shakes his head. "Don't they know what this is?"

A lot don't. Many find the red berries attractive, especially because they fruit around Christmas. Little do they know that once these plants get a foothold, especially in land that has been disturbed by farming or development, they become dictators, marching all other plant life out of the area.

In the Everglades National Park, the exotic has taken over six thousand acres surrounding the park's research center in an area known as the Hole-in-the-Donut. For most of this century farmers planted tomatoes there. The farmers were allowed to continue growing the crops even after the federal government established the park in 1947. Almost thirty years later, the land was returned to the park's managers, who had visions of restoring it to its natural vegetation of saw grass, pine, and hardwood trees.

Brazilian pepper had other plans, however. The message, "Disturbed land in Hole-in-the-Donut!" whipped along the plant hot line in no time. With a little help from its friends the robins and the mockingbirds, the pepper plant was spread via bird poop over the entire six thousand acres. Within ten years, the plant reigned so completely that the only wildlife you could find underneath its dense canopy were cottonmouths and rodents.

Part of the reason for its quick victory was that much of the land had been rock-plowed—a farming method that broke up the first several inches of limestone rock to make the soil thicker and fluffier. Once the farming ceased, these plowed lands were a few inches higher than the surrounding areas.

Not good. During the Everglades' wet season most of the land is under several inches of water. These higher lands weren't, allowing the pepper plant to take root—and causing the land managers one big migraine. But instead of throwing their hands up in despair, they hatched a plan: Take out the soil in the rock-plowed areas. No small feat, this. First, tractors with huge circular blades come whizzing down on the top of the plant to bring it down to ground level. The trunks and branches are then mulched. Other tractors are right behind, scraping the soil down to the limestone, usually about six inches underneath. One of their biggest problems is how to dispose of the soil. We're talking up to 6 million cubic yards of this stuff. While they scramble to fund roads that can withstand trucks pounding over them every day on their way to permanent disposal sites, they're dumping it into borrow pits that the U.S. Army dug up to construct a nearby missile installation during the 1960s Cuban Missile Crisis.

By the year 2000 they managed to clear only about nine hundred acres. The good news is that the method seems to be working. When the wet season comes, the land remains underwater, and the pepper plant can't grow. Instead, the saw grass has returned. Apple snails—a good sign of a healthy wetland—dot among the grasses. Red-winged blackbirds come to nest.

Perez notices these efforts when he visits Tony Pernas, who now works for the park and has an office at the research center. Perez alternates his volunteer hours between the park and the Big Cypress National Preserve, doing everything from chopping melaleuca to building shade houses for cypress and palmetto seedlings. He's motivated by a love of this land that he first encountered on a field trip in the fifth grade. While the other students held back, he was at the front of the line, walking knee-deep into the water.

"As mushy as it was," he said, "it didn't bother me."

As a young adult, he'd go camping in the Everglades with his friends about four or five times a year. But it wasn't until he did his college internship at the preserve that he began spending time out there regularly. Once he started, he couldn't stop. Long after the internship was over, he'd be out there, flying in planes with Pernas to map the melaleuca or taking wildfire training.

So far he hasn't worked with Brazilian pepper. He watches the huge tractors and the acres of scraped land and decides to leave the large-scale project to the contractors. But his itchy fingers cannot rest. Whenever he sees a Brazilian pepper in his clients' yards in Dade or Broward counties, he quickly yanks it out. If he spies one while driving through the park or preserve, he screeches to a halt, grabs his machete and herbicide, and goes to it. He believes he and others can whup this thing, even one plant at a time.

Lygodium microphyllum: Otherwise known as old world climbing fern. Characteristics: Fern with dark brown stem growing up to ninety feet. Attaches to trees. Germinates from spores within six to seven days. Spores potent for up to five months. Establishes well in pine and wetlands.

Tony Pernas, who has been a botanist for both the preserve and the park, is proud of the headway they've made on melaleuca. He's encouraged by the work underway on the Brazilian pepper. It's the old world climbing fern—the latest bad boy on the scene—that has him shaking in his boots.

"It's just being discovered," he said with a shudder.

The fern quickly twines around trees, sprouting up the bark. It can take over entire stands of cypress. The biggest problem arises during fires. In a controlled or natural fire, the flames burn only the underbrush, leaving the larger trees intact. With the climbing fern around, fire shoots straight up into the canopy, wiping out the old trees. In an aerial survey in August of 1999, Pernas found about five hundred acres of the fern in a remote part of the Everglades. He wonders where he'll find it next.

"It's scaring me to death," he said.

Brazilian pepper and melaleuca took almost a century to become power hungry. Old world climbing fern, on the other hand, has been here only since the 1960s. Already, it's sprinting across the Florida landscape. That's one of the problems with exotics. You never know which one will jump the fence and become a major problem. I feel sorry for folks on the front lines. They must have nightmares of some new plant chasing after them, tendrils snaking around their leg, dragging them down into the muck. Before they can cry for help, another exotic pops up and takes root on their head, cutting off all oxygen. They drown in a wild green sea.

The other problem that haunts people like Pernas is private land. You can eliminate as many invasive exotics as you want from federal and state land, but colonizers will always be there at the borders, ready to pounce when no one is looking. In the meantime, they'll slurp up as much private land as they can.

Some environmentalists have suggested providing incentives to landowners to eradicate invasive exotics like melaleuca. But the long-term solution depends on Floridians in general becoming aware of the problem and being willing to do something about it. Otherwise, we'll be shoveling you-know-what against the tide.

Meanwhile, concerned citizens can follow Murch's and Perez's example. I, for one, plan to volunteer with the Everglades Restoration Movement when I travel down south to visit my folks, who now live in a development right smack dab on the border of the Everglades. I can donate money to the cause. (Murch, for example, is trying to raise funds to buy a few air boats so members can get deeper into the Everglades.) I can also teach my two sons about native vegetation—or better yet, have them teach me. It was my then ten-year-old son who came home one day and demanded that we pull out all the nandina from our suburban yard.

SHARON RAUCH

"Why?" I asked naively.

"It's not native," he replied, as if stating the obvious.

Pulling those suckers out of the ground is now on our to-do list.

But I also dream of joining an ecoguerrilla movement. We would leave no invasive exotic unscathed. I can hear the TV reports now. "Last night, a group calling themselves the Mad Melaleuca Marauders struck again, slashing over ten thousand trees throughout Miami. One witness, who saw a slasher from his ground-story condo around midnight, said the Marauder was dressed in a flamingo shirt with a camera around her neck. She glanced around quickly, grabbed a sword-like object from the car and in one fell swoop toppled a melaleuca tree. Then she pulled a spray bottle from her pocket, gave it a squirt, and was gone in a flash."

I would be that woman, working on my Marauder stripes, piling up melaleuca carcasses. Someday, I hope, I'd do enough to be considered an honorary native.

―――――――――

SHARON RAUCH *is a reporter for the* Tallahassee Democrat *in Tallahassee, Florida.*

Part Four

THE WESTERN GLADES

West of Lake Okeechobee . . . the water spilled and crept out over soggy level lands, half lakes, half swamps, and so into the Caloosahatchee, the left shoulder of the Glades region. . . . West of Lake Flirt, the Caloosahatchee began in earnest, a river so remote, so lovely that even in the days when it was best known it must have been like a dream. It was a river wandering among half-moon banks hung with green dripping trees and enshrouding grapevines, green misted, silent, always meandering.

THE EVERGLADES: RIVER OF GRASS, MARJORY STONEMAN DOUGLAS

Away to the west of Okeechobee and the vast saw grass plain lies a sometimes forgotten piece of the giant mosaic Everglades ecosystem, dominated by the Big Cypress National Preserve. Its boundary is a low-lying plateau called the Immokalee Rise, which holds and shapes the disjointed drainage patterns of the extensive preserve, the Seminole and Miccosukee Reservation lands, the Corkscrew Swamp region, and the cities to the west.

To the north, the western Everglades are fed by the Caloosahatchee River, the river that Everglades drainer Hamilton Disston knew held the key to lowering Lake Okeechobee and draining the Everglades. By connecting with steam dredge and dynamite the headwaters of the Caloosahatchee to Okeechobee, he created the drainway to the Gulf of Mexico and forever fused the success and options of Everglades restoration to the western Everglades.

The name of Big Cypress National Preserve refers not to the size of the trees but to the swamp's twenty-four hundred square mile extent. The landscape consists of sandy islands of slash pine, mixed hardwood hammocks (tree islands), wet prairies, dry prairies, marshes, and mangrove forests—not simply "swamp." But the great virgin bald cypresses are largely gone, lumbered out in the 1930s and 1940s.

In the 1960s, drainage of Big Cypress began as land development and speculation schemes blossomed in this part of South Florida, and thousands invested sight unseen in land that was under water much of the year.

The heart of the Big Cypress is the Fakahatchee Strand, a one hundred thousand-acre wedge of wild but human-corrupted wilderness some twenty-five miles long and seven miles wide. The strand is a self-contained drainage basin, strung with dozens of smaller strands and sinkhole lakes whose waters eventually deliver their vital freshwater to the mangrove estuaries of the Gulf Coast. Most of the Fakahatchee's trees are tropical, as is the royal palm, but it is essentially a temperate forest with a strong canopy of bald cypress.

The biggest challenge for this region, dominated now by the rapidly developing cities of Lee and Collier counties (Ft. Myers and Naples, in particular), will be the struggle to avoid the complete urbanization of the Atlantic Coastal Ridge.

PATH OF THE PANTHER

Charles Fergus

One morning before dawn I drove to Corkscrew Swamp Sanctuary, ten thousand acres owned by the National Audubon Society on the northwestern edge of Big Cypress Swamp. The visitors' center was not open yet, so I stepped over a low wooden fence and walked along on one of the bark paths. The trail led off through pine flatwoods. The trees' arrow-straight trunks were topped by complicated crowns of twisted branches black against a faintly brightening sky. Dew lay on the ground. The air smelled sweet and pure. I sat at the base of a tree and listened: night herons croaking from the swamp, a crested flycatcher giving its strident *wheep-wheep-wheep,* a bobwhite quail whistling. A few yards away a sizable animal went rustling past. Probably it was a raccoon or a bobcat. Unlikely, but it could even have been a panther: the big cats live in and about Corkscrew Swamp and use it as a travel corridor.

As the dawn strengthened, the breeze came easing through the limber pine needles, scraping through the clustered palmetto fans. It brought from the west the faint intermittent static of highway traffic. The sky brightened to a deep rich blue, in which the last stars twinkled; another beautiful morning, the type of January day that draws so many of my friends' aging parents to Florida each winter.

I stood and continued along the path through the quiet woods until I came to a boardwalk. The walkway crossed a broad stretch of wet prairie and a band of pond cypress, then entered the swamp. Among the tall cypress trees it was still night. A clean, slightly acidic smell filled the clammy air. Birdsong ricocheted. Soon there would arrive the nature-minded retirees from nearby Naples and Fort Myers, the lifetime Audubon Society members with their sun hats, field guides, binoculars, and tripod-mounted spotting scopes—but for now I had the walkway to myself. As the light worked its way into the forest, the trees began to emerge, gray and smooth-barked, like huge concrete columns.

Corkscrew Swamp Sanctuary protects the country's largest stand of virgin bald cypress trees, seven-hundred-year-old giants like those logged in Fakahatchee Strand in the 1940s. Wood storks—Florida's largest remaining colony—build their sloppy stick nests in the tops of the trees. Around and on the cypresses grow creepers, ferns, shrubs, and air plants, the vegetation layered and dense, in every shade of green: yellow-green, blackish-green, verdigris, kelly, sea-green. Shafts of light angled in, reflecting from varnished leaves and from black water moving so slowly that it appeared to be stagnant; the sunbeams spotlighted the tips of fern fronds, loops of hanging vine, filigrees of Spanish moss, air plants plastered to trunks. From where I stood, hundreds of air plants were visible: prickly, angular ones; small, unobtrusive, lacy things; big bristling masses. An air plant is an epiphyte, requiring from its host nothing more than a reliable perch above the swamp's fluctuating water level. An air plant subsists on sunlight, rainwater, and the slow swirl of detritus in the air: bark flakes, pollen grains, leaf crumbs.

Birds flitted from bough to bough. The swamp resounded with their croaks, rasps, buzzes, chirps, trills. Pig frogs grunted. From somewhere came the heavy splash of an alligator. A red-shouldered hawk flapped into the crown of a maple a few feet from where I stood. Immediately the smaller birds in the vicinity fell silent. The hawk had a white-banded tail and rufous patches at the tops of its wings. It shuffled and settled on its perch, immobile now except for its head, which shifted up, down, left, right, in tiny increments. After a minute, it hopped off the branch and, on set wings, glided away between the trunks.

In the car, heading south from Corkscrew Swamp, I entered an area known as Golden Gate Estates.

Under a dazzling sun, Everglades Boulevard lay dead straight and north-south. At every quarter mile, a sand or a gravel road right-angled to the east and the west. No utility lines. No houses in sight, although street signs (24th Avenue, 33rd Avenue, 46th Avenue) announced the crossing roads. A thick diamondback rattlesnake lay tire-hammered and fly-attended in the northbound lane; vultures knobbed a nearby snag. A pickup truck passed me, going north, the driver wearing sunglasses and a cowboy hat, lifting a finger from the steering wheel in greeting. The country was flat. The plants were dry-land types, pines and grasses and legions of cabbage palms, stocky, rough-trunked trees whose fronds, enlivened by the breeze, caught the clear Florida sunshine and reflected it in dazzling spears and winks.

I began seeing a fair number of realtors' signs pointing off down the side roads. I turned onto one of the roads and bumped slowly along it. A few tenths of a mile brought me to another sign indicating that somewhere in the vicinity—amid the cabbage palms, wire grass, slash pines, and saw palmetto—lay a lot for sale. Golden Gate Estates is the world's largest housing subdivision. You can buy a lot in the northern half of Golden Gate Estates and build a house there. If the property lies too far from other development, and the cost of running a power line to it is prohibitive, you can install a diesel-powered electric generator; you can get a radio-telephone. You can build your own little fortress on top of the mostly drained swamp. Indeed, something of a fortress mentality is said to prevail among residents of the remoter parts of the subdivision, and there is nothing quite so embattled-looking as a split-level with vinyl siding, an attached garage, a trailered boat parked alongside, a lawn with manicured tropical shrubs—all by its lonesome in the scrubby Florida boondocks. Such an outpost may well include an alarm system and guard dogs. Or guard cats. Because, as they say, parts of Golden Gate Estates are "wide open." Drug planes use the road grid as a landing zone. Their clients on the ground find an isolated spot, switch on a couple of pairs of truck headlights, the plane touches down between them, the trucks load up, the aircraft zooms off into the night. A few years ago, a couple living in Golden Gate Estates were arrested for importing numerous tons of marijuana. Warren and Linda Stewart had surrounded their home with an eight-foot electric fence, behind which six pumas were allowed to roam. When officers of the federal Drug Enforcement Agency made the bust, they took along several Florida game wardens to deal with the pumas, most of which, fortunately, were in their cages that morning. Two of the pumas, however, were sleeping with the Stewarts, and when the officers entered the couple's bedroom, one of the pumas pounced on a warden and knocked him to the floor. The officer, unharmed, credited his bulletproof vest with warding off the puma's claws.

To the west, Golden Gate Estates resembles an actual development, with houses standing shoulder to shoulder, schools, and convenience stores; a lot on the western fringe, convenient to the burgeoning city of Naples, may sell for $100,000. Overall, Golden Gate Estates is twenty-five miles from its northern to its southern end. It varies in width from five to fifteen miles. Its grid is easily discernible in satellite photographs of Florida, like metal fencing pressed into a lawn.

Golden Gate Estates was the brainchild of two Baltimoreans, Leonard and Jack Rosen, who got their start in the world of commerce by selling refrigerators on time to poor people. They progressed to peddling hair tonic on television and, in 1957, found their true calling: selling lots in Florida. The Rosens created and sold the town of Cape Coral out of what had been mangrove swamp and miasmic coastal lowland, just across the Caloosahatchee River from Fort Myers, about ten miles west of Golden Gate Estates. My parents, like many other Northerners, bought a quarter-acre lot in Cape Coral for $2,000 plus interest, on the installment plan. (I remember thinking, every time my parents mentioned the lot, that we must be richer than I thought to have afforded land in Florida. I also felt edgy, because I didn't want to move there.) The lot was always referred to as an investment, and I do not believe my parents ever really intended to build on it. After my father died, my mother considered selling the property and asked me to check on it some time when I was in Florida. With the aid of a real-estate map, I finally found the lot, on the edge of Cape Coral, a desolate, narrow rectangle of sun-scalded weeds and sand, nowhere near a cape, a bed of coral, or a view of the ocean. A few modest tract houses were scattered about, surrounded by imported turf and planted palms braced up by two-by-fours. When one of the residents saw me, she hurried over and asked, in a hopeful voice, if we were planning on building any time soon. She was from New Jersey. She and her husband had retired to Florida not long before. A school was coming, she exhorted, a grocery store was going in down the road, and rumor had it—a bright light suffused her eyes—that a Wal-Mart was on the way.

Gulf American, the Rosens' company, projected Golden Gate Estates as a community of 400,000. The Rosens' strategy, as it had been for Cape Coral, was to buy land ($150 per acre was the going rate in the 1960s), carve it into lots, sell them, and use the payments that came flooding in to secure options on more land. Salesmen sold parcels—two and a half and five acres—over the telephone and at banquet events in Northern communities, often held during the depths of winter. Potential clients were flown for free to the developed portion of Cape Coral (at one time Gulf American owned twenty-five airliners), where deals for Golden Gate properties were struck. Few customers actually looked at their land, a practice that the sales force discouraged. The salesmen implied the presence of roads, utilities, and plenty of Florida sunshine. Usually they could deliver on the sunshine.

North Golden Gate Estates was surveyed and sold. Then South Golden Gate Estates. Speculators and retirees bought the plots. By the time the Rosens got out of the land business, their company had made them a fortune. It had built, within the bounds of Golden Gate Estates, 800 miles of road and 180 miles of drainage canals. Depending on where their lots were located, the new landowners had either made a satisfactory investment or been royally ripped off. (As with most Florida real-estate ventures, for Golden Gate Estates the dividing line between a legitimate deal and a swindle was somewhat blurry.)

Despite all the ditching, every year from May to November many of the lots lie under varying depths of water, especially the twenty thousand tracts (totaling forty thousand acres) in southern Golden Gate Estates, lower and wetter than the northern development. South Golden Gate Estates is known locally as the Blocks. The Blocks are truly wide open. To reach them, I drove south over Interstate 75, the former Alligator Alley. I stopped at a bank of eighteen mailboxes (most of them riddled with bullet holes) next to a utility pole on which was nailed a large metal sign with the message:

"ACCESS"
SATURDAY 10:00 A.M.
EVERGLADES BLV. OVERPASS
"MEETING" EVERY WEEK!

Grouped together were mailboxes for residents at 4601 64th Avenue, 5760 104th Avenue, 1655 56th Avenue, 1501 58th Avenue. The implication was of settlement widely scattered. The "Access" referred to in the sign connoted entry to Interstate 75, which, humming along below a tall overpass, no longer exchanges with Everglades Boulevard. Now residents of the southernmost Blocks must drive a circuitous forty miles to get their groceries in Naples, as opposed to eighteen miles when Everglades Boulevard met with Alligator Alley. In the Blocks, people inhabit fancy houses (generators purring), mobile homes, wood-and-tarpaper shacks, and the rusting nether portions of tractor trailers hauled off into the brush. Many of the residents are said to be squatters, with no idea who owns the land on which they live. They bathe in the canals. They trap rainwater for drinking. Some of them grow illicit crops and surround their plots with trip wires and set guns. An ornithologist I know was out looking for nests of the swallow-tailed kite (a graceful insect-eating tropical hawk, whose range extends north into Florida) in an isolated part of the Blocks, whose gridded layout is ideal for plotting out coordinates in the flat, featureless terrain. The ornithologist stepped out of the brush onto a street and saw people at work around a large U-Haul truck. He focused his binoculars. Men carrying tall, bushy, potted plants were trooping single file up a ramp into the cargo section of the truck. He noticed another man standing near the truck, exchanging stares with him through binoculars. Across the man's chest, on a sling, was a submachine gun.

Cuban-American paramilitary groups conduct training exercises in the Blocks, which sometimes resounds with the rattle of automatic weaponry. ("We hear 'em in there," a local law-enforcement agent told me, "and we just back off.") People poach game in the Blocks blatantly: deer, hogs, alligators, wild turkeys. I know a botanist for the State of Florida who worked in Fakahatchee Strand State Preserve, which adjoins the Blocks to the southeast. He once encountered a woman walking along W. J. Janes Scenic Drive (named for a member of the Janes family, who owned land in the vicinity), a road that links the Blocks with Fakahatchee Strand. The botanist said that the woman was "very hard to age, since she was so drastically weathered." She wore a cut-off shirt and cut-off trousers, had a rifle slung over her shoulder. She accepted a ride back to her home in the Blocks (the botanist asked her to unload her weapon before getting into his truck). She said that recently she had chased off, at gunpoint, "some drug people from Miami," because she did not want the feds connecting her with the marijuana the Miamians were planting. The botanist drove the woman through the maze of roads (left on this road, right on that one, left again) until suddenly she asked him to stop. She disembarked, walked down the gravel street, stepped into the brush, and vanished.

I met a family camped at a turnout next to a canal in the Blocks. Children in swimsuits were fishing in the canal and scampering about throwing rocks. A man of considerable girth sat in the sun in a wheel-chair, watching the children. He shook my hand and gave me his name. He was from Alabama. He had fixed up an old Ford panel truck as a camper. A generator and a small washing machine and dryer sat in a trailer behind the truck. His refrigerator ran on batteries, which he kept charged by driving the truck or by running the generator. His wife had long blond hair, her eyes highlighted by a generous amount of purple eyeshadow. She had once worn pop-bottle-thick eyeglasses, she told me, but the Lord had healed her ("A miracle's real sudden," she explained, "but healin' takes time"), and now she could see perfectly well without her lenses. She gave me a bologna-and-tomato sandwich made between flopped-open hot-dog buns and a cup of instant coffee. Another man with a round face, stubs of teeth, and hair that stuck out in all directions came over and offered me some vanilla creme-filled cookies in a clear plastic tray. He was the heavyset man's friend, and he was also from Alabama. He had been a truck driver and had hauled up through Pennsylvania to Caribou, Maine, where, he said, he had seen mountain goats peering down from the heights (I did not dispute his story, although there are no mountain goats east of the Rocky Mountains); and once, on a farm that he'd lived on in West Virginia, a cougar got into his chicken coop, and when he pegged a stone at the cat, it took a great bound, lit between his legs, and took off running.

The man in the wheelchair told me he had been a police officer. He had survived two severe automobile accidents, the second of which had paralyzed his legs. A white Cadillac had rammed into the side of his patrol car, leaving him beneath the wreckage, staring at the sole of one of his shoes an inch in front of his face. On the way to the hospital, he said, he died and woke up in a grave with red clay all around him, pinning his arms against his sides; worms began boring into his head through his nose, mouth, and eyes, and when he screamed, he saw a little white light that got bigger and bigger until it blinded him, and that was the Lord. Now that he had been granted an extension on his life, he regularly conducted direct conversations with Jesus and was engaged in spreading His word. He preached at revival meetings. He ran a house in Alabama where homeless people could eat and sleep, and he didn't turn anybody away, black or white. He had been in the Blocks, camped on this spot, for two months, and he liked it just fine. He said he sometimes heard panthers screaming at night. He had had no problems with anyone bothering him, although sometimes a ray, or some other kind of force, passed over his trailer, causing his battery-powered television to go blank for a while; he guessed it was the radar they used to watch for drug planes. He told me, "When you go, take this thought with you: 'Choose you this day whom you will serve. Whether the gods which your fathers served, that were on the other side of the flood, or the gods of the Amorites in whose lands you dwell. But as for me and my house, we will serve the Lord.'"

One of the keys to saving the panther lies in preserving places like the Blocks. Panthers occasionally pass through the Blocks, but none are believed to live there, perhaps because of the unrestricted and rowdy human activity. Conservationists would like to buy the Blocks and link it with other secure holdings, such as Corkscrew Swamp Sanctuary and Fakahatchee Strand State Preserve.

Big Cypress National Preserve, ten miles east of the Blocks, is the most important tract of protected habitat used by panthers today. In the southern part of the preserve are the females, numbers 23 and 55, and the two male refugees from the Everglades. In the northern sector of the preserve—perhaps cut off from the south by Alligator Alley, although its new underpasses may rectify that situation—live more than a dozen radio-collared cats, which range back and forth between the preserve and the adjacent private cattle ranches. To date, the National Park Service has not tried to make the preserve more attractive for panthers. This reluctance may stem from the fact that, even though the preserve was established twenty years ago, the government does not own all of Big Cypress: it is still buying one-, two-, and five-acre tracts that remain in private hands. Until the government buys out a landowner, it is probably illegal for the Park Service to, for instance, fill in a drainage canal, remove a road, or burn off vegetation to encourage a lush growth of grass.

In Naples I visited the Park Service's Southeast Region Land Acquisition Field Office, occupying two floors of a modern office building close to a neighborhood of expensive, manicured homes. There I met a cartographer who showed me how a modern land-acquisition system operates. In addition to buying up inholdings in Big Cypress, the cartographer told me, the Park Service is adding a tract of 146,000 acres to the preserve's northern boundary, and expanding Everglades National Park to the east. I was especially interested in the Blocks and wondered how an agency might go about purchasing land in such a place.

"South Golden Gate Estates is a state initiative, not a federal one," the cartographer informed me, while booting up a computer terminal. "That means we won't be the ones buying the land. The State of Florida—their Bureau of Land Acquisition—will decide when and how fast to do it. Actually, we'd love to go after the Blocks." Punching keys, he darted through electronic menus. "That's the kind of project you could really sink your teeth into." He whistled softly. "Ten years of acquisition work, easy." The computer hummed, made digestive noises. A map of South Florida constructed itself on the screen in blue, yellow, green, and red. "This is a vegetation map," the cartographer said. "It's a digital rendition of a satellite photograph, showing the kind of vegetation that panthers like to hang around in." Staring at the screen while guiding a mouse across a rubber pad, he boxed in a portion of the map, which suddenly leaped into enlargement, showing a grid of squares.

"Each square equals one square mile. South Golden Gate Estates has about seventy of those square-mile sections. See the number in each one? That's the total number of people who own land in that particular square mile." The numbers in the squares were 220, 260, 306. "We're talking about a whole bunch of people," the cartographer said. He changed maps, contour lines emerging like a huge green fingerprint. "These are elevations. At the top of the screen, eleven. That's eleven feet above sea level." The mouse scurried, stopped, clicked. "Here's a six right here. This is true swamp. In July this is under water." He pursed his lips and made an explosive blowing sound. "If we get a hurricane, I can't begin to describe how wet this place gets." The maps were linked to local tax rolls. The cartographer picked a tract at random and called up the owner's name: Helen O. Dwyer, of Rochester, New York.

"People from all over the world own land in Florida," the cartographer said. "Europeans, Asians, Central and South Americans— although mostly it's people like Helen here, from the Northeastern states. I'd bet that less than 10 percent of them have actually set foot on their land." According to the cartographer, real estate is still selling briskly in South Florida, including many acres (and acre-feet of water: land sold "by the quart," as the saying goes) already targeted for addition to the public domain. "In one of the more popular scams," he said, "people from Miami buy land in southwest Florida for $300 an acre, then turn around and resell it at $3,000 an acre, mostly to Hispanics, who feel that if they own land in the United States they can get citizenship more easily—and land in Dade County is way

CHARLES FERGUS

too expensive. We're hiring bilingual people to negotiate with the Hispanic owners."

Since I interviewed the cartographer, the State of Florida has bought over 15,000 acres in and around South Golden Gate Estates; it intends to buy another 27,000 acres. The tract will be called Picayune State Forest, named after Picayune Strand, a landform that perhaps still exists beneath the canals, ditches, and roads of the Blocks. I spoke with a state forester working there. One day while walking along a road, she looked off into the palmettos and saw a black object bobbing behind the vegetation. The object seemed to be moving along with her, parallel to her course. When the forester stopped and looked harder, she realized that the black object was the tip of a panther's tail. The cat was twenty-five feet away. It stood and stared at her for a moment, then faded into the brush.

In the last sixty years, Florida has lost a quarter of its forests and two-thirds of its wetlands. Since Europeans arrived, eleven species of wild animals have vanished, including the bison, red wolf, Carolina parakeet, passenger pigeon, ivory-billed woodpecker, and dusky seaside sparrow. Today, 117 species are thought to be at risk of extinction (classified as "threatened" or "endangered" by the Florida Game Commission), from the obscure, diminutive sand skink (a legless lizard that slithers through sandy soil) to the charismatic panther. Conservationists consider the panther a "landscape animal," because it roams widely across the landscape in its search for mates and food. They call it an "umbrella species," because saving the amount of natural land required by panthers will automatically save scores of smaller creatures, such as the skink, whose realms are less sweeping.

Florida, with the breakneck pace of its development, has become a proving ground for conservation schemes. One new approach is "mitigation banking": Suppose a corporation wishes to drain several hundred acres of wetlands to put up a theme park. (Since this is Florida, we might as well imagine that it is a theme park honoring the microwave oven or professional wrestling or the nation's preeminent bass fishermen.) (Fact: Wayne Huizenga, the owner of a business empire that includes Blockbuster Video and the nation's largest garbage-hauling company, proposed building his Blockbuster Park on 2,500 acres of canals, quarries, and wetlands on the eastern fringe of the Everglades. At one point, Huizenga was contemplating a billion-dollar complex to include a domed stadium for his baseball team, the Florida Marlins; a "virtual reality amusement center"; movie and television recording studios; and an indoor arena for his professional ice hockey team, the Florida Panthers. In 1994 the entertainment conglomerate Viacom acquired Blockbuster, and plans for the park are now on hold.) But before the bulldozers can roll, the corporation must first contribute, say, $10 million to a fund; the $10 million are combined with other millions paid by other corporations with similar plans, and from this lump sum come the millions needed to buy a big cattle ranch (up for sale because its dissipated heirs would rather snort cocaine in Bal Harbor than herd cattle somewhere west of Lake Okeechobee), a lonely stretch of pine, palmetto, and cypress that is home to panthers. Mitigation banking can save large tracts of land—one thousand, five thousand, ten thousand acres. There, natural processes can continue, creatures can exchange genes with individuals who are not their siblings, and offspring can disperse in the species' habitual manner rather than perishing while trying to make it from one tiny green island, across an inhospitable urbanized landscape, to the next tiny green island.

In Florida, the Nature Conservancy, a privately funded national organization, is actively buying land and giving it to the state and federal governments. A state program, Preservation 2000, enacted by the Florida legislature in 1990, provides for spending some $300 million per year during the last decade of the century to preserve wildlife habitat. As of 1991, 8 million acres of Florida had been set aside in public and private preserves; the land targeted for Preservation 2000 would add to this figure over 3 million acres. Another 6.3 million acres are coveted by conservationists, and if these could somehow be acquired, they would bring the total protected land area in Florida to 17.5 million acres: 47 percent of the state.

A man in Oregon has the clearest and most radical view of how to reshape Florida to accommodate the panther. Reed Noss is an ecologist and conservation biologist living in Corvallis. . . . Noss, who received a Ph.D. in wildlife science from the University of Florida, has also achieved stature within the scientific community as editor of the journal *Conservation Biology* and as an architect of the Wildlands Project, a plan that the journal *Science* characterized as "the most ambitious proposal for land management since the Louisiana Purchase of 1803."

The Wildlands Project would transform America from a place where nature exists as a string of redoubts in a landscape dominated by humanity into something approaching the opposite. Such scientific notables as Edward O. Wilson of Harvard and Paul Ehrlich of Stanford have endorsed the concept. The Wildlands Project is seen by many conservation biologists as the last, best chance to preserve the biotic diversity of North America. In 1993, the Pew Charitable Trusts, a respected philanthropic organization, chose Noss as a Pew Scholar in Conservation and Environment, and granted him $150,000 to begin working out the details of what has heretofore been a largely theoretical exercise: where to allow human settlement to remain, and how to integrate it with lands dedicated to wildlife.

Noss presented a blueprint for Florida in an article published in 1991 in *Wild Earth*. What he has in mind for the Sunshine State exemplifies how the Wildlands Project might work nationwide. Noss's map shows a peninsula liberally blotched and banded with natural lands. At the heart of his proposal are ten core wilderness areas. A core wilderness would be a truly wild place. People would be barred from it, except for professionals working to restore the landscape or to help out endangered species. To protect against poaching and the effects of human activities, a buffer zone several miles wide would ring each core. (The buffer zone would simultaneously shield humans and their property from fire, predation, or pests originating within the core wilderness.) In the innermost ring of the buffer zone, people could hike, canoe, watch birds, or engage in other activities that would not interfere with nature. Progressively more human influence and activity would be allowed toward the outer part of the buffer: primitive hunting (with weapons such as bows and arrows) and long-rotation

forestry; then firearms hunting and more intensive forestry and grazing use; and, at the perimeter, low-density housing, including scattered farms and small towns. Undeveloped corridors linking the wild
reserves would, for the most part, follow rivers, streams, and swamps.
These green pathways, writes Noss, would "facilitate the flow of nutrients, individuals, genes, habitat patches."

In Florida, the wilderness cores would center on public land,
such as the complex formed by Everglades National Park, Big
Cypress National Preserve, Florida Panther National Wildlife Refuge,
Fakahatchee Strand State Preserve, and the new Picayune State Forest;
the Ocala National Forest in Central Florida; the Apalachicola National
Forest farther north and west; Blackwater River State Forest and the
huge Eglin Air Force Base in the Panhandle; and southern Georgia's
Okefenokee National Wildlife Refuge, linked through Pinhook Swamp
(recently bought by the Nature Conservancy) to Osceola National
Forest in northern Florida. Buffer zones would include public and
private holdings; the private land would be bought by government
agencies or secured through conservation easements and management
agreements. Where corridors cut across roads, the roads would be relocated, fitted with underpasses, or eliminated.

If I read Noss's map correctly, he would like to see something
more than 47 percent of Florida return to its natural state. The concept of cores, buffer zones, and corridors is intuitive, commonsense,
and increasingly accepted by conservationists as a means of keeping
ecosystems intact and evolution functioning. The consensus vanishes,
however, when people start drawing lines on the map.

For the panther—top predator, landscape animal, umbrella
species—the scale would have to be grand. In the early 1990s the
U.S. Fish and Wildlife Service set as an objective five hundred panthers by the year 2000, distributed in three populations in Florida,
with at least two of those populations in the wild. (At the current rate
of bureaucratic achievement, this goal appears impossible to reach.)
Noss, in a report commissioned by the Fund for Animals, chided the
Fish and Wildlife Service for setting a goal that, if apparently unreach-
able, nevertheless remained too modest. He wrote: "It is doubtful

that any single reintroduction area will ever provide for thousands
of panthers, at least not until after the collapse of industrial civilization." To keep the subspecies genetically healthy, to let it recover from
its endangerment and become self-sufficient in the wild, the Fish and
Wildlife Service, declared Noss, must reestablish ten "subregional
metapopulations," each containing one hundred to two hundred
adult panthers. The metapopulations would be scattered throughout
the South. Each would require a huge wilderness core (or a system
of cores), plus buffers and corridors. The panther, in essence, would
become the tool with which to wrest the landscape from human influence and return it to nature.

Writes Noss: "A well-distributed, viable population of panthers
throughout the southeastern states would be a sign that the land is
reasonably healthy and that the human population has the tolerance
and humility to share resources with another large and demanding
creature."

The Fish and Wildlife Service, as part of their settlement agreement
with the Fund for Animals, looked around for places to put panthers.
They identified twenty-four candidate sites, eleven of which were
judged to be better potential homes—larger in area, with fewer roads,
fewer people, and less potential for human population growth—than
South Florida. Among these wild places were Okefenokee Swamp in
Florida and Georgia; the Smoky Mountains in Tennessee and North
Carolina; southwestern Mississippi and adjacent Louisiana; the Ozark
and Ouachita Mountains in Arkansas; along the lower Alabama River;
and along the lower Pearl River in Louisiana and Mississippi.

North Americans are not alone in their wishes to preserve and
reshape the landscape for animals. Even now, conservationists are
promoting a green corridor to run the length of rapidly developing Central America: from Mexico south to Belize and Guatemala,
Honduras, Nicaragua, Costa Rica, Panama, all the way across the isth-
mus (an overpass spanning the canal?) to Colombia. Such a passage
would link biosphere reserves, national parks, coastal bays, islands,
and lowland rainforests. It would protect the homes of native people
living in traditional ways. It would foster a continued biotic exchange

between North and South America. It is not a modest proposal, and for all the talk about it, it is still a dream. Just as the Wildlands Project for North America is a dream. Just as ten, three, and even one viable population of Florida panthers is a dream. In Central America, they call their vision Paseo Pantera, Path of the Panther.

———————

CHARLES FERGUS *is the author of* Swamp Screamer, A Rough-Shooting Dog, Gun Dog Breeds, The Wingless Crow, *and* The Upland Equation, *all nonfiction books, and the novel,* Shadow Catcher.

A GREEN HELL

Susan Orlean

You would have to want something very badly to go looking for it in the Fakahatchee Strand. The Fakahatchee is a preserve of sixty-three thousand coastal lowland acres in the southwestern corner of Florida, about twenty-five miles south of Naples, in that part of Collier County where satiny lawns and golf courses give way to an ocean of saw grass with edges as sharp as scythes. Part of the Fakahatchee is deep swamp, part is cypress stands, part is wet woods, part is estuarine tidal marsh, and part is parched prairie. The limestone underneath it is six million years old and is capped with hard rock and sand, silt and shell marls, and a grayish-greenish clay. Overall, the Fakahatchee is as flat as a cracker. Ditches and dents fill up fast with oozing groundwater. The woods are dense and lightless. In the open stretches the land unrolls like a smooth grass mat and even small bumps and wrinkles are easy to see. Most of the land is at an elevation of only five or ten feet, and it slopes millimeter by millimeter until it is dead even with the sea. The Fakahatchee has a particular strange and exceptional beauty. The grass prairies in sunlight look like yards of raw silk. The tall, straight palm trunks and the tall, straight cypress trunks shoot up out of the flat land like geysers. It is beautiful the way a Persian carpet is beautiful—thick, intricate, lush, almost monotonous in its richness.

People live in the Fakahatchee and around it, but it is an unmistakably inhospitable place. In 1872 a surveyor made this entry in his field notes: "A pond, surrounded by bay and cypress swamp, impracticable. Pond full of monstrous alligators. Counted fifty and stopped." In fact, the hours I spent in the Fakahatchee retracing Laroche's footsteps were probably the most miserable I have spent in my entire life. The swampy part of the Fakahatchee is hot and wet and buggy and full of cottonmouth snakes and diamondback rattlers and alligators and snapping turtles and poisonous plants and wild hogs and things that stick into you and on you and fly into your nose and eyes. Crossing the swamp is a battle. You can walk through about as easily as you could walk through a car wash. The sinkholes are filled with as much as seven feet of standing water, and around them the air has the slack, drapey weight of wet velvet. Sides of trees look sweaty. Leaves are slick from the humidity. The mud sucks your feet and tries to keep ahold of them; if it fails it will settle for your shoes. The water in the swamp is stained black with tannin from the bark of cypress trees that is so corrosive it can cure leather. Whatever isn't wet in the Fakahatchee is blasted. The sun pounds the treeless prairies. The grass gets so dry that the friction from a car can set it on fire, and the burning grass can engulf the car in flames. The Fakahatchee used to be littered with burned-up cars that had been abandoned by panfried adventurers—a botanist who traveled through in the 1940s recalled in an interview that he was most impressed by the area's variety of squirrels and the number of charred Model Ts. The swamp's stillness and darkness and thickness can rattle your nerves. In 1885 a sailor on a plume-collecting expedition wrote in his diary: "The place looked wild and lonely. About three o'clock it seemed to get on Henry's nerves and we saw him crying, he could not tell us why, he was just plain scared."

Spooky places are usually full of death, but the Fakahatchee is crazy with living things. Birders used to come from as far away as Cuba and leave with enough plumes to decorate thousands of ladies' hats; in the 1800s one group of birders also took home eight tons of birds' eggs. One turn-of-the-century traveler wrote that on his journey he found the swamp's abundance marvelous—he caught two hundred pounds of lobsters, which he ate for breakfasts, and stumbled across a rookery where he gathered "quite a supply of cormorant and blue heron eggs, with which I intend to make omelets." That night he had a dinner of a fried blue heron and a cabbage-palm heart. In the Fakahatchee there used to be a carpet of lubber grasshoppers so deep that it made driving hazardous, and so many orchids that visitors described their heavy sweet smell as nauseating. On my first walk in the swamp I saw strap lilies and water willows and sumac and bladderwort, and resurrection ferns springing out of a fallen dead tree; I saw oaks and pines and cypress and pop ash and beauty-berry and elderberry and yellow-eyed grass and camphor weed. When I walked in, an owl gave me a lordly look, and when I walked out three tiny alligators skittered across my path. I wandered into a nook in the swamp that was girdled with tall cypress. The rangers call this nook the Cathedral. I closed my eyes and stood in the stillness for a moment hardly breathing, and when I opened my eyes and looked up I saw dozens of bromeliad plants roosting in the branches of almost every tree I could see. The bromeliads were bright red and green and shaped like fright wigs. Some were spider-sized and some were as big as me. The sun shooting through the swamp canopy glanced off their sheeny leaves. Hanging up there on the branches the bromeliads looked not quite like plants. They looked more like a crowd of animals, watching everything that passed their way.

SUSAN ORLEAN *has been a staff writer at the* New Yorker *since 1992. Her articles have also appeared in* Outside, Rolling Stone, Vogue, *and* Esquire. *She is the author of* Saturday Night, *a* New York Times *Notable Book of 1990,* Red Sox and Bluefish, *and* The Orchid Thief.

Part Five

THE TEN THOUSAND ISLANDS
AND FLORIDA BAY

So, at the end of the saw-grass river and its bordering coasts, begins the mangrove. It shows itself in short tufts first, in green leggy rosettes far south where the saw grass is shorter over thinner muck and the emerging rock . . . Glaring under the sun or bleak in the rain, flat, with patches of scrub and bright salt weeds, this is the country of the birds.

THE EVERGLADES: RIVER OF GRASS, MARJORY STONEMAN DOUGLAS

The freshwaters of the Everglades ease southwest, finally terminating at the peninsula's end in what is arguably the most significant wilderness area in the southeastern United States. Here a dense green wall of mangrove forest twenty miles wide belts the coast from Key Largo north through the Ten Thousand Islands. Although similar forests of mangrove grow along flooded coasts throughout the tropics, the Everglades stands are among the largest, ranked by early botanist Charles Torrey Simpson "among the most wonderful vegetable growths in the State of Florida." On this coast, sandy beaches occur only on Cape Sable and the ocean side of some barrier islands fronting on Florida Bay.

Mangroves begin where the saw grass and the cypress heads are stopped by salt, and this mixing zone is the Everglades' great food-producing area, nursery for shrimp, spiny lobsters, and countless other forms of life. These forests add tons of decomposing leaves to a complex food chain that nourishes nine-tenths of the area's sport and commercial fisheries.

In South Florida, three species of these tropical trees share a common way of life at the edges of the land, using peculiar physical adaptations fitting the salty, restless environment. Walls of prop root basketry, so interlocking that it's hard to tell where one tree begins or ends, assist red mangrove trees in fracturing encroaching waves. Mangroves are land builders, advancing into the gulf, steadying the interplay between land and wind and sea, and even building land.

Because of their remote and challenging nature, few actually ventured into the mangrove fringe, save for naturalists, plume hunters, and adventurers seeking challenge or solitude. Until the middle of the twentieth century, mangrove forests were given little protection from alteration and development, resulting in thousands of acres destroyed and replaced with fill and developed land. The structural integrity, if not the water quality, of the great Everglades mangrove fringe is now largely protected under public ownership.

Beyond the mangroves, the turquoise shallows of Florida Bay, twenty-five miles long by forty miles wide, fill the triangular void between the mainland and the upper Keys. Dozens of keys—small islands fringed by mangroves—dot the seascape. An endangered population of the American crocodile, Caribbean cousin of the alligator, lives among the northern bays; sea turtles ply the waving pastures of submerged turtle grass, and manatees overwinter here as well.

Within the past twenty years, major ecological changes have disrupted Florida Bay. Large algal blooms have developed and persisted, the water has become more turbid, large areas of sea grasses and sponges have died, and changes have occurred in fish populations. Classic indicators of excess nutrients in the water are abundant in the Florida Keys, where algae have overgrown many coral reefs, coral diseases have increased, and many corals have simply died.

Scientists believe that nutrients in runoff from the Everglades Agricultural Area, more than one hundred miles to the north, are a source of these disruptions; just as phosphate from agricultural runoff has caused ecological changes in the Everglades, the nitrogen may be altering the bay. Another possible source of excess nutrients in the bay is septic tank and cesspit drainage from the rapidly growing population of the Florida Keys.

THE LIGHTNING BUG
AND THE MOTH

Jono Miller

According to the logic of schoolyard riddles, a lightning bug crossed
with a moth should produce a love-struck creature that flies in circles
around its own attractively radiant posterior. Just so, as a culture we
are infatuated with our ability to produce light—from campfires to
compact fluorescents—a habit so synonymous with civilization that
a nighttime space image of the unilluminated places is the same as
a map of the remaining wild places. Florida, with the second longest
coastline in the nation, has just two such dark coasts. The first, and
longest, is the Big Bend, the broad shallow sweep that keeps Tampa
from sprawling to Tallahassee. The second, stretching in a reverse "J"
from about twenty miles south of Miami down around the tip of the
peninsula through Everglades National Park and up to glowing Marco
Island, is the coastal wilderness known as the Ten Thousand Islands.

Over the course of the last two centuries, the Ten Thousand Islands
have morphed from an unsurveyed and challenging frontier coastal
wilderness to a patchwork quilt of publicly owned lands. Less forlorn
and less challenging today, it nevertheless remains one of those places
to which you must travel deliberately.

The Ten Thousand Islands are a landscape, or waterscape, from
a dream. If they didn't exist, speculative fiction writers would create

them—an archipelago arcing between a flat land and a flatter gulf. Attempting to convey the region without a map, chart, or aerial photograph is daunting, if not impossible. To say that there are a great many nearly identical islands of myriad improbable shapes and sizes strewn through a shallow sea is at once totally accurate and hopelessly oxymoronic. With the possible exception of Dr. Seuss, no fantasy cartographer would dare open a portfolio with islands such as these. Any publisher would toss them back as too unreal, too contrived, too impossible to be convincing. Their distribution and shapes do not lend themselves to easy metaphor. They do not look like raindrops hitting a puddle, knots in wood, blue spatterware enamel, cheap batik, or the back of a Dalmatian. It is unlikely you will doodle something like the Ten Thousand Islands while on hold with your health care provider.

About the best you can do is sit down with a draft beer in a glass mug and start drinking. Stare at the ever-morphing patterns of bubbles as the beer's head slides and anastomoses down the inside of the glass. Perhaps it is the beer, but at some point you will see an unlikely collection of improbable linear fingers and comforting more-or-less circular blobs and voids. Place yourself in a small open boat among the bubble islands and start navigating. You have found the Ten Thousand Islands.

In the beginning the only outsiders who knew about the Ten Thousand Islands were wealthy and/or obsessed recreational fishermen. Notables such as Eisenhower and Enzo Ferrari found their way to guides in tiny Everglades City. Then, in the mid-sixties, Everglades National Park opened the "Wilderness Waterway," a ninety-nine-mile recreational canoe trail from Everglades City to Flamingo. The existence of the trail simultaneously nominated and ratified the proposition that one could canoe in a subtropical saltwater wilderness, and the northernmost part of the Wilderness Waterway got people paddling in the Ten Thousand Islands. Now, after the fishers and paddlers, a new constituency, the literati, are discovering the Ten Thousand Islands.

Some Florida landscapes are known by the company they keep. Tourists find it hard to think of Key West and not of Hemingway or Jimmy

Buffet, and harder still to think of Orlando without thinking of Walt or Mickey. The Ten Thousand Islands are forever yoked to "bloody" Ed Watson. The twenty-five-words-or-less version is that a hard-working, charming, and ominous character became associated with a number of disappearances and deaths that so unhinged his neighbors that they shot him. The Watson legend has bumped about for nine decades now, passed along by Smallwood, Tebeau, and others. But in recent years the prominence of bloody Ed has been eclipsed by his dedicated chronicler, Peter Matthiessen. Matthiessen is arguably among the top writers of the last half century: persistent (he's written more than two dozen books), versatile, and a high-order craftsman. Unlike many renowned writers, he's a crossover artist equally likely to have hits on the fiction and nonfiction charts. Because he is so comfortable, so skilled, and so acclaimed in both genres, one presumes there is nothing Matthiessen could not take on. Conceivably he could write just about any book in Barnes & Noble. His books are certainly found in different sections: sociology, human rights, travel, wildlife, fiction. Yet with the whole planet before him, Matthiessen has devoted 1,320 pages over three books, *Killing Mr. Watson, Lost Man's River,* and *Bone by Bone,* to pursuing a fringe character in what must be, literally and figuratively, the most fringe landscape on the continent.

Is his exhaustive trilogy an irrational preoccupation? A compulsive reshuffling and rereading of the same salt-speckled tarot deck? Matthiessen himself concedes in the preface to *Bone by Bone* that it is "what can only be called a twenty-year obsession." When a writer of Matthiessen's caliber takes an excursion of this magnitude, literate people take notice.

It is a reality of American culture that well-told stories create their own economies. The "Field of Dreams" in Dyersville, Iowa, is a void in two cornfields where a movie happened to be shot. In summer it supports two roadside stands. *The Bridges of Madison County* spawned a tourism boomlet. One can only speculate on the movie rights to Matthiessen's trilogy, but the results would be predictable enough: tins of Island Pride cane syrup on sale in the Smallwood Store, complete with impressive dried red fingerprints; packaged trips to Watson's place to see the movie set built by special permission of the National Park

Service; and the onshore infrastructure necessary to provide a variety of tours, excursions, and experiences. Actually, the infrastructure to explore this unlikely landscape is largely in place now. Marco, Port of the Islands, Everglades City, and Chokoloskee all support businesses that depend on a wild yet accessible Ten Thousand Islands.

Instead of going to the Ten Thousand Islands to get away from something (the Ed Watson model), people now go to get closer to something, to catch the fish some celebrity caught, or to see if they can see what Peter Matthiessen sees. Some do stop at Watson's place on the Chatham River or make a pilgrimage to Smallwood's Store on Chokoloskee (now a museum), but they are not coming because of Bloody Ed. They are coming to test themselves—to explore an unfamiliar landscape and, in doing so, to better come to know themselves. If it were mere escapism they could go to Seminole Bingo.

Matthiessen's three spotlights have illuminated (or perhaps helped create) a new Ten Thousand Islands, a destination for book readers looking for the real Florida, the real America, or more likely still, their real selves. In addition to Matthiessen, Totch Brown, Randy Wayne White, and other writers have made the region more accessible and more knowable to outsiders, which makes the area easier to explore. But just as searching for darkness with a lantern eliminates any chance of success, guides to "real" places ensure that the real undiscovered areas must lie elsewhere.

The books are just the beginning. For every tourist the books bring, a handful descend as a result of engaging magazine articles. In recent years a minor cavalcade of articles has been written about this "undiscovered" tourist destination. While we might expect articles about the Ten Thousand Islands for fishers *(Field and Stream, Gulf Coast Fisherman, Sports Afield, Florida Sportsman)*, paddlers *(Canoe, Sea Kayaker)*, and park-loving environmentalists *(National Parks, Sierra, Audubon, Backpacker)*, there have also been articles in the *New York Times, Woman's Sports and Fitness, Sail, National Geographic World, Travel and Leisure*, and (slight shudder) *Meetings and Conventions*. The narrative vehicle for many of these stories is the author taking a Ten Thousand Islands paddle trip and using the experience to relate tantalizing anecdotes and necessary travel factoids. Partially as a result, nineteen canoe/kayak outfitters are now registered with Everglades National Park. Wilderness Southeast, Outward Bound, and other outdoor programs routinely run trips in the Ten Thousand Islands. And canoeing and kayaking are still dwarfed by the original hook: recreational fishing. Compare 19 paddle guides with somewhere around 350 fishing guides operating in Everglades National Park and the Ten Thousand Islands.

While fishing may have declined as a result of upstream hydrological changes, it is what passes for big business in the Ten Thousand Islands. Where paddlers see only leaping mullet, breaching dolphins, manatee noses, and an occasional Kemp's Ridley (a rare sea turtle with a fondness for the area), fisher folk see below the water, looking for the big four: snook, redfish, seatrout, and tarpon, as well as grouper and snapper offshore. Even though most visiting fisher folk abandon the area for cooler regions in summer, fishing remains good all year.

It is not coincidence that renders shrinking beer froth analogous to the Ten Thousand Islands. The islands are, generally speaking, shrinking—at least on "the outside" where the Gulf of Mexico is chipping away at them. And while rising sea level and storms erode the outside, a fascinating biological process creates new islands on the inside. The island-forming capacities of red mangroves are so well known (and overrated) that there is little need to extol their wondrous talents.

The silent partner in island building in the Ten Thousand Islands are the oysters, which flourish best when they can gather the most food. These animals, strictly nonmotile as adults, must rely on currents to bring food to them, and they prosper where flow is swiftest. The faster the current, the more food that passes them by, the more they can feed and grow. Thus, if tidal water sloshes in and out of a bay in a north-south motion, oysters oriented east-west will be better served. Intriguingly, such perpendicular bars are unlikely to block all flow, for as openings narrow, the velocity of the tide increases and prevents larval planktonic oysters from settling. By accumulating fastest perpendicular to the flow, oyster bars build up in the inside bays in a manner that ultimately has profound geologic and hydrologic effects.

While most of the Ten Thousand Islands owe their existence to storms, oysters, and mangroves, the most impressive uplands owe their existence to occupation and land building by Calusa Indians, an estuarine culture (or series of cultures) that occupied the area for at least four thousand years. Uplands areas of keys such as Dismal, Fakahatchee, Sandfly, Watson Place, and Chokoloskee were all created as either deliberate structures or accidental trash heaps—early landfills of empty mollusks. These scattered archipelagos of mangroves and mounds are divided by what are known as rivers and passes, terms more misleading than helpful. It doesn't help that there are two distinctly different types of rivers in the area: the dozen rivers that drain the marshland to the northeast, and the rivers and passes that connect the inner bays (called "the inside"), such as Chokoloskee Bay, with the outside, or gulf. These rivers and passes don't drain land, but water; they run salt, not fresh; and the flow is in two directions with the tide, not one. Other than that, they may be said to be quite a bit like rivers, in that they get wider as they approach the gulf, are unusually deep, and can move along at a good clip. In fact, the most dramatic topography in the region is unseen—some of the rivers and passes are surprisingly deep, in places ten times deeper (that is, twenty feet) than what passes for "naturally occurring" upland in the area.

The Ten Thousand Islands are not particularly on the way to anywhere, less so now that Alligator Alley (I-75) trumps the Tamiami Trail (U.S. 41) as a route across the Everglades. Faster, wider, safer, and less funky, the interstate has dried up all but the most persistent retail operations on the trail. Frog City, Orchid Isles, Monroe Station, and Big Cypress Bend are all gone, their patrons captured by the new road to the north. For four decades starting in 1928, the Tamiami Trail was both the new and the only road across the Everglades. The alignment skirted to the south of the major cypress strands (forested watercourses that lack a continuous channel), such as the Picayune and Fahkahatchee, and headed a dozen rivers (Blackwater, Whitney, Pumpkin, Little Wood, Wood, Faka Union, Fakahatchee, East, Ferguson, Barron, Halfway Creek, and Turner) that drain from the Big Cypress Swamp toward the Ten Thousand Islands. In doing so, the trail avoided the need for wide bridges and provided several trail-accessible and still-used portals to the islands.

Indisputably, the Ten Thousand Islands exist between the Tamiami Trail and the open gulf. And despite the delightfully watery confusion at Rookery Bay, few would argue that the Ten Thousand Islands extend north beyond Marco Island. In fact, ownership, development, and geography all place the northern limit of the Ten Thousand Islands along a line connecting Goodland and Horr's Island (now known, for sound marketing reasons, as Key Marco). North of that line, upscale residences, real silica sand beaches, and private land prevail; to the south, publicly owned land with skimpy beaches of mixed sand, ground shell, and rotted worm rock. What is not so clear is the south-ern extent of the Ten Thousand Islands. Some might argue they lie only in Collier County since they were owned by the Colliers at one point. Others may think that they stop around Chokoloskee, where the modestly sized islands peter out and the giant mangrove islands begin. But surely the Ten Thousand Islands reach as far as Watson's Place on Chatham River. One objective measure is the last small island on the outside, Wood Key, just north of Lostman's River. South of that point the shoreline from the outside reads as mainland, even though they are just the megamangrove islands. Of course, part of the region's charm is its ambiguity, the lack of a dashed line on a map that denotes the official end of the Ten Thousand Islands.

The one sure thing is that there are not exactly ten thousand islands. Whether the purported number is hopelessly inflated or laughably low is hard to say. An afternoon spent with NOAA (National Oceanographic and Atmospheric Administration) chart #11430 sug-gests the total number of charted islands between Goodland and Lostman's River is only somewhere around eight hundred, and cer-tainly less than a thousand. Fewer than forty appear to be named, perhaps because after Dismal Key, Buzzard Key, Sandfly Key, and

Lostman's Key someone concluded the naming, while clearly descriptive, was not likely to increase the area's marketability. In fact, the water bodies seem more likely to be named than the islands, so hundreds of keys remain to be named and many choice names remain unassigned: Cutfoot Key, Misery Key, Duplicate Key, Hardaground Key, and so forth.

The fractal nature of the landscape suggests there may be more than ten thousand islands. The number of keys fluctuates wildly depending on tide. On a full moon spring tide with the wind blowing water out of the bays, there are hundreds, if not thousands, more islands to count. And while no man is an island, perhaps each and every mangrove with its feet in the water is. In that case, the number of islands must be in the millions.

The southern half of the Ten Thousand Islands became protected within Everglades National Park in 1947. The boundary looks as though it were cut with a giant pair of pinking shears from southwest to northeast. The Collier family (of the eponymous county) donated fifty square miles of land (and water)—surely one of the more magnanimous acts in the state's history. After more than a half century of federal management, the park's approach is clear and well established. With the exception of one inholding, a modest camp on Huston Bay, the hermits, squatters, and inholders are gone, replaced with a permit system for camping. Forty-eight picnic table and portalet campsites have been established in the park, with roughly a quarter of them in the Ten Thousand Islands. Some beach campsites lack toilets and users are instructed to bury human waste at least six inches below the surface, away from shorelines and tents. Campsite numbers have been bolstered in recent years by the construction of sixteen chickees, three in the Ten Thousand Islands. The chickees, built over the water on pilings, are 120-square-foot roofed platforms with a catwalk to a portalet. While one can sleep aboard a boat without a permit, camping in the park (hence, the southern portion of the Ten Thousand Islands) requires a permit with a scheduled itinerary of campsites. The park's helpful wilderness trip planner runs four legal pages. This system, while efficient, does tend to limit spontaneous exploration and can induce a "we've got to get there by nightfall" obsessiveness about travel. Which is why many paddlers have taken to heading north from Everglades City—to get out of Everglades National Park and into a more laissez-faire camping atmosphere.

The remaining Collier-owned portions of the upper Ten Thousand Islands were unfenceable and functionally wide-open for both use and abuse. Legends of lawlessness are no doubt gratuitously inflated to fan the romantic frontier image, but it is also true that alcohol, drugs, and illegal immigrants moved throughout the Ten Thousand Islands in the course of the decades. If marriage had been outlawed, someone would have been smuggling in-laws through the Ten Thousand Islands.

While the park portion developed rules, the northern end of the Ten Thousand Islands remained as an unsupervised playground and outlaw area. There are no picnic tables here, no portalets, no designated campsites. No one needs a permit (except if they start in the park). Nor does one need to file a float plan (which is always a good idea). There is no wilderness trip planner: just launch and pray. The land is so scarce and the sea so vast that local custom contradicts park policy to the south, and beachfront campers can be seen hurling sand-weighted, partially turd-filled, long-dead horseshoe crab shells seaward, discuslike, to avoid contaminating the narrow shore. The unsubstantiated concept is that human waste poses a greater threat to the meager upland ecosystem, health, and good taste than it does entering the estuarine food chain, where it might be ecologically interpreted as just another manatee having passed that way.

The area north of the park wasn't protected until an unlikely federal event known as the Phoenix Land Swap. The Phoenix Land Swap, aka the Big Cypress Exchange (part of the Phoenix-Idaho Conservation Act) was approved by Congress in 1988. In a testimonial to the relative values of urban land in burgeoning sunbelt Phoenix and low-lying Florida coastal swampland, 68.4 acres of federal land at the former Phoenix Indian School (in downtown Phoenix, Arizona) were traded for 107,800 acres of land in Collier County and $34.9 million. Nearly one-fifth of the Florida land (19,620 acres) became the Ten Thousand Islands National Wildlife Refuge.

Operating out of a motel suite within ear shot of I-75, the Ten Thousand Islands National Wildlife Refuge (a subunit of Florida Panther National Wildlife Refuge) is an acre-rich and dollar-poor operation. The refuge must deal with an issue that the park also faces: increased visitation—also referred to as "loving it to death"—which raises the question of how many is too many for the resource to bear. As usual, the challenges of managing the new refuge have more to do with managing people than managing the ecosystem itself.

Most of the Ten Thousand Islands are now in public ownership. The gap between the new refuge and the old park is occupied by state owned lands. This raises the question of the future of the privately owned peripheral lands and the future management of the Ten Thousand Islands National Wildlife Refuge. If the recommendations of the Draft Comprehensive Conservation Plan are adopted, Ten Thousand Islands National Wildlife Refuge will enter a five-year interregnum, at the end of which some decisions may be made regarding commercial and recreational use. For the most part, this involves revisiting practices that have evolved over decades. Camping is a good example. There is so little dry land (what dry land exists is mostly Indian mounds and beaches) that recreational paddlers have traditionally headed to the few beaches on the outside. The mounds are hotter and buggier with less air movement and view. The federal government doesn't normally encourage citizens to think of camping in national wildlife refuges, but this plan acknowledges that camping in Ten Thousand Islands is both a long and nationally advertised tradition. As recreational use increases, beach campsites could take a pounding. The addition of Everglades Park-style chickees could allow the area to support more camping, particularly if they were placed to have views comparable to those from the beaches. Fortunately, a serendipitous de facto symbiosis links the nesting of summer sea turtles with peak sand fly and mosquito populations—helping to ensure campers will not be lounging on the sparse beaches when the turtles come ashore. The refuge managers will have until 2005 to assess the impacts of camping before proposing to regulate or restrict it.

The same wait-and-see, give-it-a-few-years approach will be taken with decisions regarding personal watercraft (jet skis and waverunners) and airboats. Airboats, while noisy, are the hometown favorite, and early public comment suggested that they be allowed during the purgatory period. But the same initial public comment clearly called for the banning of personal watercraft. Nevertheless, the service wants a factual basis for making decisions, and hence they will allow both airboats and personal watercraft, deciding later, based on additional research, how each impacts resources and aesthetics. The problem is that the service "cannot predict whether or not studies will be funded, occur in a timely manner, or if the research will produce the results needed to make informed decisions." Taking on any organized, economically vested industry or constituent group is akin to poking a stick in a fire ant hill. The service is no doubt wise to avoid promulgating a restriction it cannot defend. But the draft conservation plan seems to be telegraphing the news that the requisite data might not be forthcoming.

A key part of the draft plan will focus on the part of the system boaters never see—the waters that cross the Tamiami Trail and feed the rivers that flow into the inner bays. This will involve the restoration of hydrology in South Golden Gate Estates, a Nixon-era real estate scam that dug miles of canals upgradient in the Picayune Strand, with the result that the downstream Ten Thousand Island bays were made more turbid—worse for seagrass and fish. Restoration is a long-term path with numerous procedural, technical, and legal challenges along the way.

Another key goal is acquiring 1,640 acres of private land adjacent to the refuge. While the plan buoyantly states that this will "facilitate administration and management," the defensive way to view it is that private development of these lands would complicate and compromise the integrity of the refuge. Either way it is wise to acquire remaining privately held parcels when available. The alternatives are clear enough. A real estate brochure from the area encourages readers to "own a piece of Florida's last frontier." In addition to Marco and Horr's Island, there is Port of the Islands, formerly known as Remuda Ranch. Whether this resort at the head of the now straight-reamed Faka Union River is the only civilized entry to the region or an anomalous intrusion of obscene proportions is in the eye of the beholder. The plan also proposes to remove derelict boats and invasive exotic plants from the refuge and, more ambitiously, to add access features to the landscape. A nonmotorized boat trail is being contemplated as well as a walking interpretive trail with an observation tower at the end. Here the refuge runs headlong into the essential quandary of public access in natural areas. To what extent does the Ten Thousand Islands "experience" need to be packaged, made safe, and marketed? Will tinted-windowed, air-conditioned ecotour buses pull up to the future Tamiami Trail-accessible interpretive center and disgorge scores who will read sandblasted interpretive signs while the diesels drone on? What can be said of tourists who allow a half hour on their itinerary to come to know the Ten Thousand Islands? Or for that matter, one day? The more time one spends there, the more one realizes how much remains unknown. Matthiessen has spent twenty years picking at this plate and may not be ready for dessert.

Is it possible that the Ten Thousand Islands should be confusing? Maybe they should be accessible only to those patient enough to discover the secrets of moving in something other than total misery. One could argue that charts and maps allow beer-cooler yahoos access to areas that only dedicated explorers or natives should know about. This point of view is summed up by a citizen comment: "Tell the public nothing. The less the public knows about the area, the better off we will be." This may simply be the the old repackaged mindset that gave us the seven unwritten [sic] laws of the Ten Thousand Islands: "Suspect every man. Ask no questions. Settle your own quarrels. Never steal from an islander. Stick by him, even if you do not know him. Shoot quick, when your secret is in danger. Cover your kill."

The other, currently dominant school of thought holds that public agencies have been too stingy in providing diverse recreational experiences in the Everglades/Big Cypress. Access and understanding will build a constituency, it is said, and that constituency will fight off threats and lobby for an adequate budget. This quandary is recapitulated in this essay. Is the goal to intrigue and seduce the reader into wanting to visit? To convince the reader that it is not worthy of visitation? Or to argue that if you really love the area you will stay away?

Without a doubt, there are myriad special moments in the Ten Thousand Islands. Yet describing them contributes to the commodification of the islands. Thus this essay will not glamorize the Ten Thousand Islands and will not, for instance, describe as magic the flattened landscape at night on the water. It is not calm, cool, and moonless. Spill light from Miami does not create a dim horizontal glow above some distant shore. We are not drifting with the tide over shallow bottom, aggravating bioluminescent plankton that pulse with living, surging light. Islands don't slide by silently. The Milky Way is not as distinct as the moment it was expressed from Hera's breast, and no shooting stars sear our retinas, leaving lingering hypnagogic afterimages. We don't debate who was more startled, we or the offended night herons whose squawks jump us. We can't hear the dolphins and manatees breathing and we don't shiver, either at the cold or at the realization that perhaps no one has ever been in this place. Or at least at just this tide, especially with this particular sky and this nonmoon. Or perhaps someone *is* around the next bend, bent over the side of boat engaged in an activity that, if discovered, might endanger our lives. And we don't think of the first people in long dugout canoes shivering themselves, unraveling the secrets of moving through this paradoxical landless landscape.

This essay will not go there. Instead, I hope to persuade the reader that rather than being fun, it is monotonous, that instead of being challenging, it is merely difficult, and that it is exciting in roughly the same way being stranded in an airport during a blizzard is exciting—it makes a decent story afterward but is not something someone would seek out a second time. It would be hard to exaggerate how inhospitable the region can be. Visitors are unlikely to be snowbound (though hypothermia is a risk), have a rock fall on them (though you could be cut to shreds by oysters), or experience an earthquake (though even a small seafloor shift or meteor strike in the gulf would quickly translate into a heart-stopping tsunami as water piles up over the shallow bays). Aside from that, nearly any disaster seems quite likely, if not impending.

Perhaps there are boat-based tropical cultures elsewhere on the planet that could embrace the Ten Thousand Islands as a home away from home. But for people used to walking unchallenged on land, this is a sobering landscape indeed. The flora, fauna, geology, and geography all conspire to create conditions inimical to most Americans. While there are denser and spinier forests to walk through, mangroves are probably the most problematic when it comes to putting one foot in front of another. In some red mangrove forests one is forced either to climb on a jungle gym of what could pass for a coiled and looping garden hose or to step over the prop roots and back down into the muck. In addition to mangroves, spiny or otherwise obnoxious plants are in no shortage. The narrow storm-tossed beaches on the outside keys are quickly colonized by prickly pear cactus and sand spurs. Elsewhere, the only areas one could call land accrued as a result of land building; after a hundred years of more-or-less mechanized dredging, Calusa mounds probably still exceed the twentieth century's contributions in acreage. The mounds are repleat with thorny vines and the spiny and perversely named dildo cactus.

A certain lowering of expectations, or definition-adjustment, is necessary to enjoy explorations in the Ten Thousand Islands. A beach might be a narrow strip of steeply slanting gravel-sized and gravel-sharp shell fragments. A good campsite is one in which the tops of your shoes stay dry. A great place to eat your lunch might prove to be a flattened expanse of shell hash several inches above the rising tide. "Not too buggy" can mean that constant windshield-wiper-like arm waving is not necessary; intermittent flapping and swatting will suffice. "Plenty of water" means that when you look over the side of your boat you can see liquid water floating on top of the substance that has the consistency of pudding and that is simultaneously supporting and clasping your boat.

JONO MILLER

Part of the inhospitability of the region derives from the difficulty most people face in navigating the islands that deserve their labyrinthine reputation. With the exception of the few keys with shell mounds, the height and general facade of every islet seem virtually identical to a first-time visitor. On a windless sunny day the succession of similar islands rising from the flat horizon can be daunting. Longtime boaters actually do learn to recognize various keys, although the number of people who could be dropped at random and say with any certainty where they were is no doubt a modest figure.

For the rest of us, the key to knowing where you are in the Ten Thousand Islands is knowing where you were five minutes ago and making minor adjustments from there. Staying oriented involves a continuous process of successive reorientation and updating. The system is simple and reliable, and there are only two ways to get lost while using it. The first occurs when the landmarks of the previous setting become obscured by fog, darkness, or driving rain. The second, when you travel too far, too fast, without reorienting yourself. This is easy to do in a canoe and nearly unavoidable in a powerboat.

Travel in the Ten Thousand Islands reminds you that there are three states of being lost: the first, challenging; the second, annoying; and the third, potentially terrifying. The first state is to know where you are but not how to get where you want to be. Armed with maps, charts, and time, this can usually be solved, whether you are navigating the Living Seas exhibit at EPCOT or bobbing about in Fakahatchee Bay. The second state of being lost involves not knowing where you are. It's aggravating, but as long as you can backtrack successfully, you can survive. In the Ten Thousand Islands it is surprisingly easy to look up and realize you are not entirely sure where you are, a state usually referred to as being "turned around." The most pressing question to ask yourself if you are turned around is not "How did that happen?" but "Do I know how to get back to the last place where I did know for certain where I was?" Not knowing how to do that is the third type of being lost, the most sobering, the most forlorn.

Now of course, with handheld global positioning equipment and cell phones, you can determine the exact coordinates of where you are lost. But knowing where you are lost is of little comfort when you are in one of those bays that is emptying faster than you can paddle, the sun is setting, and myriad sand flies are looking for that deeply satisfying blood meal.

But I have already said too much. Having shared the secret of staying oriented, I am not at liberty to reveal any more tips or strategies that might make a visit more tolerable. You can stop reading now if you hoped to learn the secret to dealing with the bugs and the heat, or to finding a dry and private campsite. A visit here will not build character, set the stage for romance, or answer life's persistent questions. The Ten Thousand Islands, like Churchill, can promise only blood, toil, tears, and sweat—blood lost to drifts of biting insects, toil from dragging your boat through mud, tears from the frequent opportunities to get lost in the monotonous landscape, and sweat from the interminable sunlight and stifling humidity.

Despite these tribulations and the promise of public ownership, the Ten Thousand Islands remain at risk. No matter how forsaken the region can seem, more people arrive each year. Readers, fishers, paddlers, ecotourists, and egotourists read their respective magazines and add the Ten Thousand Islands to their life itineraries. In an environment that once required visitors to have extensive and arcane lore just to survive, people now feel free to set forth in a rented boat seated on their personal flotation devices with only a well-stocked styrofoam ice chest and a waterproof chart emblazoned with the simple, yet telling, credo: NOT FOR NAVIGATION PURPOSES. They are looking for the dark spots on the map. But with enough generators, camp stoves, and wood fires, the darkness of the Ten Thousand Islands—that which makes them what they are, their quiddity—can be compromised.

The national park has responded with a system that guarantees a quality wilderness experience for those who can stay on track and on schedule. Now the new national wildlife refuge will attempt to balance carefree use with careless abuse. At stake is a region whose relationship with Americans has always been strained. For the most part those strains appeared in the people who dared to live there. In ever increasing ways, the strains will now be seen in the landscape. Perhaps a toast, a haiku, a prayer to the region's future is in order.

> May your islands remain nameless,
> channels unmarked,
> your sandflies rampant.

Thanks to the internet, it is now known that there are at least three **J O N O MILLERs** *roaming the planet. If you happen to be acquainted with any of the others, this is the one that has lived in Sarasota, Florida, since Nixon stopped the jetport and barge canal. The one whose mother's father's mother's father sent the telegram from Philadelphia to Tallahassee announcing that tool magnate Hamilton Disston had agreed to buy four million acres of the Everglades for twenty-five cents an acre. And the one that accompanied Gary Paul Nabhan on the search for the Okeechobee gourd. Miller works in the Environmental Studies Program at New College of Florida and participates in local, state, and national conservation initiatives.*

THE MOST VALUABLE BIRD

Susan Diane Jewell

"I've got the signal!" I yelled to my pilot, Chuck Leverich, over the din of the Cessna 172's engine. "Keep heading north. It's getting stronger." I bounced excitedly in my seat, as much as the cramped space permitted. Three weeks ago this tricolored heron had disappeared from the nesting colony where I had radio-tagged him. I felt responsible for him, and I was afraid something dreadful had happened. As it turned out, this was a bird with a cat's nine lives.

The story of this heron began three weeks earlier in a remote mangrove swamp in Everglades National Park. The swamp was near the Lane River, one of about a half dozen tidal rivers that drain Shark River Slough into Whitewater Bay. These mangroves were home to a colony of three hundred pairs of wading birds, including great and snowy egrets, tricolored herons, little blue herons, and white ibises. My mission, as a research biologist with the National Audubon Society, was to study their movements, feeding habits, and nesting success. My colleagues and I had been enlisted by the South Florida Water Management District, the agency responsible for much of the surface water manipulation in South Florida. The water managers wanted to know how the reproductive success of the birds depended on the varying water levels in the Everglades, particularly in relation to the rainfall-driven test plan for regulating water flow that they had initiated in 1985 to help Everglades National Park. To accomplish our mission, we had to catch adult breeding egrets and herons, fit them with radio transmitters (homing devices), track the birds wherever they roamed in the Everglades, and monitor their nests.

My colleagues (project leader Dr. Tom Bancroft and volunteer Bill McKelvey) and I had arrived at our cramped observation blind that day by a long circuitous water route, as we did twice a week from March through June. We had left our dock at the Audubon office in the Upper Keys at 4:30 A.M. and crossed Florida Bay to Flamingo, a distance of more than twenty-five miles. It took three hours to navigate the shallow, tricky waters of the bay in our seventeen-foot Mako. Once we arrived in Flamingo, we floated the boat onto a large sling. A power lift hoisted the Mako over a large concrete plug and gently released it on the other side into Buttonwood Canal.

Once we cleared the plug, we motored up the canal, cruised across Coot Bay to Whitewater Bay, veered east onto the Lane River, and headed into ever-narrowing waterways, leaving all markers and any trace of humans behind. From that point, it took a practiced eye to recognize individual mangrove trees that marked subsequent turns. We idled slowly upstream until the vegetation became too thick to navigate. There we tied the boat, waded through the mangroves to our stashed canoe, and paddled the rest of the way to the colony. All of our gear, including observation blinds and towers, had been laboriously transported to our study site in this fashion.

When we arrived at the colony, we would have only a few hours to do our work, since our presence invariably startled the parents from their nests and exposed the eggs and chicks to the killing sun. When it got too hot, we'd withdraw from the colony until cooler temperatures allowed us to resume our work, later in the afternoon. During the interim hours, we would observe the birds' flight patterns from a distance. From Tavernier to the colony, it was about forty miles and another world away.

From a small plane, I could always spot this rookery among the endless green sea of mangroves, even when the wading birds were not present. Decades of nesting had contributed a rain of nutrients onto the trees from the birds' defecation and regurgitation, inducing those trees to grow taller and brighter green than the surrounding trees. It's a good thing wading birds have no appreciable sense of smell—unfortunately, wading bird biologists do.

We had selected the Lane River colony to study for three reasons. First, it was located where the effects of changes in Everglades hydrology would show. Second, we needed a colony that we could expect to appear each year in the same place for the duration of our four-year project. Colonies in the saw grass area of Everglades National Park tended to be ephemeral. They would appear on one tree island one year and another the next. How could we set up our blinds, or map and monitor particular colonies, if they constantly shifted? The Lane River mangrove colonies stayed put, probably because they were located on the transitional edge between freshwater and saltwater habitats. Here the birds could choose from a variety of feeding habitats within short flying distances. And the third reason we selected this site? It was relatively easy to get to.

Historically, South Florida's largest wading bird colonies were located in the headwaters of the rivers along the mangrove fringe on the western edge of what is now Everglades National Park. Their peak nesting was between March and May each year. During the early part of the nesting season, which coincided with the end of South Florida's dry season, the river of grass would slowly dry, offering wading birds a moving edge of shallow water and concentrated aquatic prey. In wet years, they could forage in the mangrove estuaries of Whitewater and Rogers River Bays, instead of the flooded saw grass marshes. The varying water depths along the drying edge and the estuaries allowed wading birds of different leg lengths to forage efficiently and provide for their hungry chicks.

Mangroves live in the netherlands—neither land nor sea, but somewhere in between. Only where the ocean's ample energy dissipates languidly and the waters are always warm will you find them growing. No waves crash on the mangroves; only gently creeping tides ebb and flow, carrying some nutrients in and others away. Three species—red mangroves, black mangroves, and white mangroves—occur in the Everglades. Closest to the sea grow the reds, closest to the land live the whites, and in between are the blacks. Mangrove seeds have such a tough time getting started that they have evolved a special trick: their seeds germinate while they are still hanging on the tree. The seeds then drop into the water feet first, ready to set their roots into the muck. The long seed pods of the red mangrove are weighted like bowling pins. Drop a ripe one into loose muck and it will land with its fat end down, roots already sprouted, leaves already poking out the top. At the fringes of mangrove colonies, the gentle tides allow a soup of nutrients to collect around the proplike roots, creating a smorgasbord for small fish and invertebrates. It's no wonder the herons like to hang out there.

The real challenge for our study was to safely catch the adult birds as they incubated eggs on their nests, so that we could correlate their movements with the stage in their nesting cycle. Did the adults feed in one area when they were incubating, then switch to another when the eggs hatched? If we could answer this question, we might learn how the man-made shifts in hydrology were affecting the success of the colony.

Our method of capturing the adults involved stuffing a gelatin capsule filled with a measured amount of a sleep-inducing drug inside a small fish, and then slipping the fish onto a nest. Oddly, although herons and egrets normally catch fish alive in shallow water, they will recognize a dead fish on the nest as food. Once the bird ate the fish and succumbed to the drug, usually within an hour, I'd radio from the blind to Tom and Bill, who were waiting out of sight in the canoe, and they'd retrieve it. We'd weigh the bird, band it, and attach the radio transmitter. The bird would sleep through the entire ordeal and be returned to the nest without ever seeing a human.

The fish—our birds' prey—were an important part of our studies. Part of my job was to collect and identify regurgitated meals to learn what species the birds normally ate. Regurgitation, or vomiting, is a defense mechanism (probably involuntary) used by wading bird chicks when a predator threatens. The theory is that the predator will turn its attention on the regurgitated meal and leave the bird alone. Birds in the Everglades colonies eat the typical wader diet of small fish, crayfish, freshwater shrimp, frogs, tadpoles, and aquatic insects.

These prey are all dependent on the hydropatterns of the water—that is, the timing, depth, location, and velocity of the water—as well as the water quality. Changes in any of these can alter the food chain and starve the birds. Every time we entered a nesting colony, a symphony of plops echoed through the mangroves as the regurgitated fish dropped into the water or onto branches. I "caught" sailfin mollies, mosquitofish, flagfish, sheepshead minnows, Everglades pygmy sunfish, least killifish, marsh killifish, and other fish. Ordinarily, fish biologists identify their subjects alive or preserved shortly after death. But by the time I would get the fish, they were somewhere between death and fertilizer. I learned to identify them without scales, fins, or color.

As I peered from a slit in the cramped blind on this sweltering day, twenty-five feet from a nest on a red mangrove branch, I saw a parent tricolored heron pick up and swallow the spiked fish. It was 3:13 on an afternoon in early May. Twenty-one minutes later, the now-wobbly heron tried to shift one of the three eggs around in the nest, but instead knocked it into the water. He had gotten so groggy. As I watched, he teetered too far and fell into the water.

No time to call for the canoe! Frantically, I pushed through the chest-deep murky water toward the floating heron, ignoring the omnipresent gators. Alligators love to hang out in wading bird colonies. What could be more inviting than an easy meal of an occasional chick falling out of a nest and into your waiting maw? And for dessert, a few choice morsels of marinated fish? I *had* to beat the waiting gators to the booty. Running in slow motion through the water, I reached the splash point and scooped up the limp body.

The heron had fallen into such a deep sleep that Tom, Bill, and I were certain we had fatally overdosed him. As with most drugs, the dosage depended on the body weight of the patient, which we had to estimate. We had an approximate idea of tricolored heron weights from previous research (about one pound), but the weights of individual birds can vary up to 30 percent, especially between males and females.

We brought our comatose patient back to the cottage we had

rented in Flamingo for this intensive field work phase. How vividly I recall the three of us standing over the limp body, poking and prodding, looking desperately for signs of life late into the night. There were none. Finally, depressed, we left the lifeless corpse in a cardboard box and retired for the night.

I slept on the couch in the living room, near the cardboard coffin on the coffee table. Sometime during the night I awoke to the sounds of weak scratching emanating from the box. I switched on a lamp and peeked in. There, to my astonishment and joy, was the heron, sitting up, looking up at me.

By the next day he had recovered, so we fitted him with a half-ounce solar-powered radio transmitter that emitted a signal detectable only with a special receiver. The radio was attached to a backpack harness designed to allow the bird complete freedom for flight and all other activities. The signal was an individually identifiable frequency for that bird, which was very helpful since I subsequently caught and radio-tagged seven other birds from that same colony.

We called our bird "151" (the frequency of his radio signal) and released him near his nest at the Lane River colony. Unfortunately, during his absence, fish crows had consumed his two remaining eggs. We weren't too worried, since other researchers had documented herons and egrets laying replacement clutches in the same nests after a first clutch was destroyed. But, unexpectedly, 151 disappeared from our search area in southwestern Everglades National Park.

I continued to spend about fifteen hours a week in the air, learning which feeding areas were important to this colony as I tracked the other radio-tagged birds and searched for 151. We had to track by airplane, due to the lack of roads through the Everglades and the maze of nonnavigable waterways and frequency-absorbing mangroves. I studied the radio-tagged birds so intensively that I discovered how their habits varied, even between individuals of the same species. For example, I almost always found one particular tricolored heron foraging alone in the mangrove region, while another regularly foraged in open marshes with a mixed flock of wading bird species. I could not make many generalizations about the herons' or egrets'

movements. They all had their preferences. Day after day, I kept
searching for 151.

Wading birds have served as a barometer of the environmental health
of South Florida, particularly the Everglades, for a century. Before the
end of the nineteenth century, when few white people lived in South
Florida, wading birds were so abundant—very roughly estimated at
2.5 million birds of seventeen species—that they came to symbolize
the Everglades. The numbers and variety of wading birds were greater
there than anywhere else in the country.

However, a thousand miles away, in crowded northern cities like New York and Boston, people were deciding the birds' fate.
Fashionable women wore hats decorated with long soft plumes from
great egrets, snowy egrets, reddish egrets, tricolored herons, roseate
spoonbills, and other species, most believing (because they were told
by milliners) that the birds shed the plumes and were not harmed in
their collection. While it is possible to collect shed feathers harmlessly,
in fact the birds were slaughtered when their plumes were the showi-
est—during the breeding season. And of course, the easiest place to kill
large numbers of plumed birds was around their nesting colonies. And
when one of a nesting pair was shot, its mate was forced to abandon
the nest because it could not care for the young alone, resulting in
the deaths of chicks as well as their parents. Plumes could bring up to
thirty-two dollars an ounce, even more than gold. It was a big business, exterminating hundreds of thousands of birds and causing such
massive disturbance in the South Florida colonies that reproduction
plummeted.

Every National Audubon Society employee in Florida knows the
story of how the birds were saved. In 1901, the State of Florida banned
plume hunting, a first but insufficient step. The next year, the National
Association of Audubon Societies (precursor to the National Audubon
Society) hired Guy Bradley, a young resident of the fledgling settlement of Flamingo, as the warden to protect the birds. After three years
of making arrests and trying to educate people about the effects of
plume hunting, Bradley was shot to death in his boat by a neighbor

who was illegally harvesting plumed birds. The news of Bradley's heroic action spread to the fashion industry, and women in distant cities began to comprehend the deadly price of their vanity. Many stopped buying plumed clothing. New York state banned the sale of plumes in 1910. When the demand dropped, so did the price of feathers, and eventually, so did the poaching.

During the next few decades, wading bird populations began to rebound, and by the 1930s their numbers had reached 180,000 to 245,000. But just as most species had begun to recover, threats to their habitats ensued as the slow torture of the Everglades accelerated. Dredging for canals caused productive marshes to ebb into farmland. Earthen levees, some as long as seventy miles, sprang up like a network of giant mole tunnels and blocked the vital sheet flow of the remaining marshes. Development mushroomed along the east coast. Water was diverted from the Everglades to quench the irrigation and municipal needs of the new tenants. Dirty water was pumped back in, loaded with pesticides, fertilizers, mercury, and other toxins. This caused chain reactions of all types, including a rapid expansion of nuisance plants, like cattails, that disrupted the food chain for all Everglades creatures. By the 1970s, the population of wading birds in the Everglades had crashed again. Everglades biologist John C. Ogden estimated that from 1934 to 1976 the wading bird population in the central-southern Everglades declined by 75 to 80 percent. It has declined further since then.

Even small threats add up. One day in the late 1980s, when our boat landed at a wading bird colony on an island in Rogers River Bay (in western Everglades National Park), my crew and I discovered dead white ibises floating on the water, wounded ones limping on the ground or caught in branches, and an eight-foot alligator sprawled on the shore with a bullet hole through its head. Shotgun shells littered the ground and water. We were shocked, and more than a little nervous, halfway between Flamingo and Everglades City, as far from civilization and park rangers as we could be. Judging by the vigor of the wounded birds, the poachers could still have been nearby. And we were in a boat with a big Audubon logo on the side! We were out of communication with the rangers until we returned to Flamingo. It was a nerve-racking day of field work, but we finished our tasks without seeing any other boats. We surmised that some locals from Everglades City had boated by that morning, using the winging birds for target practice as they left or entered the colony. Modern poachers don't even do it for food or money—these show-offs didn't even take the gator's tail.

Chuck aimed the little Cessna north toward Everglades City. The signal was getting stronger—I was getting closer to 151. Finally, I located the beeps coming from a clump of mangrove islands in a borrow pond next to the Tamiami Trail, just south of Naples. As I peered through my binoculars (not a recommended activity for those prone to airsickness), I began to distinguish dozens of tricolored herons winging in and out of the trees. So he was alive! Could 151 be starting life anew?

Then I remembered another radio-tagged bird that had recently disappeared from my search area. As Chuck skillfully circled the colony, I quickly dialed the second frequency on the receiver. "Beep, beep, beep . . ." came the second signal. So *another* tricolored heron (known as "370") from Lane River colony had wandered fifty miles northward. This was getting very interesting.

Early the next morning, I drove two and a half hours from my home in the Florida Keys to the colony just south of Naples. On the roof of my truck was the sixteen-foot canoe I needed to get to the mangrove islands where the nests were in Fakahatchee Strand State Preserve.

I waited nearby for several hours until the radio signals told me that both birds had returned from foraging. Silently I paddled to the nest islands and quickly found them on separate nests. Both nests contained eggs. To my relief, the drugging incident had not harmed 151. This time I had to sit perfectly still in the canoe while my insides were jumping with excitement. Previously, biologists didn't know whether tricolored herons were loyal to one colony, not nesting if local conditions were unfavorable, or if they would seek alternate colonies. This was the first time anyone had documented that tricolored herons do change colonies, even if their original one is still thriving. In the world of ornithology, this was big stuff.

I visited the Fakahatchee Strand colony once a week that summer until the chicks fledged and left the colony. During the following winter, I wondered whether the two birds would return to the Lane River colony or the Fakahatchee Strand colony. Slowly, the radio signal from 370 weakened over the winter until I could no longer track it. Thus, when the next year's nesting season began, it was 151 that I sought.

The bird surprised me once again by appearing in April of the second year at a colony on Frank Key near Flamingo in Florida Bay, about fifteen miles south of the Lane River colony. It was a much larger colony than either Lane River or Fakahatchee Strand colonies, with several thousand pairs of herons (great blue, great white, tricolored, little blue), egrets (great, snowy, reddish), brown pelicans, and double-crested cormorants. Here it was inappropriate for me to locate 151's nest, since my search would disrupt too many nesting birds. I left him alone.

In a few weeks, 151 amazed me further by leaving his apparently good nesting situation for the mangrove colony in Rogers River Bay, located between Lane River and Everglades City. There he stayed for the rest of the season with a new mate and two chicks. For a third time, I could document a tricolored heron switching colonies.

The second winter left me guessing: of the four colonies that 151 had visited in the past two years, which would he choose to set up housekeeping in next? My National Audubon colleagues were equally curious. To ease the subtropical doldrums, we set up a pool of wagers around the office, all betting a dinner on which colony 151 would choose that spring. Our office included some of Florida's most experienced wading bird biologists, but no one guessed right. Wouldn't you know that 151 would make fools of us all?

During the third May, tricolored heron 151 appeared in a fifth colony, a bald-cypress swamp along the Tamiami Trail near 40-Mile Bend, about thirty miles northeast of Lane River, and well inland.

Almost two thousand great egrets, snowy egrets, and tricolored herons had already established their nests. Luckily, I was able to locate 151's nest relatively easily, and I visited him periodically by canoe to watch him raise two more chicks. The radio that 151 carried gradually lost signal strength and I was not able to track him after that year.

During four years of radio-tracking thirty-three adults and many juvenile birds, I documented six tricolored herons and two little blue herons changing colonies. But 151 was my favorite. None was so transient, so reproductively active, or so long-lived (radiowise) as 151. Thus he became our "Most Valuable Bird."

The significance of our discovery, that tricoloreds and little blues may change colonies even if the original colony still thrives, is both good and bad. On the positive side, if a colony suffers from human disturbance, the birds may find another place to nest and still reproduce that year. Wildlife managers may even be able to lure wading birds to a new colony site, using decoys and fish ponds. On the negative side, the seemingly haphazard wanderings of some birds during the nesting season may mean that surveys of nesting wading birds are not accurate. If surveys are conducted periodically through the nesting season, as most are, there is potential for counting some birds twice, thus inadvertently inflating their numbers.

It's a relief to know, however, that wading birds can be adaptable. They will respond to our attempts to heal the Everglades. And they will be a necessary part of the healing, for they have a function, too. Without wading birds to keep the small aquatic life in balance and move nutrients around the ecosystem, the Everglades will be an empty and ill place. If we can restore the water flows and water quality at least in some parts of the Everglades, the wading birds will return. Maybe this time they will stay.

From 1986 to 1998, wildlife biologist **SUSAN DIANE JEWELL** *roamed the Everglades by motorboat, airboat, airplane, canoe, and soggy foot to study wading birds, alligators, and dirty water. Her work for the National Audubon Society in the Florida Keys, Everglades National Park, and A.R.M. Loxahatchee National Wildlife*

Refuge brought her experience in all parts of the Everglades. She has published two books, Exploring Wild South Florida *and* Exploring Wild Central Florida *(both published by Pineapple Press). She is a Certified Wildlife Biologist, pilot, and scuba diver, and is employed as a biologist for the U.S. Fish and Wildlife Service in Washington, D.C., where she writes about endangered species.*

THE MOST VALUABLE BIRD

THE LAST DAYS OF FLORIDA BAY

Carl Hiaasen

On a gum-gray June afternoon, between thundershowers, my son and I are running a seventeen-foot skiff through the backcountry of Florida Bay. The wind has lain down, the water is silk. Suddenly, a glorious eruption: bottle-nosed dolphins, an acre of them, in a spree of feeding, play, and rambunctious lust. From a hundred yards we can hear the slap of flukes and the hiss of blowholes. We can see the misty geysers, the slash of black dorsals, the occasional detonation as a luckless bait fish gets gobbled.

No matter how often I witness the sight, I'm always dazzled. A stranger to these waters could only assume he was traveling in authentic wilderness, pure and thriving. If only it were so. It's easy, when surrounded by dolphins, to forget that the bay is fatefully situated downstream from the ulcerous sprawl of Florida's Gold Coast. Four-and-a-half million people live only a morning's drive away.

The river that feeds the backcountry is the Everglades, sometimes parched and sometimes flooded. Water that once ran untainted and bountiful is now intercepted and pumped extravagantly to sugarcane fields, swimming pools, golf courses, city reservoirs—and even the Atlantic. What's left is dispensed toward the bay in a criminally negligent fraction of its natural flow. The water isn't as clean as it once was, and it doesn't always arrive in the right season.

That the bay is sick is hardly a surprise. The wonder is that it has survived so long and the dolphins haven't fled to sea forever.

I fell in love with the Florida Keys by staring at a road map. I was about five years old. My grandfather was a storyteller, and my father was a sportfisherman, and I had listened to their exciting tales long enough. I wanted them to take me.

Outdoor magazines extolled the Keys as jewels or gems or a string of pearls dangling languidly from the continental flank. From the map I memorized the islands transected by U.S. 1. They had lyrical, funky names—Sugarloaf, Saddlebunch, Ramrod, Big Coppitt, Lower Matecumbe. To a boy growing up on the steamy, iron-flat apron of the Everglades, it seemed fantastic that an exotic undersea paradise existed only three hours away—maybe less, the way my dad could drive. This I already knew: The Keys were surrounded by water—the Atlantic, the Gulf of Mexico, Florida Bay—and the water was blue, by god. All you had to do was look at the map.

Except the map was misleading, as I discovered when we rode down the Overseas Highway, me in the backseat, my father and grandfather up front. The water of the Keys was beyond a map-printer's blue; it was a preternatural spray of indigo, emerald, turquoise, and violet. And the hues changed with each passing cloud.

Another thing I knew about the Keys: The great Ted Williams lived there! In certain sporting circles he was more revered for his flycasting than for his batting. Riding through Islamorada, I pressed my face to the window in hopes of glimpsing the legendary slugger. He was bound to be at one of the charter docks or tackle shops, grinning that newsreel grin, posing for snapshots next to a gaping one hundred-pound tarpon.

It was a much different era, before jet skis and time-shares and traffic signals came to the Keys. Now they're trying to four-lane U.S. 1 all the way from Florida City to Key Largo. Ted Williams has moved away, and the water isn't always as blue as it should be. Florida Bay is a thousand square miles of hard-bottom shallows, grassy banks, and mangrove islands that stretch from the Upper Keys to the rim of the

Gulf of Mexico. On low tide the flats become exposed, pungent, and crunchy, revealing the labyrinth of spidery ditches by which the backcountry must be navigated. Casual boaters seldom venture here more than once. Getting beached on the banks is no fun; getting lost can be worse. Despite its smooth and placid face, the backcountry sometimes roils to a murderous fury.

In 1948 a promising young jockey named Albert Snider won the Flamingo Stakes at Hialeah. To celebrate he and some friends took a fishing trip to Florida Bay. They anchored their yacht off a small island named Sandy Key. Snider and two pals got in a rowboat to go redfishing. They were still within sight of the yacht at dusk when a storm blew up out of nowhere. The next morning the Coast Guard launched an extensive air-and-sea search, which lasted for days. Snider and his companions were never found.

The racing world was shocked. Snider's mount in the Flamingo, a horse named Citation, was given to one of Snider's best friends, a rider named Arcaro. That year Citation won the Triple Crown, and the famous jockey gave part of his winnings to Snider's widow. Eddie Arcaro had considered joining his buddy on that fishing trip to Florida Bay but had gone to Santa Anita instead.

Historically the backcountry has belonged to fishermen, smugglers, poachers, bootleggers, fugitives, and the occasional professional adventurer. Its gallant snook and tarpon attracted Zane Grey in the 1920s. Its imposing eagles, ospreys, and herons caught the artistic eye of John James Audubon in the 1830s.

Early this century, plume hunters in Florida Bay wiped out many thousands of wading birds because rich ladies on Park Avenue fancied white feathers in their hats. When the law cracked down and plumed hats went out of style, the egret and heron populations slowly rebounded—only to be ravaged again as wetlands dried up, victimized by drought and greedy water "management" practices. Today most of the backcountry lies within the boundaries of Everglades National Park, so the birds, manatees, and crocodiles enjoy a modest degree of protection. The water itself is under no such stewardship.

The decline of Florida Bay has spanned the terms of several park superintendents, who have displayed widely varying degrees of concern and influence. Blame must also be assigned to the State of Florida. It boasts strict pollution laws for rivers and coastlines, but enforcement is a farce in the Everglades, which is used as both a cistern and a sewer by industry and agriculture. By the time freshwater reaches the bay, scientists can do little but draw samples and hope for the best.

To be sure, some of the bay's natural spectacles still appear unharmed by man: A fire flash of roseate spoonbills high in the black mangroves. Or the sparkle of jittery bonefish tails among mangrove shoots at dawn. Or a steep tannic creek so teeming with snappers that you can't see the bottom for the fish. Here's the heart of the riddle: How can the backcountry look so robust in some places and so moribund in others? How can it change so fast? One day the water is as clear as gin; the next it's like chowder.

Nobody truly knows why. The maddening riddle is now pursued by biologists, ecologists, hydrologists, and a wagon load of other Ph.D.s. Cheering them on are business leaders, tourism promoters, and once-indifferent politicians.

Not so long ago only fishermen and a handful of scientists gave a damn. One of the first to spot the trouble was captain Hank Brown, a dean among the guides of the Upper Keys. Impassioned but quiet spoken, Brown has spent more time in the backcountry—roughly eight thousand days—than all the attending academics combined. "The only thing I have going for me," he says, "is that I look at it every day."

In the late 1980s Brown noticed patches of turtle grass dying in the western and central parts of the bay. Soon entire banks went bald, and the water turned muddy. The effect upon backcountry fishing, a major industry of the Keys, was instantaneous. Flycasting for tarpon, permit, and bonefish depends on relatively clear water. Hard-core anglers won't pay $325 a day to flail blindly in the mud. They want to see their quarry; it's the essence of the sport, an indescribable high. As the backcountry got murky, Brown and other guides began losing clients to the still-crystal flats of the Bahamas, Belize, and Mexico.

In the fall of 1990, Florida Bay suffered a staggering fish kill in Garfield Bight and other coves. Administrators of Everglades National Park showed scant interest in the problem until Brown and others began directing the media to the scene. For a place that depends on tourism, the only thing worse than the sight of bloated rotten fish is front-page headlines about bloated rotten fish. The kill was investigated. Lack of oxygen was blamed but not explained.

But by far the most shocking symptom of the bay's collapse was the massive floating clouds of algae that seemed to bloom wherever the sea grasses died. Phytoplankton mixed with wind-stirred sediments to transform healthy water into a bilious, rank-smelling broth. "First came the turbidity," Brown recalls. "Then the grass died. Then the root systems disintegrated, and the banks of the channels literally caved in." In twenty-nine years on the water he had never seen anything so ominous. Hank and his wife, Joy, videotaped the fish kills and the rotting sea grasses and sent out copies on cassettes. Hank went to government meetings to warn about what was happening in Florida Bay. Other guides, young and old, sounded the alarm, too.

One important tourist who heard about the crisis was George Bush Sr. That the president loved fishing in the backcountry was a cause for great optimism by many Keys locals. If he couldn't do something to save the place, they reasoned, nobody could. And they made a point of telling him about it. During one bonefishing expedition, a guide scooped a handful of foul mud off the flat to show the president how the sea grass was dying.

But nothing happened after Bush went back to Washington. Nothing. Meanwhile Florida Bay got sicker.

The problem is fresh, clean water. There's not enough of it moving down the peninsula. Getting more will require prompt, stouthearted action, for which Florida's lawmakers are not famous. When nature controlled the plumbing, good water ran south in a sheet from Lake Okeechobee through the Everglades, finally emptying from Shark River and Taylor Slough into the brackish estuary called Florida Bay. It was a perfect system, except that it did not anticipate the demands of reckless, unchecked urban growth. As Fort Lauderdale and Miami boomed in the forties, the Army Corps of Engineers built fourteen hundred miles of levees and canals. Pump houses were installed to prevent flooding of farms and newly developed subdivisions (real estate brokers still being somewhat sensitive about their image as tawdry swamp peddlers).

In the ravenous euphoria of a land stampede, no thought was given to the possible adverse effects of gouging deep trenches across Florida's wetlands. For engineers the mission was a simple one: Move the water.

Now the federal government and the State of Florida are spending millions trying to fix the mess. In theory the restoration plan would mimic the ancient pattern of Everglades drainage while reducing pathogenic levels of mercury, nitrogen, phosphorus, and pesticides. But in fact there's still no official commitment to replenish the total annual volume of freshwater once sent to Florida Bay. Without that, many scientists say, the backcountry will never recover.

So much water has been purloined for urbanization that the bay today receives about one-tenth of its historic flow. In the 1980s successive seasons of brutal drought and exceptionally high temperatures conspired with dumb flood-control practices to hasten the crash. No longer brackish, the bay was becoming a hot, briny lagoon—in some places, twice as salty as seawater. Most experts think huge algae blooms in the backcountry are related, at least indirectly, to the ultrahigh salinity. They believe too much salt in the water can kill sea grasses, triggering a cycle of decay. Dead grass loads the water with nutrients, which in turn gorge the plankton. As the algal mass spreads, it damages more grasses in its path. "Thus a positive growth loop, similar to a cancer cell's, is born," explains Dr. Joseph Zieman, a University of Virginia scientist who has studied Florida Bay extensively.

A minority view is that the blooms are caused by phosphates and other waste swept into the bay from distant cities and farms. Whatever the cause, the effect is arresting. Although the phytoplankton isn't toxic to sea life, it blocks sunlight essential to the habitat of larval lobsters, shellfish, corals, and sponges. The onset of the algae was followed by a drastic slump in the Gulf of Mexico's pink-shrimp harvest.

By 1992 the bloom was so prolific that a 450-square-mile area of the bay had been dubbed the Dead Zone. Mark Butler, a biologist at Old Dominion University in Virginia, was conducting a field study of spiny lobsters when a 100-square-mile blanket of algae settled for three months around the Arsnicker Keys. Underwater visibility dropped from twenty-five feet to six inches. In a letter to the Florida Keys National Marine Sanctuary, Butler wrote, "When the bloom finally dissipated, we were awed at the devastation. . . . Over 90 percent of the sponges at our study site were either killed or severely damaged."

I was out in the bay on a day when it was happening. With the plankton clogging their membranes, sponges were dying by the hundreds and floating off the bottom. The surface became a bobbing gantlet of brown, decaying clumps of sponge; the water was greenish and grungy. The sight put a knot in my gut.

So widespread and thick was the algae that it could be tracked by satellite photography. Currents eventually carried the inky plumes out of the bay through the bridges of the Keys, toward the Atlantic. There the algae settled on reefs, causing an uproar among dive-shop operators and charter captains. Traitorous winds also puddled the crud around Islamorada, in plain site of tourists on the Overseas Highway. It was not a pretty postcard.

Once a preoccupation of guides, lobstermen, and shrimpers, the worsening conditions in the backcountry suddenly became an establishment crusade. That's because the Keys' economy depends entirely on water as clean, blue, and inviting as it appears in the travel brochures. (To say the aquatic balance of the Keys is fragile isn't a cliche, it's an understatement. Recently scientists flushed a viral tracer into a residential septic tank in Port Largo. Only eleven hours later the virus emerged in a nearby canal; in another twelve hours it turned up offshore.)

As soon as the decline of Florida Bay was identified as a major threat to tourism, the obligatory task forces and blue-ribbon panels were convened. Politicians from Key West to Washington, D.C.—some in dire need of proenvironment credentials—adopted the bay as their ward, their Walden Pond.

Even George Bush Sr. finally got on board. A few summers ago, he hosted a celebrity bonefish tournament, with proceeds to benefit the Everglades. For those who waited in vain for Bush to do something during his presidency, it's sourly ironic that the gesture came when he was out of office and out of power.

But any newfound support must be welcomed, because time is so precious. Between sixty thousand and one hundred thousand acres of sea grass are dead or damaged in the bay. The die-offs and algae blooms continue to advance across the backcountry in two prongs, one from the gulf and one from the interior.

The worst-hit area remains the so-called Dead Zone, the bay's northwestern quadrant. There, near the once-fabled tarpon grounds of Oxfoot Bank, the marine bed is tundra. Redfish, trout, and pompano have been displaced by mud-loving bottom feeders such as catfish and mullet. A slight breeze churns the lakes and basins to marl; on each incoming tide the silt-filled water rolls eastward from Sandy Key toward Ninemile Bank and beyond.

From far away it's visible—a march of yellowish muck on the horizon. In July it breached Rabbit Key Basin, clouding one of the backcountry's most pristine lakes. One day you could count the blue-black slabs of tarpon resting along the banks, and the next day you couldn't see your own fingers in the water.

SAVE FLORIDA BAY! plead the bumper stickers. Theories, models, and plans abound. One thing virtually every expert agrees upon: The bay is doomed without a pure, dependable flow of freshwater. That's only the beginning of recovery, the baseline. Reclaiming that water means rechanneling some canals, filling others, and displacing some farmers and homeowners who have moved into the wetlands bordering Everglades National Park. Unfortunately, less controversial options haven't worked.

For instance, the Army Corps of Engineers and the South Florida Water Management District have been trying to transfuse water from the problematic C-111 canal toward Taylor Slough. After two years of experimental pumping, the results are discouraging. "There's no evidence any of that water is making it to the bay," concedes Steve Davis, an ecologist for the water district. Davis and others suspect that what's being pumped toward the backcountry is cresting at the upland marshes and retreating downhill into the same holding canal from which it came. Even in a swamp, gravity rules.

No fewer than fifteen government agencies and private conservation groups are working on the mystery of Florida Bay. Support has been strong and bipartisan, but folks in the Keys are nervous about the antienvironment mood in Congress. Meanwhile scientists are lining up for about $5 million worth of grants earmarked for studying the bay.

The camps are sharply divided between those who believe years of further research are needed and those who advocate swift action. Davis says that well-grounded science is important, but the clock is ticking for the backcountry: "We want to move ahead. We don't want to study this thing to death." So many bureaucracies are involved in the saving of Florida Bay that it's inconceivable that the process would go smoothly, and it hasn't. After a long, heated battle with vegetable growers, the State of Florida this year finally agreed to condemn and purchase the Frog Pond, a tract in southwest Dade County deemed critical to the replenishing of the bay. But no sooner was the deal done than the state offered to lease the disputed land back to the very farmers it had evicted. (Applying the same logic, General Norman Schwarzkopf should have allowed Saddam Hussein to reoccupy Kuwait after the Gulf War and pay rent.)

The upgrading of Florida Bay from a problem to an emergency has also spawned predictably petty turf guarding and bickering about who's running the show. In July, for example, scores of scientists met in the Keys to offer strategies for reinvigorating the bay. Conspicuously absent were the staff and biologists of Everglades National Park, wherein the bay is situated. Incredibly, park staffers were forbidden to attend the summit. The brass didn't like the way the meeting had been arranged, so they ordered a boycott.

Nothing like team spirit in a time of crisis.

The last eighteen months have been blessedly wet. Loads of rain, including a deluge from tropical storm Jerry, drenched the Everglades and continue to nourish Florida Bay. Some shallow banks show a stubble of new sea grass—a promising sign, even if it's only a few meager inches. Salinity in the bay's northeastern reaches has fallen to predrought levels. Another good sign: The algae blooms aren't as stubborn as in recent summers. Prevailing breezes have kept the discolored waters away from the shorelines of the Upper Keys—a relief for the Chamber of Commerce, because not even the most dogged tourists will snorkel in pea soup. In some basins and inlets the backcountry looks amazingly healthy. It was a good spring for tarpon, and guides say snook fishing is the best it has been in twenty years. An air of cautious hope has returned to the docks. "The water," says Hank Brown, "is absolutely gorgeous in places. But every time you get your hopes up, a storm comes through, and everything looks like crap again." All of us who live here would love to think that the worst is over, that Florida Bay is rebounding for good. But most scientists don't think so. The rains are fickle, and by winter the water might be too salty again. That's why it is imperative that a natural flow be restored as soon as possible, while the political will and funds exist to do it. The engineering isn't as daunting as the politics. Powerful special-interest groups are demanding a say in where the lifeblood of the Everglades goes, how much they get to keep and what they're allowed to dump in the water on its way downstream.

The battle begins up at Lake Okeechobee, where Big Sugar finally (and reluctantly) has agreed to filter phosphates from the runoff of the cane fields. Farther south, the cities siphon heavily from the diked "conservation areas"—cheap, accessible reservoirs that help fuel the breakneck westward growth in Palm Beach, Broward, and Dade counties. Even below Miami, on Florida's still rural southern tip, water policy is disproportionately influenced by private interests. In the dry months, what would otherwise trickle through the Glades to the bay is diverted instead to a small cluster of tomato and avocado farms. Conversely, in the wet season the surplus water is pumped off the fields to protect the crops. The canal network was absurdly designed to flush millions of gallons not into the Everglades (which were made to absorb them) but into Manatee Bay and Barnes Sound, which are saltwater bodies. The effect of such a copious, sudden injection of freshwater is an overdose—lethal on an impressive scale to fish, corals, and other marine life.

But it's all for a good cause. Upstream the avocados are plump and safe.

During all my days in the Keys, I met Ted Williams only once. It was several years ago, at a gas station in Islamorada. He noticed my skiff on the trailer and stalked up to inquire about the bonefishing. Understand that Williams's reputation in the backcountry was as fearsome as it was at the ballpark, so I was a jumble of nerves. But he was as pleasant as anyone could be. We talked about the tides, the wind, where the fish were feeding. Then he got in his station wagon and said good-bye. It wasn't so long afterward that he sold his place and moved away.

I understand why he left, but I wish he hadn't. His unshy temperament would have made him a valuable ally in this battle for Florida Bay: a glaring, impatient presence before county commissions, water boards, and legislative committees.

Fortunately the Keys have other fiery defenders. One is Mike Collins, who spends almost as much time haggling in the back rooms of Tallahassee as he does poling the backcountry. Twenty years ago Collins fled Wall Street to become a fishing guide in Florida, the sort of madcap impulse of which urban daydreams and Jimmy Buffett lyrics are made. Changing latitudes, I'm happy to report, did not transform Collins into a laid-back guy. He has been a tenacious and refreshingly bluntspoken advocate for Florida Bay. So, given the many exasperating obstacles to saving the place, I was mildly surprised to hear Collins say, "I'm pretty optimistic. There's enough will to get it done. And there are some very good people working on it."

We were in his nineteen-foot skiff, tearing a frothy seam across a glass-calm morning, when he stopped to explore a redfish bank near Buoy Key. The scene was disheartening. Only months earlier the bottom had been lush and green. Now there were silty craters where the turtle grass had died. Leaning hard on the push pole, Collins agreed: It looked bad. But it could bounce back, he said. With a little luck and a little help.

You'll hear this over and over from those who spend their lives in these waters—a firm, almost spiritual confidence in the recuperative power of nature. "What this does," Collins said of the big rains, "is buy us some time." But he, too, worries that budget cutters might pull the plug on the Everglades, murdering it once and for all. For Collins, who happens to be a Republican, saving Florida Bay isn't an ideological choice, it's a moral one. There is simply no honorable argument against it.

"Look, I've been all over the hemisphere looking for someplace else that compares—the Bahamas, Belize, you name it," he says. "But I always end up back here in the Keys, doing battle with these bird-brained bureaucrats. You've got to fight for it, because there is no place else that comes close."

A few days later I travel to the source: Taylor River, a tributary of the aortal slough through which the Everglades delivers essential freshwater to the eastern bay. At the boat's helm is Frank Mazzotti, a University of Florida scientist who has spent eighteen years with endangered crocodiles along the backcountry's most remote coves and beaches. It has been a banner season for the crocs, Mazzotti reports, and a good year for most wildlife, thanks to the rains—which could end tomorrow, or next fall, or five years from now. Another drought is inevitable; the only uncertainties are when it will come and how long it will last.

Mazzotti is no less ardent than Collins, but he's a bit more diplomatic. "It's not that we've killed Florida Bay, though we're damn close," he says. "It's that we've compromised its resilience." For today, there's water enough to navigate Taylor River, which at its mouth is but a jungly creek—overgrown, slender as a mine shaft, mosquito choked, strung with ornate, dewy spiderwebs. A whispering current, southbound and strong, puckers around the mangrove roots. Reaching over the gunwale, I touch two fingers to the surface, then to my mouth. No trace of salt.

The water is warm, absolutely fresh. It tastes like hope.

———————

CARL HIAASEN *is a syndicated columnist with the* Miami Herald *and author of several novels, including* Lucky You, Tourist Season, Stormy Weather, Skintight, Double Whammy, *and* Striptease.

SAVING OUR TAILS

June Wiaz

"How come we don't get no respect?" complain members of the spiny
lobster community of Florida Bay.

In the summer of 1999, at least two restaurants in touristy, lobster-
loving Key West, Florida, installed machines where customers paid
two dollars each to try to grab a lobster. The arcade-style machines
allowed patrons a limited amount of time to use a dangling metal claw
to nab a lobster and drop it down a chute. The contraptions not only
gave new meaning to the expression "grabbing a bite to eat," but were
in violation of Key West property codes. City officials shut down the
practice. And for the spiny lobsters of Florida Bay, this was just one
more in a series of insults to their own integrity and to that of their
watery homeland.

In the mid-1980s, there was a notable downturn in the quality of
water in the bay—the spiny lobsters' habitat. Between 1987 and 1992,
large swaths of sea grass, some even visible by satellite, died off. Algal
blooms proliferated, virtually wiping out sea sponges—the favored
protective hangout of juvenile lobsters—in a one hundred-square-mile
area of the south-central bay.

Increases in the salinity of Florida Bay in the late 1980s corresponded with a slime mold infection that produced sea grass die-off.
The increased salinity was due to a combination of drought and a
reduction in the amount of freshwater reaching Florida Bay from the

Everglades—an estimated siphoning of 30 to 40 percent or more due to development and diversion of water to the east. The well-being of the open waters of Florida Bay clearly is bound to the vitality of the Everglades and subject to the biological influence of big dairy, sugar, avocado, tomato, and sugar farms, as well as roughly six million residents "upstream."

Florida Bay is home to spiny lobsters and more than 250 species of fish, numerous bottom-dwelling organisms such as sponges, corals, and shrimp, as well as alligators, crocodiles, green sea turtles, West Indian manatees, fish-loving birds, and wind-surfing, lobster-eating humans. This giant lagoon is roughly eight hundred square miles of placid and productive, clear blue-green water between the Keys and the squishy shoreline of the southern tip of Florida. From an airplane window, the bay looks like a rarified fish tank and plays tricks with viewers' depth perception due to its startling clarity. That's the usual case, anyway.

Well before the early 1990s, the decline of all sorts of Everglades animals and plants was well documented. Environmentalists had known for many years that something drastic would have to be done to revitalize the river of grass. But it took the offshore events of algal blooms and the subsequent die-off of sponges and spiny lobsters to lift all boats to the point of action on the Florida Bay front.

FSU'S LOBSTER AMBASSADOR

In February 2000, Bill Herrnkind shared his life's passion, the Caribbean spiny lobster, with an evening class of students at Florida State University. The rangy Herrnkind, attired in a busily patterned orange, black, red, and sepia-colored shirt, could almost pass for a cryptic and anthropomorphized spiny lobster.

Herrnkind, who received his Ph.D. from the University of Miami, is a specialist in the behavior of marine invertebrates. He's traveled with Jacques Cousteau and is perhaps best known for his research on the phenomenon of lobsters queuing up under certain conditions. Herrnkind jests that the title of his talk is "Florida Spiny Lobsters: So Delicious, So Easy to Catch and to Over Fish." It seems a miracle that there are any left at all, he says, until you learn a bit about the fascinating and fortuitously mobile life cycle of the creature.

The major difference between a "lobster" and a "spiny lobster" is that the spiny variety has no claw meat. Like some people who are noted most for one body part—Elizabeth Taylor for her violet eyes or Jimmy Durante for his nose—*Panulirus argus* is prized simply for its tasty tail. The Florida fishery reports a substantial yield of between 5 and 8 million pounds per year. Cuba produces around twice that amount, and that's without the complete exploitation of the island nation's lobster-laden southern shore.

"There simply aren't enough lobsters in the world to meet the human craving," Herrnkind says.

The queuing up phenomenon is one that Herrnkind seems to want to downplay, but to the uninitiated, it offers insight into the complex behaviors of spiny lobsters. In sufficient population densities, lobsters walk in single file. The animals in the rear expend less energy by drafting. "It's a drag-reducing formation," Herrnkind explains. The lobsters may be triggered to migrate by severe storms, which usually occur in the fall. They move from shallow into deeper water and thereby avoid the shock that a sudden influx of cold water will produce during a severe storm. Migration gets them out of an area most liable to have problems. Spiny lobsters also organize themselves into formation in the face of a predator such as a trigger fish. There is safety in numbers.

Spiny lobsters inhabit the waters from Brazil through the Caribbean and up to Bermuda and Cape Hatteras. Some males can grow to about fifteen pounds, but that's rare in Florida Bay, other than around the remote Fort Jefferson at the Dry Tortugas Islands. The animal's primary "predator" is the wood slat trap. Lobsters enter the traps looking for food, shelter, and occasionally companionship, for these are social beings, and the most effective lure is another lobster. Lobster fishers sometimes keep undersized lobsters, or "shorts," in the traps to attract others, although there is a fairly high rate of mortality and injury in these traps. This amounts to an ironic and counterproductive process wherein lobstermen often kill some of next year's catch to bag this year's. Moreover, by the late 1990s, there were about

530,000 traps in Florida Bay and along the eastern side of the Florida Keys as far north as Miami (down from almost a million a decade ago). The Florida Marine Research Institute—with the collaboration of the lobstermen—is attempting to further curtail this number via a passive reduction program. Lobster takers must pay twenty-five hundred dollars for a permit and one dollar per trap and receive a certificate. The traps are thus regulated as though each is worth one share in a company. Lobstermen generally have several hundred traps that they check weekly.

Herrnkind offers this astounding statistic: that each year an estimated 80 to 90 percent of all "catchable" lobsters in Florida Bay are indeed captured. How is this sustainable?

LIFE CYCLES OF THE RICH AND FAMOUS

Lobster lovers in the Keys mainly have the wide distribution and fecundity of the species to thank for saving our tails. Sexually mature female lobsters may produce as many as one million eggs, most of which are fertilized and become larvae. The larvae of spiny lobsters generally spend six to nine months floating with the currents before settling among the larger algae or sea grass for cover. Likewise, the larvae from Florida Bay's spiny lobster population drift northward and many probably die in the North Atlantic. If you set a bottle adrift from Key West, it would take the same northerly route, float across to Africa, and then make its way back to the Caribbean. The lobsters would have to stay in their larval stage for a year for them to float the full circuit, if doing so were possible. Studies suggest, however, that some larvae sink deep and reverse direction via opposing currents; some float up and sink down and therefore remain fairly stationary.

After months of drifting, spiny lobsters enter the postlarval stage. The postlarval stage lasts several months, and during this time the creatures' greatest needs are for shelter from the dozen or so other sea creatures that might eat them. At this stage, the lobsters have the instincts of Navy Seals (or perhaps it's the other way around). They migrate inshore only during the darkest lunar phase, stay close to the surface, and settle in vegetated habitats to reduce their risk of predation. Highly branched red algae offer lots of interstices, and this is where spiny lobsters reside for several months before emerging as an early benthic juvenile, the lobster equivalent of a bottom-dwelling preteen. They begin to develop cryptic coloration, like a zebra, like Herrnkind's shirt.

When the carapace of the lobster is about one inch long they make another ecological transition. By day, the small juvenile lobsters begin to inhabit the crevices of sponges. Vase sponges and loggerhead sponges together account for roughly 70 percent of the habitat for small lobsters as they duck from gray snappers, pompano, and inshore shark species. Juvenile spiny lobsters also hide out among the sheltering spines of sea urchins, rocks, and corals.

"To a lobster, there is no such thing as a sponge," Herrnkind says in a way that is existential and provocative. "A crevice is a crevice."

As the junior crustaceans grow, they become extremely social. They congregate with other lobsters and move out of the shelter of the bay to areas in which they will mate in the spring. All the while, lobster larvae are entering and exiting Florida Bay in an inexorable swim of life.

In November of 1992, a mass of dark green water appeared in the north-central part of Florida Bay. The algae had grown explosively. By the time the bloom dissipated after about three months, virtually all the sponges in a one hundred-square-mile area had succumbed. The sponge die-off meant a housing shortage for juvenile lobsters. Scientists responded by experimenting with artificial shelters in the form of concrete blocks that could be inhabited until the sponges grew back. Herrnkind and colleagues put out the blocks, then measured the recruitment, or occupancy rate, at the sites. What they found after backbreaking labor was that the recruitment rate in the spongeless areas was about the same as in areas where they had placed the artificial habitats.

"There's lots of talk about artificial reefs. But one artificial reef is not as good as another," Herrnkind said. It turned out the larger spaces of concrete blocks just attracted lobsters with carapaces that were generally larger than fifty millimeters, or about two inches. Blocks with smaller gaps provided protection. Artificial shelters can effectively replace lost natural shelters, but Herrnkind wisely concludes, "The best thing is not to allow the natural habitat to get messed up in the first place." Perhaps the whole bottom of Florida Bay will one day be strewn with cement block lobster tenements. That would be fine for the cement block manufacturers—Florida Bay is the one niche in the state that builders and developers have not yet targeted directly.

The algae that went berserk in the early 1990s is naturally present in various portions of the Florida Bay ecosystem, such as the more protected embayments. There is no strong evidence that a similar event had happened before, and years of above-normal rainfall after the bloom lowered the salinity of the bay. But the sheltering sponges have not come back. "Some sponges have returned," says Herrnkind, "but not the kind the lobsters need."

Herrnkind draws an analogy between car repair and ecological research. You might be riding in a car when a warning light goes on. The car is still functioning, so you might not take immediate action. But if a piston shoots through the hood of the car, then you know something has to be done. Now that Florida Bay has thrown a piston, there's lots of research money. At least fifteen agencies are involved with Florida Bay research efforts.

One of the important areas of research is establishing the historical fluctuations of nutrients and conditions in the bay. Nineteenth-century naturalists reported clear tropical blue waters dotted with white sand keys. Researchers have taken shallow cores from Florida Bay to determine the historical changes in flora and fauna. Research by Lynn Brewster-Wingard and others at the U.S. Geological Survey shows that salinity and sea grass distribution in the past one hundred to two hundred years have fluctuated considerably but consistently with natural cycles. Since 1940 (around the time that the Army Corps was constructing canals in the Everglades) the variability has been much greater, and the fluctuations no longer match natural cycles.

Although the connection of the algal blooms to the output from the Everglades is not well established, there seemed to be scientific support for the theory that the changes in Florida Bay are due to elevated salinity and/or increased nutrient loads from South Florida and possibly the Keys. The model that was developed to illustrate the causes and effects of sea grass die-off provides a hint of the complexity of the Everglades and Florida Bay ecosystems. The droughts of 1987 through 1990 created hypersalinity in the bay. That, combined with high water temperatures, made the turtle grass susceptible to disease. As huge swaths of sea grass died off, dissolved oxygen levels dropped and plant decomposition released nutrients such as nitrogen and phosphorus that led to blooms of cyanobacteria, or brushlike alga. Sediments that had otherwise been anchored by the sea grass were now mixing into the water column, adding to the turbidity. The feedback loop continued as the pea soup killed even more of the turtle grass, as well as the sponges and corals in those areas.

There is a long history of direct human manipulation of the natural environment of the Florida Keys and the bay to the north, beginning with the construction of the causeways of Henry Flagler's Overseas Railway from 1906 to 1914. The railway beds and, later, the filling in of parts of the Keys to build the Keys highway effectively reduced the exchange of water between the Atlantic Ocean and Florida Bay and led to a decline in coral growth rates in southwestern Florida Bay.

Assessing the deterioration of water quality in the bay is complicated. Certainly the flow from the Everglades is the dominant factor, but the flow of nutrients from the overinhabited Keys and the destruction of natural habitats that grace these islands also is a consideration.

The summer of 1999 raised the awareness of Key residents and locals as Monroe County health officials closed public beaches due to unacceptably high levels of disease-causing microorganisms. Most of the locals—from a waitress at the restaurant Margaritaville to a bicycle rickshaw driver—thought the water quality seemed no different that particular summer than it had in the recent past. It was just that someone had finally tested the water for the obvious, given the high failure rate of septic tanks and the rapid trip that partially treated sewage makes from wastewater injection wells to surface waters in the Keys.

Another factor is population. From 1980 to 1998, the population of Monroe County—the jurisdiction that encompasses the Keys—increased by roughly 35 percent, reaching more than eighty-five thousand. In addition to the year-round residents, a healthy tourism industry raises the inhabitants by another twenty-five thousand on any given day during the winter tourist season.

With people come the aftereffects of so many consumed lobster tails and piña coladas. Only within the last ten years have population centers in the Keys begun to employ a system of centralized sewage treatment. Before that, raw waste from places such as Key West flowed directly through pipes into the Atlantic—one of the last places in the continental U.S. to discontinue the practice.

Many scientists view Florida Bay as a classic estuary with fluctuations in clarity and algal blooms depending on rainfall. The bay needs freshwater, but it has to be relatively clean water that passes through the "sentry" red mangroves, which actually generate their own nutrient loads. Florida Bay is a system that naturally tolerates a higher level of nitrogen and phosphorus than the Everglades. But Shark River Slough, which eases into western Florida Bay after draining the farmlands at the northern end of the spongiest part of the state, brings with it ample nutrients that some research suggests is the biggest threat to the health of the bay. Some scientists worry that restoring flow to the bay will speed up the choking of the ecosystem by contributing more nutrients; others such as Interior Secretary Bruce Babbitt have been ardent supporters of restoring freshwater flow.

Draft legislation circulated by the staffs of Florida's U.S. Senators Mack and Graham in the spring of 2000 dropped guarantees of new water for Everglades National Park and for Florida Bay. Big sugar and the Miccosukee Tribe don't want their interests sacrificed for restoration; developers want to have access to future allocations. Research will continue, but in the end, politics may prevail. For now, the goal is to increase freshwater flow into the bay via Taylor Slough, which empties into eastern Florida Bay. Whether this will benefit the southern and western segments of the bay is not clear. After all, the Gulf of Mexico is thought to be the greatest source of phosphorus to the Florida Bay system.

The lack of international consistency complicates management of the spiny lobster fishery. Minimum size limits largely have been established by arguments put forth by the lobster fishermen, not necessarily by what makes ecological sense. The U.S. minimum is seventy-six millimeters, and Cuba's legal "langosta espinosa" is sixty-nine millimeters. Since the influx of larvae from the Caribbean and elsewhere into Florida Bay still is rather healthy, the most obvious ecological bottleneck is the quality of habitats for the settlement stage of the spiny lobster.

"In Mexico, they take everything that moves," says lobsterman Gary Nichols. Nichols recounts a recent trip to Mexico, where he and his wife were served undersized lobster tails in a restaurant. Enforcement of legal size limits is more lax in third-world countries, but where there are fishing cooperatives, as there are in several bays south of Cozumel, the lobster trappers are much more rigorous in protections for undersized lobsters. Cuba also strongly enforces minimum size limits.

Nichols, who also owns a seafood company, calls Everglades National Park his backyard. He has been plying the waters of South Florida and Florida Bay for more than twenty-five years. Lobsters were once so plentiful that their antennae could be seen jutting from the shallows. Nichols has served on various action groups and committees on behalf of the lobster industry and protection of lobster habitat, and points out that because Everglades National Park includes considerable offshore acreage, there really is not a large area of Florida Bay from which lobsters can be caught. But Nichols understands and appreciates the value of protected waters as a nursery and safe haven for his quarry.

If you ask Nichols what the biggest threat is to the lobster fishery, the first thing he might tell you about is the black market for lobster meat. Trap robbing is a huge problem for legitimate fishermen, and is also a threat to propagation of the species, according to Nichols. Sometimes lobster boats pull up a trap with literally thousands of baby lobsters perhaps two to three inches long. Licensed fishermen happily return the young lobsters to the sea anticipating a future harvest. The "bad guys," many of whom come down from Miami, take everything. The thieves seem to be well organized, and the lobster fishing industry is desperate for more involvement from the Florida Marine Patrol. Several years ago the Marine Patrol organized a sting operation to find which restaurants in the Keys were supporting the black market lobster trade. They went to the back doors of scores of restaurants. They even bleached rotten lobster tails that could be shredded for enchiladas or salads. The undercover vendors couldn't find anybody who wouldn't buy the illicit crustacean meat.

"We're at a time where the social impacts are greater than the environmental impacts," Nichols says.

Scientists and fishermen often don't have the same perspectives and motivations; they use their antennae quite differently. John Hunt, a spiny lobster expert and research administrator with the Florida Fish and Wildlife Conservation Commission says that, yes, trap robbing occurs, but "it isn't the death knell of the industry."

LIFE AT THE BOTTOM

The greater threat is the change in the habitats of juvenile lobsters through the loss of sponges and other alterations in the bottom-dwelling community. The 1999–2000 lobster season (which runs August through March) brought between seven and eight million pounds for the Monroe and Dade County lobster fishery—an excellent haul. "Either these lobsters are much more resilient and adaptable, or the areas are less important than we thought . . . or the harvest would be even greater," Hunt said. Some have attributed the increased yields to the cleansing power of Hurricane Georges. Georges blew away many of the lobster traps, but it also scoured the scum from the recesses of the bay while transporting sea grass from east to west, where it has rooted itself nicely. In fact, the banner lobster hauls started two years before the hurricane.

Gary Nichols is far from sanguine about the state of the fishery. "I have tremendous concerns about the Everglades restoration," Nichols says, expressing trepidation about burgeoning development in western

Broward and Dade counties. "By restoring freshwater flow [to Florida Bay] what really is being accomplished?" Nichols also raises the global warming issue, and how increased water temperatures make Florida Bay that much more accommodating to algal blooms.

The comprehensive Everglades Restoration Plan offers some curious language that may ease Nichols's worries but cause consternation in others. The Army Corps of Engineers states that its fundamental goal is to "capture most of the freshwater that now flows unused to the ocean and gulf to deliver it when and where it is needed most." Vague language such as this feeds the concern by some that the Everglades advocacy of Governor Jeb Bush is motivated far more by the desire to quench the thirst of future residential and commercial developments than to restore habitat for wading birds.

There seems to be no guarantee that the multibillion dollar restoration effort will mean greater freshwater inputs to Florida Bay. Meanwhile, the bay has been rebounding nicely since the cascade of ecological events that took place starting almost fifteen years ago. The spiny lobster has likewise shown itself to be resilient, even if the sponges have not. But the next extended dry spell will tell us whether the recent depredations were merely an unfortunate blip, or a foreshadowing of future decline.

JUNE WIAZ *is among the legions of transplanted northerners who have settled in Florida and been captivated by the state's lush beauty. June lives and writes in Tallahassee with the support of her two girls, husband, and dog. Her work has appeared in the* Tallahassee Democrat, *Florida State University's* Research in Review, *and other regional publications. June also has had commentaries air on the local National Public Radio affiliate, WFSU. She and coauthor, Kathryn Ziewitz of Lynn Haven, Florida, await the public birth of their book,* Green Empire *(University Press of Florida), the story of the St. Joe Company's relationship with the land and the people of the Florida Panhandle.*

A SNAIL'S RACE

Renée Ripple

It's hard to hate airboats when you're riding on one. Wind and gravity anchor you against the vinyl seat as you fly across the surface of the water, an arrow, taut and set free, hurtling toward some unknown mark. With earphones cupped close to your head, sound diffuses into motion. It's a rush.

When the boat stops, quiet reasserts itself, settling over the sounds of the wake slapping the shoreline and scattering herons. Breathing slows. Between the humid heat rising off the water and the sharp glare of the sun bearing down, your body seems to hover and then seep out beyond tangible boundaries of skin and bone, melting into the atmosphere.

At least these were my inner musings as the airboat cruised to a stop and I awaited my companions' next moves. Deb Jansen and Rob Bennets, the biologists in charge of today's expedition, were embroiled in a discussion over the best way to secure the boat, fondly named the *Lady Liguus*. Steve, a significantly more seasoned volunteer than I, was already over the side, waist deep in water, aimed in the direction of the island hammock we'd come to survey.

The island was in Big Cypress National Preserve, near its border with Everglades National Park. I was there to help with an ongoing study of the liguus tree snail populations on this and similar tree hammocks in the preserve. The day was steamy with the temperature closing in on ninety degrees, so rather than linger onboard I slipped over the side after Steve. The water was hot and viscous, like a strong chicken consommé. Struggling for a foothold, I regretted my choice of lightweight nylon pants as they congealed against my legs in the waist-deep water.

Deb shouted a warning. "Watch out for the caprock. It's slippery."

Rob chimed in. "It's the pinnacle rock that's the problem."

I couldn't decipher their geologic terminology at first but did catch a phrase about one of the last volunteers, who'd ended up with a broken ankle. That slowed me down. I stood still, then cautiously inched my right foot over the rocks. What they meant became obvious, painfully so. Pinnacle rock composed of sharp points of rock jutting upward along the edges of the slippery, flat surface of caprock, all hidden beneath the water's surface.

I figured out how to slide one foot forward across the rock, then drag the other one behind it—a surreal sort of wedding march. I slipped once, pitching forward into the water, but quickly righted myself.

Up ahead, Steve was working his way through the shrubby trees at the island's perimeter, a mix of swamp bay, pop ash, and wax myrtle. Excited, he turned back to look at me. "Can you hear the baby gators?" he asked. "They're swimming around right up here in front of me."

I considered bolting back to the airboat, but Deb and Rob were closing in from the rear. I had a quick word with the Creator about keeping mama gator at a distance, bent my head, and sloshed my way toward Steve. With his help, I made a not too ungraceful landing on shore.

It was dead summer, and the interior of the island was a leafy sauna, the dense vegetation spongy with humidity. Sunlight spilled into the hammock in fluid shafts and droplets, and mosquitoes buzzed, heavy with the island's lethargy. After a quick application of bug spray, our search for tree snails began.

Liguus tree snails have an extremely limited distribution—South Florida, including the Everglades and the Keys, Cuba, the Isle of Pines, and Hispaniola. These creeping jewels occur in color varieties that range from drab brown to brilliantly striped pinks and yellows, some found in only one particular hammock. No one knows how many hundreds or thousands of years worth of evolutionary transition it took to create the nearly sixty color variations of the liguus tree snail that are known today, but it has taken only a few generations of human intervention to nearly devastate the entire species.

Weather events, such as hurricanes, and natural predators, including the usual suspects—possums, raccoons, native and nonnative rats, birds, and the carnivorous snail *Euglandina rosea*—once dictated the distribution of liguus tree snails in the tree hammocks. Over time, and with the aid of natural selection, each variety evolved to fit into its own niche and to deal with expected occurrences. *Euglandina,* which lives on the ground, has been seen scaling hardwoods in hot pursuit of this species—known locally as ligs—high in the trees. Devastation wrought by hurricane or fire spurs rapid growth of vegetation and discourages species succession. But, to my knowledge, no one has even guessed at the survival strategy behind the ligs' color variation, or if there is any strategy at all.

It was that whimsical diversity of colored shells that made the ligs irresistible to human collectors. Had human tastes and peccadilloes ever been factored into the evolutionary track of these lovely little gastropods, they would surely sport only one shade of bark brown, which would afford them the same camouflage as a fence lizard on an oak tree. If the lizard doesn't move, it effectively disappears into the tree. Unfortunately, ligs evolved their colorful carapaces well before humans made it to the top of the food chain.

From the early days of settlement in South Florida and the Keys until they were named a species of special concern in the seventies, it was open season. Certainly the challenge of harvesting arboreal snails was greater than picking up seashells off the beach, and the element of adventure intrinsic in picking one's way through a tropical hammock must have made for exciting conversation in homes and bars near and far.

Had these adventurers really looked around they would have seen habitat unlike any other, fertile oases of hardwoods and vegetation offering respite to birds and wildlife that might not otherwise exist. Unimpressed, a few collectors were known to torch a hammock on exit, so that they would possess the sole specimen of a color variety. Others played God and distributed their own hybrids from hammock to hammock.

The biologists outfitted Steve and me with an extendable pole (scavenged from a boat or pool house) with a paper cup duct taped to the end. Our task was to locate liguus snails in the upper levels of the trees, scoop them into the cup, and examine their shells for engraved numbers. If they had numbers, we recorded the number and location and replaced the snails at the base of the tree.

Snails with unmarked shells we took to Deb, ensconced in the center of the hammock on a camp chair, and set them in a container that corresponded to the tree from which they'd come. With her hair pulled back into a ponytail and a red bandana headband tied above her magnifying goggles, Deb resembled some otherworldly jeweler crafting precious gems. Her task was to engrave identification numbers on the snails' thin shells. We carried the marked ligs back to their trees of origin, hooked the cups onto a bit of branch or bark, and allowed the snails to crawl out at their own pace.

Looking up into the treetops, neck craned and eyes squinting from jabs of sun, at first I couldn't see a darned thing. I was supposed to be the scout and Steve the picker, but in most cases before I was able to focus, Steve would shout, "There's one."

I could stare for minutes on end at a tree limb and see nothing. Then I'd look back a little while later and, voilà. Eventually my eyes became sufficiently trained to pick out the small shells from among the leaves and bark, but Steve was our star. I learned later that he had gained his expertise as an avid Liguus collector. Volunteering for this project allowed him to feel like he was making restitution while still enjoying the pleasure of the hunt.

At the bases of some of the trees we found the empty shells of dead snails, and those were recorded as well. Some, caught in an earlier portion of the study, had engraved numbers, and a look back over the records could reveal an entire lifetime spent on one tree—or a certain wanderlust. If a tree remained healthy, a snail had no reason to move to another. If, however, the host tree died, snails would search out a new home.

The greatest excitement came when we found a snail dug an inch or so into the soil, laying eggs. Liguus tree snails mate and lay eggs from about the middle of May through November. Although hermaphroditic, mating still takes two, with both snails often becoming impregnated. Then the snail hollows out a small tunnel and lays up to two dozen pea-sized eggs.

The eggs hatch with the first rains of the season, and the new ligs, or "buttons," emerge fully formed. Over time, the shells grow swirling to the right, although there have been a few "left-handed" ligs recorded. You can estimate the age of a lig by the size of its shell and the number of whorls. They can live as long as six years. Each year, as the winter dry season approaches, a snail will find a protected spot and seal itself to the tree's bark with mucus. There it estivates until the spring rains return.

Tree snails feed on the algae, molds, fungi, and lichens that grow on trees. The most popular host tree in Florida is the wild tamarind, but poisonwood, gumbo-limbo, mastic pigeon plum, and other smooth-barked hardwoods common in tropical hammocks also accommodate the snails. Our hammock had the typical array of tropical hardwoods, and most of the ligs we collected were found on wild tamarind branches.

The hammock's location was fortunate. Its inaccessibility and minimal land mass made it unsuitable for human habitation. Others haven't fared as well; more than 41 percent of the hammocks in the upper Keys alone already are gone. The remainder are considered severely threatened.

Landscape devastation in Florida has been generally viewed as progress. At a watchable wildlife conference some years ago, I slipped out into the parking garage of the hotel to sneak a cigarette. A man in a business suit joined me, and we shared the usual smokers' banter. Then he asked what the conference was all about. With the enthusiasm of an emotional optimist, I blathered for awhile about educating people about the environment and promoting ecotourism as a means of preserving what was left of the wild Florida.

He leaned back, looked at me, and with a good dose of Florida cracker in his voice, said, "You should have seen the Florida I grew up in." Then he shook his head. "But there's nothing you can do about it. It's progress."

Writing about South Florida in his 1920 book *In the Lower Florida Wilds,* naturalist Charles Torrey Simpson lamented, "Today most of its hammocks are destroyed, the streams are being dredged out and deepened, the Everglades are nearly drained; even the pine forests are being cut down." Something about our state, perhaps the allusions to paradise, seems to inspire a binge mentality—dredge, build, plant, poison, reap—that works contrary to any logic.

For years, scientists and land managers have been working on the concept of carrying capacity: How much can the land sustain? How many people can live here? When will the water run out? An aerial survey of the spread of concrete and asphalt, the insult of exotic plants and trees, and the insistence on right angles and ease of access makes me wonder why the entire lower end of the state doesn't just sink under the weight. Or why the earth doesn't just rebel and toss it all off as I do shoes and hose returning home on a hot, summer day?

Most folks scoff and yawn at government and independent reports decrying overpopulation or overdevelopment, the same people who, when looking into an elevator with a posted carrying capacity of nine hundred pounds, would not join a three hundred pound man and his six hefty friends. And in a nation where people wrinkle their noses at sprinkling their lawns with reclaimed water, I doubt many of those people would choose to swim in a pool/septic tank combo. Yet the Keys sewage system is one of the few in the developed world with a high and low tide.

The remarkable thing about the Florida found by the Spaniards was that everything worked. Water levels rose and fell. Food sources swelled and dwindled. Natural wildfires, floods, and storms, what we call natural disasters, allowed for regeneration and new growth.

Creatures, plants, and trees flourished. Underwater landscapes of coral and sea grasses thrived.

But after only a few generations of the dredge-and-fill philosophy still espoused by some who would "grow" more Florida to suit their needs and fill their pockets, one thing is painfully clear. We broke it. Our rivers are choked with hydrilla, the Everglades are clogged with cattails, and the algae bloom in Florida Bay looks like a toxic spill. The reefs are dying. Only a fraction of the native Florida vegetation and wildlife remains, while noxious exotics spread like the wildfires that can't be controlled after so many years of fire suppression.

With the day's survey over, we rested while waiting for a team that had been at another hammock. Steve was by the water trying to call the baby gators in. I ran an inventory of my new scrapes, cuts, and insect bites. Hot and tired, I desperately wanted a shower. I picked up one of the empty shells and cupped it in my hand. It was mostly brown with random milky white markings, one of the most common varieties.

In early printings of *In the Lower Florida Wilds* are color plates of thirty or so liguus tree snails. By the time the second edition came out, some of the varieties were already extinct. I returned the shell to its spot beside the tree and wondered what would be left should there be a reprint.

––––––––––––––

RENÉE RIPPLE, *a writer for University of Florida Foundation publications, including* Florida *and* Today *magazines, has been published previously in* The Wild Heart of Florida *and aspires to be a voice for wild lands and creatures everywhere, but especially in her adopted home—Florida.*

A CALL FOR RESTORATION

Paul N. Gray

Now Mack, if you can pull yourself away from that dad blamed television for a pair of minutes, maybe I can spin you some yarns as good as what you are seeing between commercials, except that what I'm fixing to tell you really happened. Folks have said that the Everglades and Lake Okeechobee were the last frontier in the United States, and I reckon that may be true, but it was dad blamdest frontier you ever heard tell of. It sure was a heap different from what my old grand daddy ran into out west . . . it wasn't many years ago when it was about the wildest and most inaccessible region in the whole United States. Of course, other places have been wild, but there has never been another Everglades, nor nothing even like it.

So began Lawrence Will in his 1964 classic, *A Cracker History of Okeechobee.* His words remain largely true, except that this wilderness is slipping away. It doesn't have to, but it is.

We arrive at the year 2000 with about half of the Everglades drained. We have only one-tenth of our wading birds, indicating the sickness of the remaining half of the Everglades. Eighty-eight percent of our native prairies have been converted to tame-grass pasture, or something similar. Essentially all of our ancient forests are felled. The soils of the Everglades Agricultural Area have dropped as much as eight feet in some areas—the muck rots away in the dry conditions that we now farm—and a precious resource of America, our soils, are being destroyed by corporations that call themselves farmers, encouraged by government incentives. Everglades National Park and Florida Bay cannot get enough freshwater, while the St. Lucie and Caloosahatchee estuaries are periodically overwhelmed by too much of it.

Even the Everglades plant communities that are in "protected" areas, where nary a bulldozer or trackhoe is allowed, are profoundly changed. Dirty water is overrunning them and pulling a carpet of new, pollution-loving plants with it. Thanks to our water management system, the Everglades often are too wet in the dry season and too dry in the wet season.

Perhaps the greatest irony of all this progress is that we don't have enough water anymore. We get between fifty to eighty inches of rain across the greater Everglades ecosystem, yet we have engineered a system that cannot retain enough water to meet environmental needs, or human needs either.

People believe that "long-ago" activities drained the Everglades, that somehow all those bad things happened far in the past. Yes, the largest canals were dug before 1950, but for the Everglades ecosystem, the greatest changes have come in the last fifty years, relying on the infrastructure of those canal ways and benefiting from a suddenly mechanized post–World War II America. We plan our growth, but we never cap it. We don't stop developers from putting people's homes in flood-prone areas—also known as wetlands. We do not support low-intensity agriculture. Following the arrival of air-conditioning, the line graphing South Florida's rising population has the accelerating slope of an aberrant and terrifying ski jump. We are almost out of Everglades, or at least the wild glades that were so recently here with us.

When we review the chaotic collection of plans and projects that comprises the history of South Florida's development, it is no mystery why we have been unable to balance our competing needs. I am reminded of the television commercial where a toddler pulls a large butcher knife off a chair. As a viewer, you know the baby is unaware of what that knife can do, of the power the knife has to change things. Unsupervised, the baby proceeds. It seems to me that our development has unfolded with about as much foresight as that baby could exercise. Can we recognize ourselves as that child, wielding our own dangerous tools—bulldozers, draglines, pumps, pesticides, fertilizers, blueprints, legislatures, governing boards, and lawsuits? We have no wise parent to take our knives away until we are mature enough to use them. Would we even listen?

The good news today is that we seem to have realized our tools have created profound problems. Recently, the state and federal governments and various interest groups have embarked on the next chapter in South Florida development, called the Comprehensive Everglades Restoration Plan (CERP). This plan came about as the result of the Restudy, in which we tallied our problems and made a consensus plan to fix South Florida. We seem now to understand that this is the chapter of our story where our heroes—wilderness and wild things—either live on, or don't.

It is difficult to overstate the magnitude of the restoration plan. Its basic goal is to restore as much of the great Everglades ecosystem as possible. Today, we send about two million acre-feet of water into the ocean instead of through the Everglades and toward Florida Bay. Today, an estimated 30 percent of the water in our system flows correctly for the environment. After the restoration plan is completed, we will capture an additional 1.1 million acre-feet of water, of which 80 percent is earmarked for the native ecosystems. The restoration plan is intended to send this water once again on its proper path: clean water in the right spots, in the right amounts, and at the right times.

Much of the captured water will exist in water storage and treatment reservoirs and injection wells in all regions of South Florida, but some of it simply will be rehydrating overdrained areas. In the Everglades proper, about 240 miles of internal canals and levees will be removed to allow sheet flow to resume. In the Kissimmee River Valley, much of the C-38 canal will be refilled, restoring about 75 percent of the thirty-five thousand acres of marshlands that were lost in the original drainage project. To get an idea of the scale of the Everglades Restoration Plan, we can look at the largest river restoration ever attempted in the world: the Kissimmee River restoration, projected to cost about half a billion dollars. The overall Everglades Restoration Plan will cost an estimated $7.8 billion, and will take thirty years to complete.

The Restudy has paralleled an interesting progression for the United States Army Corps of Engineers, accurately labeled in one book as "the river killers." The role of the corps has evolved from that of the original destroyers to strong advocates for restoration. Assistant Secretary of the Army Joseph W. Westphal recently wrote, "Over half the Everglades have been lost forever. The remaining half is dying."

He continued, "Most of the negative changes in the ecosystem are a direct result of water management activities designed to reduce flooding and provide for urban and agricultural water supply. If we do not act now, we may very well lose the opportunity to save [the Everglades] for future generations." A similar change in thinking and rhetoric has occurred in the South Florida Water Management District, formerly called Flood Control. Cynics argue the corps and the district merely are funded to construct yet another project, but I wonder how reconstructing such a sensitive thing as a functioning ecosystem might affect them. In my house, we have a scared little black cat. He reminds me to walk gently lest I upset him. Can the job of restoring our Everglades teach our agencies how to tread gently upon our land?

There are many who fear the restoration plan cannot live up to our hopes. Indeed our best and brightest scientists and engineers disagree, in good faith, about the best ways to implement these fixes. Although the Restudy is more than four thousand pages (nine inches tall on its side), it is considered conceptual. The plan for some areas, such as Florida Bay, the Florida Keys, and southwest Florida, is merely to draft a feasibility study. We enter this great plan with many uncertainties and past proof that our best plans and tools still can lead us into unexpected problems.

For example, in 1987, when the legislature passed a plan to remedy polluted Lake Okeechobee (after huge algal blooms developed), they planned to reduce phosphorus inflow to the lake from about seven times more than natural to about four times more than natural. Scientists predicted that the extra phosphorus would settle and become buried at the bottom, allowing the lake waters to grow progressively cleaner. It didn't happen. The lake is so shallow that even moderate winds create waves that stir the bottom, and all that extra phosphorus-laden mud kept getting stirred. After twelve years of attempting to restore the lake, its water quality is worse than ever. Now scientists have recalculated phosphorus movements and essentially concluded that if we want the lake returned to a healthy 40 parts per billion phosphorus, the inflow needs to be about the same—40 parts per billion, genuine clean-water standards. But the computer models also predict that even if such clean water were again to flow into the lake, about sixty more tons of phosphorus will accumulate in the lake each year. Considering the lake is six thousand years old, if this rate had been happening all along, the lake now would be mostly filled in with muck. What's wrong?

The answer may be found in the tragic, hurricane-related floods south of the lake, in the town of Belle Glade. When unfortunate souls in that town were swept off their roofs by the twelve-foot storm surge of the 1928 hurricane, they didn't have time to think about how much muck was being carried out of the lake. They knew they had moved there to farm deep, organic soils. They knew Lake Okeechobee had a sandy bottom without much muck, but they apparently hadn't realized that the muck soils of the Everglades came largely from Lake Okeechobee—either as dissolved nutrients in the annual outflow water, or as physical muck being periodically flushed from the lake by grand ecosystem events, such as the very hurricane that took their lives. Today, the Hoover Dike contains the lake's water and muck, and even if we put clean water in Lake Okeechobee from now on, it will continue to muck-in at an accelerated rate.

Not only is the lake prevented from periodically flushing, but it also has accumulated one thousand years worth of fertilizer-derived, phosphorus-laden muck on its bottom in the past fifty years. Phosphorus concentrations in the lake's water column have risen from 40 parts per billion in 1970, to more than 130 parts per billion in 2000.

PAUL N. GRAY

Even if we could stop all phosphorus inflows to the lake (which we can't, since the phosphorus in the lake is perhaps one-tenth of what has been spread in its watershed and is still on its way to the lake), it might take centuries for phosphorus levels to drop back to 40 parts per billion. To restore the Everglades, we must have water at 10 parts per billion phosphorus, or lower. We plan to use Okeechobee's water for this task—but can we clean it? This is an example of the formidable obstacles to successful Everglades restoration.

Another is the plan to store water that presently escapes to the ocean by building huge reservoirs and underground injection wells all around South Florida. We will build larger canals to transport this water to where it is "naturally" needed. How ironic that our wetland wilderness stored and cleaned water for free, and we spent billions draining Florida. Now we will spend billions more trying to get the water back. These construction projects will truly help the vast, continuous areas of the Water Conservation Areas, Everglades, and Big Cypress. But reservoirs are not wetlands, and by themselves cannot replace lost ecosystem functions.

For example, a healthy duck population requires a thousand small wetland ponds to sustain its thousand duck families. Similarly, any wetland dependent species needs many suitable wetlands to maintain a large enough population to ensure its persistence in the face of periodic calamities (disease, drought, hurricanes, predation, humans, whatever). And if a local wetland experiences an extinction of certain species, we need a nearby wetland that can supply organisms to recolonize when conditions become favorable again. This idea of needing whole regions to remain intact, or at least connected, to retain species over the long run is one of the fundamentals of conservation. Reservoirs cannot keep the greater Everglades intact. Neither can injection wells.

Even as I worry that the great ecosystem machine we are tinkering with is more complicated than we can ever understand, weaknesses inherent in the huge restoration plan are not my greatest concern. The restoration's ultimate success lies not in our intention, but rather in our willingness to stick to a plan once we have it. Gardeners know that planning, and even planting, a garden is the least of the work. The real success, and most of the work, comes in the tending.

Our South Florida garden will need continuous tending, and it must involve more than the Everglades and wilderness. The impermanent design of South Florida development tells us more about ourselves than we may notice. Mobile homes, abandoned strip malls, and gas stations reflect a society that doesn't plan on sticking around very long. We cut our trees without regard to long-term forestry. We farm our muck soils until they are destroyed and farming must stop. We need a longer vision.

We are creatures of stories. No matter what culture of humans, we tell ourselves stories that embody important life lessons. In America, we read books for their stories, watch that dad-blamed television for its function as a story machine, and play our video games for their unfolding tales (the addictiveness of these machines may be the strongest evidence of our inherent reliance on stories).

Perhaps the most important job of this generation will be to place firmly in the hearts and minds of our people the story of returning South Florida to health and balance, wild areas as well as our own neighborhoods. Everyone, I mean everyone, sees that wilderness is disappearing. Once gone, we cannot rebuild it. Economists must argue the value of natural areas for tourism and water storage. Medical people, agricultural and materials scientists, pest control and erosion control experts, and climate watchers can remind us of the value of biodiversity. Citizens need to argue about the value of a nice place to live, with clean water, fish in our lakes, crickets singing from the wood pile, foxes by the creek, panthers in the woods, eagles in the air, and beautiful communities.

Human history in South Florida is one big story, full of tragedies and triumphs. If we consider historical triumphs, as we hope the Everglades story will be, a common theme of triumph is of a group of people who told an inspiring story. They shared a common vision and imbedded this vision deeply enough into their souls and the souls around them that their civilization was able to confront the inevitable obstacles and to prevail. We must have a public waking up to the importance of our natural systems. All of us must make it a priority to tell the Everglades story. And if we do, I think we will restore to our rapacious civilization something more than an ecosystem.

PAUL N. GRAY *comes from an area of the Midwest where the prairies and wetlands were more than 90 percent lost by the time he was born. He hopes Florida can protect more than that. He obtained degrees from Missouri University and Texas Tech University, and a doctorate from the University of Florida. Paul presently works as a sanctuary manager for Audubon of Florida and lives in the country with his wife, where they like the quiet, and seeing the critters and flowers.*

PRAYER FOR THE EVERGLADES

Lola Haskins

A gumbo-limbo swoons in the arms of an oak.
A royal palm, smooth as sunless skin, rises
against blue. In this whole untouched world
there seems only wind, the grass, and us.
Now silent lines of wood storks appear,
their white wings edged black. Here is
a mathematical question for your evenings.
How many moments like this make a life?

But if it were not true? What if the Glades
were a dream, ancient, written on the walls
of caves, so anthropologists peering into
the darkness could say only, *it must have
been lovely then, when grass flowed under
the sun like a young woman's falling hair.*
What if none of it were true? What if
you and I walked all our afternoons under
smoke, and never saw beyond? What if
the tiny algae that velvet the water, the
gators that pile like lizards on the banks,
the ibis with her sweet curved bill? What
if the turtles that plop off their logs like little

jokes? What if the sheltering mangroves?
Oh what if? Look up, friend, and take my
hand. What if the wood storks were gone?

———————

LOLA HASKINS *is a two-time Pulitzer nominee whose most recent (of six)*
books of poems are The Rim Benders *(Anhinga, 2001) and* Extranjera *(Story*
Line, 1998). Her collection Hunger *(University of Iowa Press, 1993) won the Iowa*
Poetry Prize in 1992. Her work has appeared in the Atlantic Monthly, Christian
Science Monitor, London Review of Books, Beloit Poetry Journal, Georgia
Review, Southern Review, *and* Prairie Schooner *and elsewhere. Ms. Haskins*
enjoys collaboration; her most recent venture was a ballet for which she both wrote
a libretto and performed it (as "the speaking Mata Hari"). Ms. Haskins has taught
computer science at the University of Florida since the 1970s.

EVERGLADES ORGANIZATIONS AND RESOURCES

The Everglades Coalition includes forty-two organizations that advocate for Everglades restoration, each in their own way. The coalition does not have a website or an office, but does convene each January for a multiday conference, a "must" event for Everglades advocates to attend. The organizations listed below are among the prime Everglades activists; on their websites you will find many more links, as well as information about the annual coalition conference.

Friends of the Everglades
7800 Red Road, Suite 215K, Miami, FL 33143
(305) 669-0858
www.everglades.org

Friends of the Everglades was founded in 1969 by Marjory Stoneman Douglas, a pioneer conservationist and author of The Everglades: River of Grass. *Members pay annual dues of $10.00 a year and receive a periodic newsletter, the* Everglades Reporter.

Audubon of Florida
444 Brickell Avenue, Suite 850, Miami, FL 33131
(305) 371-6399
(305) 371-6398 fax
www.audubonofflorida.org/leadership/eadvocacy.htm

Audubon has created the Everglades Conservation Network, a citizen's advocacy network, to push forward the restoration and protection of the greater Everglades ecosystem. You can keep up-to-date with the Everglades newsletter Restore, action alerts, and event announcements through the Everglades Conservation Network and the ECN-GENERAL Listserv. To subscribe, send an email to LISTSERV@LIST.AUDUBON.ORG with the message: SUBSCRIBE ECN-GENERAL.

Everglades Field Office/National Wildlife Federation
2590 Golden Gate Parkway, Suite 109, Naples, FL 34105
everglades@nwf.org
(941) 643-4111
(941) 643-5130 fax
www.nwf.org/everglades/

A newsletter, the Everglades Growler, *helps Everglades activists keep up-to-date.*

A SELECTION OF ONLINE RESOURCES
FOR EVERGLADES INFORMATION

National Park Service, Everglades National Park
www.nps.gov/ever/home.htm

The Everglades Information Network (a collaborative project of Florida International University libraries and numerous other libraries and information sources)
everglades.fiu.edu/

South Florida Water Management District
www.sfwmd.gov/

South Florida Ecosystem Restoration Task Force
www.sfrestore.org

The Everglades Village—An Electronic Community
www.evergladesvillage.net

This website bills itself as the virtual South Florida home for all the individuals and nongovernmental and governmental organizations that are working to sustain the environments and the communities in southern Florida. This is a good site to browse to find directories, services, and resources related to the Everglades.

EVERGLADES MUST-READS

Here is a sampling of some of the best that's been written and published about the greater Florida Everglades ecosystem, in a variety of genres, from natural history to mystery.

Brown, Loren G. Totch. *A Life in the Everglades*. Gainesville: University Press of Florida, 1993.
Carr, Archie. *The Everglades*. New York: Time-Life Books, 1973.
Davis, Stephen M., and John Ogden, eds. *Everglades: the Ecosystem and its Restoration*. Boca Raton: St. Lucie Press, 1994.
Douglas, Marjory Stoneman. *The Everglades: River of Grass*. Sarasota: Pineapple Press, 1997.
Douglas, Marjory Stoneman. *Voice of a River*. Sarasota: Pineapple Press, 1987.
Fowler, Connie May. *River of Hidden Dreams*. New York: Fawcett Books, 1995.
Hogan, Linda. *Power*. New York: W. W. Norton, 1998.
Hurston, Zora Neale. *Their Eyes Were Watching God*. Chicago: University of Illinois, 1978.
Johnson, Lamar. *Beyond the Fourth Generation*. Gainesville: University Presses of Florida, 1974.
Jumper, Betty Mae. *Legends of the Seminoles*. Sarasota: Pineapple Press, 1994.
Matthiessen, Peter. *Lost Man's River*. New York: Random House, 1997.
Matthiessen, Peter. *Killing Mr. Watson*. New York: Random House, 1990.
McCally, David. *The Everglades: An Environmental History*. Gainesville: University Press of Florida, 1999.
Robertson, William B., Jr. *Everglades: The Park Story*. Homestead: Florida National Parks and Monuments Association, 1989.

Smith, Patrick. *A Land Remembered.* Sarasota: Pineapple Press, 1998.

Tebeau, Charlton. *Man in the Everglades.* Miami: University of Miami Press, 1968.

Toops, Connie. *The Florida Everglades.* Stillwater, Minn.: Voyageur Press, 1998.

White, Randy Wayne. *The Mangrove Coast.* New York: Prime Crime, 1999.

Willoughby, Hugh L. *Journey Through the Old Everglades.* Philadelphia: J. B. Lippincott, 1898.

ACKNOWLEDGMENTS

Thank you to Emilie Buchwald, publisher of Milkweed Editions, and writer Janisse Ray, who together settled on the Everglades as a vital area to portray in Milkweed's Literature for a Land Ethic series. Janisse was originally recruited to edit this work, and even after she withdrew to return her poet's heart and activist's attention to Georgia longleaf, she helped select and edit many of these essays. In all my writing, and in my life, I am always gratefully intertwined with Janisse. Thank you to Emilie for the privilege of preparing this book, also to Greg Larson at Milkweed for the answers to essential questions.

Any good Florida collection should begin with several days picking the prodigious brains and bookshelves of Jono Miller and Julie Morris in Sarasota, and that's what I did. Throughout the twenty years we have worked the cause of conservation in Florida together, I have taken refuge often with these dear and committed friends, in their home, on rivers, and in endless motel and meeting rooms around our state. Jono enlivened this project in particular with brilliance and enthusiasm. Good friends and writers Ann Morrow, Jan Godown, Bill Belleville, Julie Hauserman, and Jeff and Renée Ripple also searched their libraries and their long immersion in the literature of Florida for just the right pieces and authors for this book.

I was privileged to work under the tutelage of the wise and experienced Don Snow, of the Northern Lights Institute, as my editor. If Florida had a Don Snow to shine the light of excellent writing on its landscape and people, we'd be the better for it. A great joy in preparing this anthology was the chance to reconnect with its writers, who in many cases reshuffled their workloads to accommodate our tight deadlines. I salute their generosity, wisdom, and general good humor. Special appreciation to Paul Gray and Bill Hammond for important contributions. Thank you to Mimi, Chuck, and David Carr for trying to get the necessary permissions to include the work of Archie Carr in this volume.

Gratitude, always, to Marjory Stoneman Douglas, Art Marshall, Bill Robertson, Richard Coleman, and Carl Hiaasen for their fearless, matter-of-fact, and passionate advocacy, even in the darkest times, watching their most beloved places be annihilated, and still standing to demand restoration, with eloquence. And thanks to hundreds of others under the umbrella of the Everglades Coalition, and in state and federal agencies, who go to work every day on behalf of our beautiful and battered South Florida. Mary Ann Poole, of the Florida Fish and Wildlife Conservation Commission, especially comes to mind.

Thanks to Loisa Kerwin and Paul Gray for so graciously guiding Jeff and me in the Kissimmee Valley, opening our eyes to the river's restoration. I also owe many thanks to Lora Silvanima for technical assistance, last-minute document preparation, and constant support, and to Norine Cardea for the comforts of home, for feeding the animals while I traveled, and for believing in my work. My son, David, spent most of a year listening to the travel diaries of early Everglades explorers and the wonderful Florida fiction of Patrick Smith, at bedtime, and it wasn't always his first choice. It is to him and all of our children— the born and unborn of every wild species—that I offer this book.

I so appreciate my parents, Charles R. and Janet Isleib, for taking me to wild places and teaching me to love them. Even that endless summer night in 1964, camped at Flamingo in a tent full of siblings, no-see-ums, and a panting German shepherd, informed my love and respect for Florida.

My greatest debt is to my partner, Jeff Chanton, who lived and thought and talked this book every single day with me, for his keen scientific perspective, willing editorial pen, and pleasure of his companionship in the Everglades and in life; this is his book, too. Our days boating, biking, slogging, and investigating together in Florida are always a joy.

CONTRIBUTOR
ACKNOWLEDGMENTS

Al Burt, Foreword. Copyright © 2002 by Al Burt. Printed with permission from the author.

Archie Carr, "The River and the Plain," excerpted from *The American Wilderness: The Everglades*, 24–27. Copyright © 1973 Time Life, Inc. Reprinted with permission from the Editors of Time-Life Books.

Marjory Stoneman Douglas, excerpts from *The Everglades: River of Grass* (Sarasota, Fla.: Pineapple Press, 1997), 10–11, 19–20, 20–21, 41, 53. Copyright © 1997 by Marjory Stoneman Douglas. Reprinted with permission from Pineapple Press, Inc.

Charles Fergus, "Path of the Panther" from *Swamp Screamer: At Large with the Florida Panther* (New York: North Point Press, 1996), 158–172. Copyright © 1996 by Charles Fergus. Reprinted with permission from North Point Press, a division of Farrar, Straus and Giroux, LLC.

Jan Godown, "This Path Don't Lead to Miami: Everglades Treks of the 1800s." Copyright © 2002 by Jan Godown. Printed with permission from the author.

Paul N. Gray, "A Call for Restoration." Copyright © 2002 by Paul N. Gray. Printed with permission from the author.

Juanita Greene, "Losing Ground: Soil Subsidence in the Everglades." Copyright © 2002 by Juanita Greene. Printed with permission from the author.

SUSAN CERULEAN *has written and advocated for wildlife conservation from her home in Tallahassee, Florida, since 1981. She edited* The Wild Heart of Florida *(with Jeff Ripple, University Press of Florida, 1999), and coauthored* The Florida Wildlife Viewing Guide *(with Ann Morrow, Falcon Press, 1993). In 2002,* The Guide to the Great Florida Birding Trail: East Florida *(edited by Cerulean with Julie Brashears for University Press of Florida) will be published.*

Her essays have appeared in several collections, including Intimate Nature: The Bond Between Women and Nature *and* The Woods Stretched for Miles: New Nature Writing from the South, *and many publications, including* Orion Afield, Miami Herald, Gainesville Sun, Tallahassee Democrat, Defenders, Florida Naturalist, *and* Florida Wildlife. *In 1997, she was named Environmental Educator of the Year by the Governor's Council for a Sustainable Florida.*

Cerulean teaches writing workshops for women and records occasional commentary for Florida Public Radio. She is a founding council member and newsletter editor for the Heart of the Earth (www.heartoftheearth.com) and is the mother of a thirteen-year-old son, David.

MORE BOOKS ON THE WORLD AS HOME
FROM MILKWEED EDITIONS

To order books or for more information, contact Milkweed at
(800) 520-6455 or visit our website (www.worldashome.org).

WILD EARTH:
WILD IDEAS FOR A WORLD OUT
OF BALANCE
Edited by Tom Butler

SWIMMING WITH GIANTS:
MY ENCOUNTERS WITH WHALES,
DOLPHINS, AND SEALS
Anne Collet

THE PRAIRIE IN HER EYES
Ann Daum

BOUNDARY WATERS:
THE GRACE OF THE WILD
Paul Gruchow

GRASS ROOTS:
THE UNIVERSE OF HOME
Paul Gruchow

THE NECESSITY OF EMPTY PLACES
Paul Gruchow

A SENSE OF THE MORNING:
FIELD NOTES OF A BORN OBSERVER
David Brendan Hopes

THIS INCOMPARABLE LAND:
A GUIDE TO AMERICAN NATURE
WRITING
Thomas J. Lyon

A WING IN THE DOOR:
LIFE WITH A RED-TAILED HAWK
Peri Phillips McQuay

THE BARN AT THE END OF
THE WORLD:
THE APPRENTICESHIP OF A QUAKER,
BUDDHIST SHEPHERD
Mary Rose O'Reilley

ECOLOGY OF A CRACKER
CHILDHOOD
Janisse Ray

OF LANDSCAPE AND LONGING:
FINDING A HOME AT THE WATER'S EDGE
Carolyn Servid

HOMESTEAD
Annick Smith

THE *CREDO* SERIES

BROWN DOG OF THE YAAK:
ESSAYS ON ART AND ACTIVISM
Rick Bass

WINTER CREEK:
ONE WRITER'S NATURAL HISTORY
John Daniel

WRITING THE SACRED INTO
THE REAL
Alison Hawthorne Deming

THE FROG RUN:
WORDS AND WILDNESS IN THE
VERMONT WOODS
John Elder

TAKING CARE:
THOUGHTS ON STORYTELLING
AND BELIEF
William Kittredge

AN AMERICAN CHILD SUPREME:
THE EDUCATION OF A LIBERATION
ECOLOGIST
John Nichols

WALKING THE HIGH RIDGE:
LIFE AS FIELD TRIP
Robert Michael Pyle

THE DREAM OF THE
MARSH WREN:
WRITING AS RECIPROCAL CREATION
Pattiann Rogers

THE COUNTRY OF LANGUAGE
Scott Russell Sanders

SHAPED BY WIND AND WATER:
REFLECTIONS OF A NATURALIST
Ann Haymond Zwinger

LITERATURE FOR A LAND ETHIC

ARCTIC REFUGE:
A CIRCLE OF TESTIMONY
Compiled by Hank Lentfer and
Carolyn Servid

THE BOOK OF THE TONGASS
Edited by Carolyn Servid and
Donald Snow

TESTIMONY:
WRITERS OF THE WEST SPEAK ON
BEHALF OF UTAH WILDERNESS
Compiled by Stephen Trimble and
Terry Tempest Williams

***STORIES FROM WHERE WE LIVE,
EDITED BY SARA ST. ANTOINE***

For Middle-Grade Readers

STORIES FROM WHERE WE LIVE—
THE CALIFORNIA COAST

STORIES FROM WHERE WE LIVE—
THE GREAT NORTH AMERICAN
PRAIRIE

STORIES FROM WHERE WE LIVE—
THE GULF COAST

STORIES FROM WHERE WE LIVE—
THE NORTH ATLANTIC COAST

LITERATURE FOR A LAND ETHIC is an anthology series that addresses the need to preserve our last wild places. These books offer prismatic portraits of endangered landscapes across our continent through the various perspectives of some of the best of each region's writers.

THE WORLD AS HOME, the nonfiction publishing program of Milkweed Editions, is dedicated to exploring our relationship to the natural world. Not espousing any particular environmentalist or political agenda, these books are a forum for distinctive literary writing that not only alerts the reader to vital issues but offers personal testimonies to living harmoniously with other species in urban, rural, and wilderness communities.

MILKWEED EDITIONS publishes with the intention of making a humane impact on society, in the belief that literature is a transformative art uniquely able to convey the essential experiences of the human heart and spirit. To that end, Milkweed publishes distinctive voices of literary merit in handsomely designed, visually dynamic books, exploring the ethical, cultural, and esthetic issues that free societies need continually to address. Milkweed Editions is a not-for-profit press.

JOIN US

Since its genesis as *Milkweed Chronicle* in 1979, Milkweed has helped hundreds of emerging writers reach their readers. Thanks to the generosity of foundations and of individuals like you, Milkweed Editions is able to continue its nonprofit mission of publishing books chosen on the basis of literary merit—on how they impact the human heart and spirit—rather than on how they impact the bottom line. That's a miracle that our readers have made possible.

In addition to purchasing Milkweed books, you can join the growing community of Milkweed supporters. Individual contributions of any amount are both meaningful and welcome. Contact us for a Milkweed catalog or log on to www.milkweed.org and click on "About Milkweed," then "Why Join Milkweed," to find out about our donor program, or simply call (800) 520-6455 and ask about becoming one of Milkweed's contributors. As a nonprofit press, Milkweed belongs to you, the community. Milkweed's board, its staff, and especially the authors whose careers you help launch thank you for reading our books and supporting our mission in any way you can.

Interior design by Dale Cooney
Typeset in Stone Serif 9.5/14
by Stanton Publication Services, Inc.,
on the Pagewing Digital Publishing System.
Printed on acid-free 55# Frasier Miami Book Recycled paper
by Friesen Corporation.